Virginal Sexuality and Textuality in Victorian Literature

SUNY Series, The Body in Culture, History, and Religion
Howard Eilberg-Schwartz, Editor

VIRGINAL SEXUALITY AND TEXTUALITY IN VICTORIAN LITERATURE

edited by

LLOYD DAVIS

University of Queensland

State University
of New York
Press

Published by
State University of New York Press, Albany

Printed in the United States of America

For information, address State University of New York
Press, State University Plaza, Albany, N.Y., 12246

Production by Susan Geraghty
Marketing by Bernadette LaManna

Library of Congress Cataloging-in-Publication Data

Virginal sexuality and textuality in Victorian literature / edited by
Lloyd Davis.
p. cm. — (SUNY series, the body in culture, history, and
religion)
ISBN 0-7914-1283-0 (alk. paper) : $49.50. — ISBN 0-7914-1284-9
(pbk. : alk. paper) : $16.95
1. English literature—19th century—History and criticism.
2. Virginity in literature. 3. Body, Human, in literature. 4. Sex
in literature. I. Davis, Lloyd, 1959– . II. Series.
PR468.V57V57 1993
820.9'3538—dc20 91-45286
CIP

10 9 8 7 6 5 4 3 2 1

For Julia

CONTENTS

ACKNOWLEDGMENTS

This collection developed from a Special Session at the 1989 MLA Convention entitled "Virginal Ideals: Sexuality in Victorian Literature." The papers given at that session form the nucleus of the volume, and I thank those speakers for persevering through what became a more involved project. The other authors whose work is included here have all shown commitment to the collection over the last two years, for which I am also grateful.

Howard Eilberg-Schwartz, the editor of State University of New York Press's *The Body in Culture, History, and Religion* series, offered appreciated support to the project, and Lois Patton, the press's editor-in-chief, gave much long-range assistance in getting the collection together.

I am grateful to the University of Queensland for a special project grant in 1990 which aided in my work and research for the volume. Thanks are also due to Lori Lefkovitz, to Susan Geraghty, John Leonard, and Ruth Barcan for helping to prepare the manuscript, and to Julia Duffy for her support.

PART 1

Virginal Texts

CHAPTER 1

The Virgin Body as Victorian Text: An Introduction

Lloyd Davis

> The high value which her suitor places on a woman's virginity seems to us so firmly rooted, so much a matter of course, that we find ourselves almost at a loss if we have to give reasons for this opinion.
>
> Sigmund Freud, "The Taboo of Virginity"

> The question of chastity, both of mind and body, is of the greatest interest and complexity.
>
> Virginia Woolf, *Three Guineas*

I

Virginity exemplifies paradoxes of the body. It signifies a pre-cultural state that seems to indicate the natural origins and to ensure the value and propriety of sociosexual codes. Virginity helps keep the system going, as Julia Kristeva suggests in noting that, when linked to the maternal, it is able "not only to calm social anxiety and supply what the male lacks, but also to satisfy a woman, in such a way that the community of the sexes is established beyond, and in spite of, their flagrant incompatibility."[1] In this process, virginity both displays hierarchies and orders of sexuality and works to naturalize them through offering the "illusion" of an ideally pure "attribute which one, particularly a woman, *has* rather than a socially constructed attribute into which a person is socialised."[2] Virginity is one of the means through which societies generally translate "sexuality as a natural and *moral* fact of life" into a commonsense, unquestioned mirage that becomes "a natural fact of life."[3]

When analyzing such so-called natural facts, it is notable that each is positioned at the intersection of many social texts. Virginity is an important topos in a context comprising discourses of nature, patriarchy, the family, economics, morality, religion, metaphysics, psychology, medicine, literature, even politics and royalty. In *The History of Sexuality,* Michel Foucault writes that through the eighteenth and nineteenth centuries, western "sex became an issue, and a public issue no less; a whole web of discourses, special knowledges, analyses, and injunctions settled upon it."[4] The essays in this collection examine the ways that virginity is central to representations of sexuality and the body in Victorian literature and culture. What is significant about the texts that are discussed, and about the ways that they are discussed, is less their literary and thematic treatments of virginity than their use of the virginal to disclose different dimensions of this broader "public issue." Through representing the virginal, these texts reflect upon and participate in the "web of discourses" which articulated ambivalent Victorian conceptions of the body "as either valuable or problematic."[5]

As Foucault has also examined, the nineteenth century was a crucial period in the development of a system of "power-knowledge" through which "a productive body and a subjected body" could be set into social action.[6] The discourse of virginity in Victorian culture operates as one means of constructing such a body. In depicting virginity as cultural *ideal,* the period's literary texts reproduce this discourse and its effects of subjection. Yet as the essays in this collection reveal, in inscribing the virginal as cultural *process* these texts also question the origins and effects of Victorian "power-knowledge." The virgin body discloses the interplay between a cultural icon and social process; as Herbert F. Tucker remarks in his essay, "virginity belongs among those ideals that culture posits in compensation for its own belated derivativeness." As an ideal state, virginity would reside prior to any knowledge; yet in being recognized and valued as the virginal, it implies an extensive construct of social rules and beliefs. Virginity seems to efface the cultural and sexual system that produces it. In Foucauldian terms, the virgin body hides power-knowledge behind a pure, corporeal intactness that is itself produced by power-knowledge. The ideal, natural state of virginity in fact signifies the practical, social process of the virginal. If *virginity* names a mythical, originary physical state, then the term *virginal* can be used to name the productive, subjected virgin body that virginity would conceal.

As will be discussed in more detail in the second half of this introduction, these essays consider the virginal as central to many aspects of society and sexuality in nineteenth-century England. Through readings of literary texts, they examine the virgin figure's varying effects on and roles in the Victorian cultural imagination. Before proceeding to introduce those readings, however, I will discuss the virgin as a social, sexual, and literary phenomenon by trying to locate the virginal figure in a range of Victorian discourses of gender, social structure, and power. The approaches of the individual essays, and of the volume as a whole, will then be related to critical theories of the body, gender, and representation. For all the essays here, the Victorian virgin exemplifies historical and cultural interactions between sexuality and textuality.

II

One of the key episodes in Lytton Strachey's biography of Victoria comes with the death of William IV and the new queen's initial council. The young monarch emerges from her mother's "extraordinary watchfulness," a "mental atmosphere . . . almost entirely feminine," into a world of old and commanding men.[7] This transition is full of social and personal significance; in entering the red saloon at Kensington Palace, Victoria is committed to a fateful construction of character. Recounted at the nexus of Strachey's second and third chapters, which record the shift from childhood through early sovereignty to imminent marriage, her entrance represents a personal passage from one social level to another, a rite of selfhood that incorporates crucial values of a culture. The continuity of political rule and power is staged through the site and sight of Victoria's person. In the moment of its affirmation and reinforcement, however, this power becomes complicated and uncertain in view of a figure it expects and recognizes, yet fails wholly to anticipate. The young queen both meets and exceeds speculation:

> at half past eleven she went downstairs into the red saloon to hold her first Council. The great assembly of lords and notables, bishops, generals, and Ministers of State, saw the doors thrown open and a very short, very slim girl in deep plain mourning come into the room alone and move forward to her seat with extraordinary dignity and grace; they saw a countenance, not beautiful, but prepossessing—fair hair, blue prominent eyes, a small curved nose, an open mouth revealing the upper teeth, a tiny chin, a clear complexion, and, over all, the strangely mingled signs of innocence, of gravity, of youth, and of composure; they heard a high unwavering voice reading aloud with perfect clarity; and then, the ceremony over, they saw the small figure rise and, with the same consummate grace, the same amazing dignity, pass out from among them, as she had come in, alone. (62)

Strachey's account underlines the way in which an expectantly masterful scrutiny would frame and size this "girl" up. The assembled males wait for her to enter, not so much submitting to sovereign audience as assuming priority and control over it. They anatomize the new queen physically and culturally. Their perception oscillates between distinguishing her individually, in the image of girlhood, and as a ceremonial, queenly persona, each alternative a determination of social value. Her youthfulness, gender, and isolation reinforce through contrast their male solidarity. The synthesized perspective conveyed by Strachey's "they saw . . . they heard . . . they saw" suggests the enduring dominance of a patriarchal political vision.

In relating this episode, Strachey's text duplicates that framing of Victoria. The footnotes reveal that his version is based on both the autobiographical jottings of *The Girlhood of Queen Victoria* and the *Memoirs* of the "cold and caustic" Lord Greville (63). The "girlhood" perspective takes us up to the moment of entering the council, and the episode is then completed through references to Greville's work. The transition from body natural to body politic is reflected by this shift in the informing source of Strachey's account, from ingenuous autobiography to the reminiscence of a knowing subject. In addition, a significant change in the text's temporal orientation is represented. Up to this point, the narrative has been suspensefully projected toward the future, to what Victoria will become. Strachey's text has exercised a careful supervision over its princess, almost matching that solicitude maintained by her mother, the Duchess of Kent—"An extraordinary watchfulness surrounded every step: up to the day of her accession, she never went downstairs without someone beside her holding her hand" (46–47). The entrance to the saloon, in itself a seemingly simple, everyday step, ends this process of becoming, definitively characterizing Victoria as a historical personage and a cultural symbol. While her reign is to continue for over six decades, with vicissitudes of popularity, personal happiness, and political power, from this point on she will always be acting within "the history of Queen Victoria" (203), a participant in a sociopolitical system that, though named after her, commands her cultural value.[8] In assuming this symbolic place, she is circumscribed by a historical and political ethos.

Through these ideological and symbolic effects, Victoria's accession reveals changing constructions of virginal selfhood that come into play as she passes from one identity to another. At first it would appear that youthfulness and gender make her particularly susceptible to cultural determination, exemplified by the gaze of the patriarchal council: the virgin as sociopolitical and feminized object. It is also apparent, however, that Victoria's virginal status realizes a type of political authority which is more effective because of its surprising and unexpected intervention. Although the council members envision her status as the weaker opposite of their own familiar powers, it becomes one of the key means of imposing her sovereignty. Her virginity is not objectifiable, nor does it merely resist speculation. It commands the scene, reworking the conventions of authority through its "strangely mingled signs of innocence, of gravity, of youth, and of composure." The virginal mystery which veils Victoria translates into a charismatic social power:

> it was not only the public at large that was in ignorance of everything concerning her; the inner circles of statesmen and officials and high-born ladies were equally in the dark. When she suddenly emerged from this deep obscurity, the impression that she created was immediate and profound. Her bearing at her first Council filled the whole gathering with astonishment and admiration; the Duke of Wellington, Sir Robert Peel, even the savage Croker, even the cold and caustic Greville—all were completely carried away . . . . Among the outside public there was a great wave of enthusiasm. Sentiment and romance were coming into

> fashion; and the spectacle of the little girl-queen, innocent, modest, with fair hair and pink cheeks, driving through her capital, filled the hearts of the beholders with raptures of affectionate loyalty. (63)[9]

The accession of Victoria may serve, in Kenneth Burke's terms, as a "representative anecdote" for the workings of virginity in nineteenth-century England. In passages like the ones discussed above, Strachey represents some of the significant effects virginity could have. More importantly, the biography demonstrates the means through which virginity is related to and represented in other social practices. Generally, this factor suggests that within the singular noun *virginity* we might recognize *virginities,* the different sociosexual meanings, values, and effects that the virginal assumes as it moves and is resituated, by the virgin and by others, in different contexts.

In the first place, the portrayal of Victoria's rise and of the charismatic sway her virginity exercises has a historical reference. Allowing for the weighted interpretations that a subsequent era may produce about the preceding one, Strachey's modernist text nonetheless suggests the intensified sociosymbolic power that virginity could carry with a queen on the throne. Recalling the overdetermined imagery through which Elizabeth I was depicted and through which she ruled, where the virgin body became a key topos in the political, sexual, and discursive relations between sovereign and subjects, the accession and persona of Victoria set into play a cultural emphasis on things virginal.[10] (In subsequent years, this emphasis extended to things maternal, though as Kristeva's "Stabat Mater" underlines, these two emblems of woman are frequently reconciled: "We see in the maternal the highest conception of womanly purity," counsels one Lady Cook late in the 1890s.[11]) This symbolic fusion reverberates through the period that bears Victoria's name. Analogous to the way in which queenness itself becomes the ontological goal of Ruskin's idealized image of woman—"queens you must always be"—virginity is used to signify and reflect upon a variety of sexual, cultural, philosophical, religious, and even textual issues and traditions, which the Victorian period both inherited from previous times and reworked in relation to prevailing social, economic, and political conditions.[12]

The accession of Victoria endows virginity with an added impact in texts of nineteenth-century England, the biological concept working as recurrent sign in social discourse.[13] The council episode in Strachey's biography draws out distinct meanings of this sign, ones that were frequently represented and reconceived in other texts. In the first place, at a social and an interpersonal level, the virginal is a topos through which relations of cultural and economic power are played out. The meeting between Victoria and her council propels peers, political factions, and bishops into contests for a hold on the power and status that she embodies in the renewed sovereign order. The underlying sociosexual links between the struggle for influence, if not control, over the virginal queen are suggested in the father-daughter imagery used by Strachey to depict the relationship between Victoria and her first prime minister, Lord Melbourne: "His manner towards the young Queen mingled, with perfect facility, the watchfulness and the respect of a statesman and a courtier with the tender solicitude of a parent" (74); "She found him perfect; and perfect in her sight he remained. Her absolute and unconcealed adoration was very natural" (75). As Strachey tells it, such mutual and "natural" attractions carry a range of consequences, from changes in court behavior—"after-dinner drunkenness began to go out of fashion" (79)—to political decision-making, as seen when Victoria uses a dispute over her household attendants to keep Melbourne's Tory antagonist Peel from government (90–95). The interpersonal, oedipal relation converts to sociopolitical power.

At the same time, as noted earlier in the new queen's charismatic success, the virginal figure is not unequivocally passive. Victoria's sovereignty draws upon a social force that may be exercised by the virgin toward those around her, "she had come suddenly, in the heyday of youth, into freedom and power" (75). Such power might be conceived ideally and transcendentally (often under the guise of moral constraint), as is shown by Lady Cook: "if purity elevates man, it absolutely glorifies woman. It lifts her to majestic heights. It invests her with ethereal grace." Yet even here the contrast between an "active" purity and a "passive" innocence allows for the expression of the efficacy of virginity, in regard to both the benefits it may bring for the virginal figure, and its practical and symbolic effects upon those who would control it.[14] Freud ponders this latter reversibility at one point in his essay on taboos that surround virginity. The various constraints on woman's behavior may signify man's fearful subjection to, not his social mastery over her: "a generalized dread of woman is expressed in all these rules of avoidance. Perhaps this dread is based on the fact that woman is different from man, for ever incomprehensible and mysterious, strange and therefore apparently hostile. The man is afraid of being weakened by the woman, infected with her femininity and of then showing himself incapable."[15] This hypothesis points to the politicosexual power and awe that figures like Victoria and Elizabeth could realize amidst a male-dominated setting.

A second implication of Strachey's scene is what could be called the *temporality* of virginity. In terms of social and personal sexuality, virginity marks the point when past turns toward future. Acceding to the throne, Victoria embodies an existing pattern of chaste conduct that, having been carefully constructed by her mother and minders rather than instinctively followed by herself, becomes oriented to her impending role. The effects of her virginity are in part orchestrated through a revelation which is *timed,* in the sense both of having been scheduled and of being presently full of significance for future events. Especially in the case of a queen, this temporal significance suggests links between personal and social experience.[16] Such links are tied to a process of *defloration.*

Defloration condenses the temporality of virginity. The process is dramatized in Strachey's text not through the marriage to Albert but as Victoria enters the red saloon. This passage ends her pregnant innocence by concluding her past and projecting a now-sovereign virginity onto future events. Defloration is a temporally ambiguous process that effaces and sustains the sociosexual value of virginity; after the event, it re-marks what is lost or passed. Lady Cook's image of a tested, Miltonic purity resolves this ambiguity by sublating it into moral terms: "purity is not the untried innocence of childhood, but the sustained virtue that passes unpolluted through the temptations of maturity . . . we cannot say of a woman that she is pure until she has passed through the fire."[17] Lost innocence becomes experiential gain. In his comments on defloration, Freud charts a similar movement, but one in which the gain is not solely personal or to the virgin's benefit. He suggests that defloration leads to "a state of bondage," sexual bondage of the deflowered to another, and thus sets up the future of a relationship based on dominance. At the same time, the demand for virginity is a masculinist attempt to survey and control a woman's past. Defloration is here being conceived in terms of a climactic present or happening through which personal and sexual authority may or may not be realized. Freud suggests that one of the motives for the taboos surrounding virginity is the traditional "fear of first occurences," experienced by both virgin and would-be "deflowerer," and in this suggestion we might additionally see an anxiety that awaits the outcome of this bid for socialized dominance over the virgin.[18]

Part of the symbolic importance of the virgin body thus derives from its role as a social site where the timing, meaning, and consequences of sexual actions, desires, and power interact. Discursively, it works as a spatial and temporal trope that figures links between personal and cultural histories and destinies. As Mary Douglas has pointed out, the virgin body functions synecdochically in symbolic transfers between self and society. It can become a vehicle for communal experiences, with "the powers and dangers credited to social structure reproduced in small on the human body."[19] Control over virgin defloration becomes a symbolic enactment of control over communal integrity and purity. The body-vehicle's features may in turn influence the communal tenor, first through the rituals that are performed on or with the body and become part of social practice, and then through the understanding of the tenor that those practices afford: "The rituals enact the form of social relations and in giving these relations visible expression they enable people to know their own society. The rituals work upon the body politic through the symbolic medium of the physical body."[20] The virgin body may be specially valued because it signifies a closed social form, as in the case of early Christians attempting to distinguish themselves from surrounding groups: "The idea that virginity had a special positive value was bound to fall on good soil in a small persecuted minority group . . . these social conditions lend themselves to beliefs which symbolise the body as an imperfect container which will only be perfect if it can be made impermeable."[21] This sort of idealized impermeability underlies various Victorian representations of the virginal discussed in this collection of essays—the interpersonal rapport of lovers, in Herbert F. Tucker's study of *The Ring and the Book;* the cultural defensiveness of a colonizing empire against the colonized that Kelly Hurley traces through the fin de siècle gothic novel *The Beetle;* the wish for textual wholeness that Susan David Bernstein shows preoccupying Hardy through *Tess of the D'Urbervilles.* Once conceptualized, even as an ideal, the virgin body contributes to the imposition and reinforcement of social rules and dispositions; its symbolic value is constantly practical.

The temporal ambiguity that virginity represents is paralleled by its uncertain visual status. As Virginia Woolf notes in *Three Guineas,* in Western traditions the question of virginal visibility emerges from Paul's "famous pronouncement on the matter of veils [made in one of the letters to the Corinthians], upon which the theory of woman's chastity seems to be based."[22] Victoria's entrance into the council chamber and before the people at large recalls this equivocal visual impact. As noted above, the expectant male gaze seems to exemplify a controlling speculation that, as Luce Irigaray has mapped out, is "caught up in the dream of identity . . . the autological or homologous representations of a (masculine) 'subject'," wherein the virginal queen reinforces the phallocratic sociopolitical structure.[23] Yet in nineteenth-century England, to see the queen is, if not entirely to succumb to her authority, at least to be surprized and shifted from one's vantage point. The unveiling has unforeseen consequences. It puts an end to an otherworldly ideal of virginity by revealing an ambiguous virginal power through which observer and observed interrelate. This equivocal visibility recapitulates and exposes the Pauline tradition which would mystify the virgin's cultural functions in either an aura of transcendent innocence, when the virgin performs to prescription, or a shadow of lapsed experience, when the virgin performs to proscription.[24]

The political, temporal, and visual implications, conveyed through the impact of Victoria's virginity upon her subjects, suggest that against Freud's materializing and objectifying definition of virginity as "the state of a woman in being untouched," the virginal functions as a process that reflects and helps impose differing interests within a social system.[25] Although through the notion of taboo Freud does direct his study of virginity toward social rituals, he assumes that these rituals conform to a pattern which remains consistent from the old cultures he initially cites to recent cases from his own analytic practice. This consistency derives from the abstract definition of virginity in a priori stasis, as a natural origin, with which his paper begins. Once framed in this way, virginity assumes a universal value which is continually perceived from objective, that is, "hidden," masculinist perspectives, first as "the right to exclusive possession of a woman, which forms the essence of monogamy"; next, as taboo, to express "a generalized dread of woman"; and last, in the "lives" of Freud's patients, as a function of the castration complex: "The danger which is thus aroused through the defloration of a woman would consist in drawing her hostility down upon oneself," where the final pronoun reveals the character-fusion of "Freud," the imagined reader, and the male deflowerer.[26]

Freud's paper rests on a trans-historical male sexuality, whose sociopsychical features—monogamy, dread, and the castration complex—are taken as indices of the essential state of virginity. Hence, while virginity is defined and posited as prior to any sexual economy, it is depicted only through the features of masculinist systems that take this idea of virginity, which has been generated in their own image, as natural proof of the validity of their structure. The shift Freud makes at the end of the essay, from considering primitive cultures to considering his own, exemplifies the continuity of this process whereby virginity is constantly reinvented to suit the sexual status quo. Having referred to various patients, Freud concludes that postdefloration frigidity in women is a function of penis envy. The loss of her virginity underlies "woman's hostile bitterness against the man, which never completely disappears in the relations between the sexes, and which is clearly indicated in the strivings and in the literary productions of 'emancipated' women."[27] His comment reveals, as it would efface behind psychoanalytic truth, the sort of immediate social reference and impact that conceptions of virginity (and of psychoanalysis in general) might have.[28]

It is through the work of one such "emancipated" woman that the implications of Freud's notion of virginity are revealed in social as well as theoretical action. In note 38 of the second chapter of *Three Guineas,* Virginia Woolf both records and questions the traditional construction of the virginal by "detouring" through its cultural background and political economy, especially as they functioned in the Victorian period. The note seems to begin in the "objective" manner of Freud's paper, accepting and using the pronouncement of St. Paul to explain the traditional values of virginity. Yet this discursive logic of objective and historical exposition is gradually undermined through various double-voiced tropes (repetition, excessive modifiers, understatement, parody) which effect a switch in interpretive focus that Freud's essay defensively refuses to make. The virginal is revealed not as the preexisting subject that the Pauline—and Freudian—text seeks to elucidate but as the constructed object of a lasting and motivated cultural discourse. It is that discourse which Woolf would have us understand:

> Chastity then as defined by St. Paul is seen to be a complex conception, based upon the love of long hair; the love of subjection; the love of an audience; the love of laying down the law, and, subconsciously, upon a very strong and natural desire that the woman's mind and body shall be reserved for the use of one man and one only. Such a conception when supported by the Angels, nature, law, custom and the Church, and enforced by a sex with a strong personal interest to enforce it, and the economic means, was of undoubted power.[29]

A seemingly archetypal male desire manifests itself in a physical, intersubjective, and discursive demand for the virginal. This demand is cloaked in a reification of nature through which religious, philosophical, economic, and political myths of a patriarchal ideology are installed. Woolf intimates the interlocking and reinforcing imposition of these myths on historical and cultural consciousness; and in the personal example from Victorian England of Gertrude Bell, she shows the direct and multiple effects of the masculinist demand for virginity. The historicized ideal weighs upon the single self. Not only are obvious cultural, intellectual, and vocational constraints imposed, but the covert ideological process of constructing the body—through limits upon what can be seen, heard, and touched, upon how she may move and what postures assume, upon where she may pass and with whom, and upon whether solitude or company may be sought—such processing of selfhood is carried out in the name of virginity:

> Chastity was invoked to prevent her [Gertrude Bell] from studying medicine; from painting the nude; from reading Shakespeare;

> from playing in orchestras; from walking down Bond Street alone.[30]

The diversity of circumscribed practices suggests at once the convertibility of virginity's meanings across official social codes and the continuing attempt of the virginal figure, once marked as such and from within this pervasive network, to rework and contest the codes and limits of "virginal" behavior and identity. Virginity is revealed as a cultural motif through which numerous social myths and institutions may jointly seek to fashion a determinate personal identity: "Not only was the social stigma strongly exerted on behalf of chastity, but the Bastardy Act did its utmost to impose chastity by financial pressure."[31] And while set up to be a subjected body, the virginal also affords a social identity under the guise of which apparently fixed social myths and institutions may be questioned, revised, or even evaded. The veil works both ways.

III

In studying nineteenth-century literary representations of the virginal, the essays in this collection employ a range of contemporary critical practices. The ideal of virginity is analyzed and unraveled in various, often interlinking, ways—in psychoanalytic terms as the impossible origin and goal of desire, in poststructuralist terms as the foreclosure of discursive reference, and in feminist terms as a paradoxical absence that subverts finality of patriarchal identity and discourse. Through focusing on writers from throughout the century, shifts in cultural estimations and textual uses of the virginal are also traced. The virginal is not a singular, unified concept through the Victorian period. The way it changes can be partially related to a broader social and historical backdrop, as dominant Victorian culture moves from celebratory heights in the 1850s and 1860s to various forms of cultural interrogation by the 1890s. This pattern of change is then reflected in shifting paradigms of representation, as the virginal moves from signifying creative transcendence to becoming a site of personal, social, and textual cancellation.

By marking the discontinuities in Victorian culture's mythmaking, the virginal acts as an index to a "genealogy" which, as Foucault suggests, would be "situated within the articulation of the body and history." In this light, the discourse of the Victorian virgin represents a significant historical corpus, a "body [that] is the inscribed surface of events (traced by language and dissolved by ideas)." Like Foucauldian genealogy, these essays would "expose a body totally imprinted by history," but in addition, they examine attitudes and beliefs that are molded to and through the changing possibilities suggested by the virginal.[32] The virgin body is both culturally produced and textually generative.

This collection is divided into three parts which are chronologically based as early, middle, and late Victorian. This periodization is not rigid or absolute. Its first aim is to underline the intertextuality of a virginal figure that relates to a widening range of cultural issues and texts through the period. Secondly and more importantly, the distinctions are set up to show the absence of a purely linear development of social thought and literary practice: there is no resolution to issues which circulate around and are represented by the virginal, no final meaning which it can be taken to have. In different contexts and for different texts, the virgin means different things. The essays in the first section, *Virginal Texts,* deal with the ways in which some nineteenth-century works use the virginal to rework and interrogate generic patterns and values in eighteenth-century and Romantic texts. If the essays in the middle section, *Virgin Poeisis,* show mid-Victorian writers capitalizing on these generic shifts in order to fashion romantic, creative, and spiritual mythologies through the virginal figure, then the papers in the final section, *Virgin de Siècle,* discuss the contradictory limits of these myths, by considering the social, sexual, and discursive investments that produce such virgin ideals and texts.

The relationships among the three sections are, then, interactive rather than discretely contrastive (or, to echo Thaïs E. Morgan's recent formulation, dialogic as well as chronological[33]). Taken together, these essays examine the ways that texts from different times and settings through the Victorian period react to and contest cultural values signified by the virginal. The essays in each section consider a "history of morals, ideals, and metaphysical concepts . . . as they stand for the emergence of different interpretations" of the virginal.[34] Through the collection, two main critical moves are made in order to review these differences: to examine the contrasts between different Victorian interpretations of the virgin body, and to trace the relationships these interpretations have with previous discourses of virginity. The essays discuss the intertextual processes through which works as varied as the paintings of the Pre-Raphaelites, the odes of Patmore, or the gothic narratives of Mary Shelley, Bram Stoker, and Richard Marsh cite and revise conventions of virginal representation. The diversity of these nineteenth-century texts reveals that the concept of the virginal is used to review and represent changing historical and generic positions in relation to various traditions of cultural, sexual, and literary discourse.

In the opening essay, "Virginal Sex, Vaginal Text: The 'Folds' of *Frankenstein*," Gerhard Joseph explores a primal narrative scene for nineteenth-century discourse on the virginal. Beginning with Victor Frankenstein's disturbing dream of his bride-to-be Elizabeth, Joseph traces Victor's recurrently ambivalent efforts to keep both himself and this "more than sister," mother-substitute virginal. Victor does so through a process of displacement, burying objects in the folds of women's dresses, which themselves etymologically figure the "woven" text. These thematic folds and displacements supplement the text's series of structural foldings or invaginations, the story's compounding tales-within-tales. Joseph suggests that rather than presenting presocial ideals of asexuality or instinctual sexuality, Shelley's staging of Victor's dream recounts the deferral of desire through the incest taboo. The ambivalent loss and sustainment of, plus the attraction to and revulsion from the virginal, are revealed within the deep structure of Shelley's narrative.

L. J. Swingle examines a network of references and allusions that extends from eighteenth- to nineteenth-century British texts, wherein virginal characters are also used to problematize responses to narrative forms. His essay "The Reader and the Virgin: What Next?" outlines two patterns of reader manipulation that run through this network and intersect in Tennyson's *The Idylls of the King*. The one pattern, dependent upon traditional notions of value (and so itself traditional, whatever its nineteenth-century metamorphoses), plays upon the thrills and chills range of moral, psychological, and sexual responses which the witnessing of the virgin's trials can generate in the reader who thinks in conventional ways. The other pattern, which Swingle suggests is an emerging nineteenth-century countermovement to the former, reflects preoccupation with the question "What next?" How can the narrative be resolved? This question puts in danger ideas of value and threatens the very notion of the virginal both in the text and in the reader. It unveils a conceptual threat to cultural and textual values that is more devastating than any immediate phallic pressures exerted by mere sexual seducers against individual virginal figures.

Joseph's and Swingle's essays also note the reader's voyeuristic involvement in deflowering the virgin body. Such involvement seems to exemplify Peter Brooks's account of narratives that "both tell of desire—typically present some story of desire—and arouse and make sense of desire as dynamic of signification."[35] From early in the nineteenth century, however, these representations of what Swingle calls the "Virgin's Tale" also unsettle and displace the conventions of literary and social desire that Brooks points to, by forestalling their neat resolution. Diane Elam's paper, "White Narratology: Gender and Reference in Wilkie Collins's *The Woman in White*" questions the notion of cultural closure through considering the contradictions of narrative structure and reference that the virginal may represent. Collins's novel is read as an interrogation of mimetic narrative. Rather than taking the woman in white as the quintessential Victorian figure of woman as innocent virgin, Elam considers the ways in which the woman in white poses a problem for the referential premise of the realist novel. First of all, the title figure genders the problem of referentiality and truth, but not simply in the sense that the body of the woman in white functions univocally as a blank page, as virginal space, to be inscribed by the pen of an authorial and authorizing male. Instead Elam suggests that the woman in white inscribes the figure of reference itself, uncannily haunting the mimetic claims of the realist novel and upsetting its vision of presenting truth. As a result, we find that the essentialist image of woman in virginal whiteness paradoxically reveals her as a gap or absence in representation. Her virginal sexuality and textuality thus pose a fundamental riddle for any ideal of discursive presence: to what might *woman* refer?

As the four essays in the second section of the volume, *Virgin Poeisis,* examine, in the mid-Victorian period a number of writers use the above types of discontinuity, signified by virginal repetition, suspension, and absence, to create their own myths of personal and poetic presence. Revisionary notions of defloration and temporality take on a constructive textual function. In "Representation and Repristination: Virginity in *The Ring and the Book,*" Herbert F. Tucker traces this movement from absence to affirmation in Browning's epic. Noting that virginity is hard to discuss because it belongs among the idealizations of natural origins that a culture posits to compensate for its belatedness, Tucker asks whether this difficulty is as much an effect of an ideal construction of discourse as it is of virginity itself. In *The Ring and the Book,* which begins with and repeatedly turns on virginal tropes, it is Browning's purpose to expose this doubled idealization, to challenge unthinking socialization, and to restore, in the fallen present, a quantum of culturally originative power. The poet's notorious ring-figure from Book 1 centers attention on his larger subject, the verbal and imaginative processes that generate meaning to begin with. Then, at the heart of the poem in Books 6 and 7, the reciprocal repristination of Caponsacchi and Pompilia as freely loving souls proceeds from a shared mythology of a belated virginity, which they invent—discover and create—within the inimical cultural ambience that the poem represents. This heroic, mutual rescue figures the poet's historicist stance vis-à-vis the text's problematically original sources and the pristine epic tradition that his work renovates for modernity.

In Browning's account, virginity becomes a shared experience of self-fashioning that involves self and other, rather than being an individual state. This concept of the virginal as interpersonal process may be represented by other mid-Victorian poets in terms of a mixture of rivalry and mutuality. Dolores DeLuise and Michael Timko's paper, "Becoming the Poet," traces such a mixture through the verse of Elizabeth Barrett Browning, where a female voice comes to transcend a traditionally male poetic persona used in the earlier poems. Although in her 1838 and 1844 volumes of poetry, Barrett Browning demonstrated a preoccupation with the figure of a male poet-genius, she started to endow the figure with female characteristics. After this time, she feminizes one male poet in particular, Robert Browning, who reappears as the poet-hero in *Sonnets from the Portuguese*. In the *Sonnets,* this poet-hero and the feminine speaker attain equality. When the poet-genius again appears in the work of Barrett Browning, it is as a transformed female figure, Aurora Leigh, who synthesizes the qualities of both the male poets and the female speakers who preceded her.

Barbara Garlick's "The Frozen Fountain: Christina Rossetti, The Virgin Model and Youthful Pre-Raphaelitism" examines the opposing perspectives of Rossetti and the Pre-Raphaelites on the virginal woman and the way in which this conflict fed into Rossetti's own work. The female figure played a central role in the early Pre-Raphaelite aesthetic credo, featuring in their literary journal *The Germ* and in their drawings and paintings. Garlick notes, however, that this textual figure, in contrast to the Brotherhood's professed iconoclasm, was depicted entirely in accord with prevailing beliefs and attitudes toward sexuality. Christina Rossetti's writing against the Brotherhood's dominance is evident in her interrogation both of important elements of their pictorial method and of the traditional use of women within and in relation to nature. In her poems, moreover, Rossetti indicates the possibility of retaining the inviolability of the virginal self after lived knowledge through the exercise of a poetic creativity, which increasingly celebrates a sexually charged relationship with a male godhead. Virginal absence leads to a spiritualized self-fulfillment.

A related notion of a virginal *telos* emerges in John Maynard's study, "Like a Virgin: Coventry Patmore's Still-Unknown Eros." Maynard argues that virginity, not as a form of antisexuality but as a marker of potential consummation, is Patmore's central concern in numerous poems that place religious chastity and the myth of the Virgin in relation to sexual desire, especially the odes of the too-little-known *The Unknown Eros*. Within Patmore's corpus, these poems reverse the celebration of married love and sexual fulfillment represented in the too-popular *The Angel in the House* and return the poet to the anxious issues of sexual loss, or unfulfilled desire, or satiation raised in his virtually forgotten early work. Written after his first wife's death, the sequence moves from observing sexuality in its absence (a story of love and loss by death) in the external world, to a more direct focus on virginity itself. In increasingly mythic and religious poems, the poet invokes the sexual experience now lacking in his world by creating a language of virginity as desire removed from its object. Religious subjects, such as the nuns and their dream of the love festival of the Lamb of

"Deliciae Sapientiae de Amore," become potent symbols by which the speaker expresses and hopes to realize his disappointed desire. Eventually the text itself is the locus of a new poetry of sexuality, as a sexual myth created by the celebration of a lack. Yet Maynard concludes by noting that eventually Patmore must recognize the limits as well as the force of this unleashing of desire, and the ode series ends by focusing on the human virgin as a sign of our need rather than on the fulfilled figures of Eros (God) and Psyche (the human as God's lover).

The acknowledgement of limits that Maynard discerns even in Patmore's ecstatic rendering of virginity becomes dramatically marked in the late-Victorian works considered in the volume's final section. The personal and discursive affirmations discussed in the essays of *Virgin Poeisis* give way to darkened notions of culture, sex, and textuality. A number of texts from the 1890s seem to revive the sort of questions about narrative and textual closure raised earlier in the century by works like *Frankenstein, The Idylls of the King,* and *The Woman in White.* Unlike the virginal poetics of Browning and others that could be built upon this discontinuity, for later works the impossibility of closure seems to figure a lapsed cultural mythology. These fin de siècle texts represent virginity as an ideal which involves its own loss, and thus signifies the period's sense of the incompleteness of its prolonged discourse of virginal innocence.

In "What Lily Knew: Virginity in the 1890s," Adrienne Auslander Munich focuses on the dissolution of a virginal semiotics. At the end of the nineteenth century, the lily, a traditional emblem of virginity, begins to turn into a more equivocal sign. Not only does it no longer signify absolute virginal purity, as referring to the Virgin Mary, but its gender also carries a power generally defined as "phallic." Flowery maidens, represented as knowing more than a true virginity allows, connote a challenge to binary oppositions and to a Victorian sexual economy. In such various texts as Oscar Wilde's *Salomé,* Henry James's *What Maisie Knew* and *The Turn of the Screw,* and Freud's paper on anxiety neuroses, the boundaries separating virginal innocence from carnal knowledge are challenged, though not without an anguish associated with ultimate loss. The age "knows" that the virgin center can no longer hold. Knowing virginity, lilies unflower themselves.

In further contrast to the realizable goals of virgin poeisis,

Susan David Bernstein notes a cycle of narrative repetitions that lack the sexual and spiritual *telos* of Rossetti's and Patmore's verse, by examining Thomas Hardy's efforts to reinscribe a virginal narrative, when inscription itself would seem to forestall that possibility. Bernstein's essay, "Confessing and Editing: The Politics of Purity in Hardy's *Tess,*" examines the novel's revised prefaces and plot, through which Hardy attempts to preserve the "purity" and moral rectitude of a text whose narrative recommends an essential purity of its sexually "fallen" protagonist. The author struggles to recover Tess's and the text's bodies from interpretive and substantive violations, to reinstate and protect the pure text as a corollary to a pure Tess. Yet like Tess's admission to Angel Clare, Hardy's compulsively repeated, prefatory confessions disclose that neither in the editing history of *Tess,* nor in the narrative history of Tess, does an "original," virginal body exist. Nonetheless, the image of the presexually pure body determines a demand for the virginal through Hardy's prefaces and narrative.

In his essay, "Gender and Sexual Dis-Ease in *Dracula,*" Jeffrey L. Spear studies the psychosexual undertones of this revised knowledge of the limits of virginity. Stoker's text posits a radical duality between a self-sufficient manliness that threatens to slide into dependency and a pristine womanhood whose ostensible purity, gender without sexuality, has no power to resist the vampiric possession that inverts those characteristics. *Dracula* works as a perfect projective screen for theories of unconscious motivation that can explain what the surface of the text seems to deny, particularly the sexuality of the pure woman and the nature of masculine desire. Spear contends that all the sexuality in *Dracula* can be understood as projections of forms of male fantasy that represent male desires and fears, especially fantasies of dominance, of the "omni-available woman," and of lesbian sex. Underlying these fantasies, which are depicted through the characterizations of Jonathan and Mina Harker, Lucy Westenra, and the vampires themselves, is an extreme fear of male sexual desire. Desire is treated in terms of contagion, thus associating the text with the late-century fear of syphilis, quite likely the cause of Stoker's own death. The end of the novel removes the mark of contagion from Mina's brow at the expense of her agency and turns her into a revirginalized maternal icon in order to restore conventional gender distinctions. Like Dracula and the potentially nonbinary sexuality he represents, the ideal of a virginal motherhood as a male psychic refuge from sexuality refuses to die.

The fin de siècle emphasis on the paradox of virginal knowledge questions virginity as transcendent ideal of sexual absence and cultural origin. Its temporality and chastity are complicated through simultaneous loss and sustainment. The cultural and discursive work that goes into preserving the natural ideal becomes increasingly apparent. This paradox extends to different social practices which would use the virgin body to figure their wholeness—literary discourse in the case of Hardy's *Tess,* heterosexuality in the case of *Dracula.* Kelly Hurley's reading of Richard Marsh's 1897 novel, *The Beetle,* reveals that the virginal ideal might also be used to attempt to shore up the sociosexual politics of imperialism. Marsh's narrative is saturated with perverse sexualities, particularly in its representations of a monstrously gothic and oriental female sexuality. Yet the text will not implicate itself in its own perversities, maintaining a certain virginal reticence through the strategies of euphemism, indirection, and displacement it deploys to describe this sexuality. Hurley's essay is particularly concerned with one crucial displacement that occurs within *The Beetle,* by means of its conflation of gothicized female sexuality and a gothicized Orient. Paranoiac representations of aggressive femininity slip imperceptibly into paranoiac representations of the aggressive Easterner, so that anxiety about female sexuality becomes covered up by anxieties about racial conflict and the sexual vulnerability of the white Anglo body. Marsh's text represents an extreme effort at cultural defense through virginal myth.

Hurley's paper discloses a process where representations of virginal impermeability can suggest the sexual undercurrents of a sociopolitical phenomenon like Victorian imperialism. In addition, Marsh's gothic narrative becomes a final example of a generic opposition between depictions of the virginal that is drawn through these essays. Narrative representations tend to problematize the virginal by revealing its presuppositions of cultural and literary closure and their conflictual effects. In contrast, poetic accounts, though not naive about an unequivocal virginal ideal, nonetheless move toward disclosing the affirming powers of a virginal origin and supplement to sociosexual discourse. As we have seen, these generic contrasts are also related to shifting sociohistorical outlooks, from early- to late-Victorian values concerning the possibilities of cultural integrity and progress.

In both narrative and poetic texts of the Victorian period, the virgin works as a figure able to cite orthodox ideals from different historical and cultural traditions and so become a starting point for reworkings and revaluations of the notions involved. As the essays in this volume show, the virgin body plays an ambiguous role in Victorian literature. The apparent certainty of its sexual absence triggers discursive strategies that seek to comprehend and depict both this absence and the social and sexual presence which frames it. The figure of the virgin is one of the central literary tropes through which complex relations in the Victorian discourse on sexuality can be articulated. The virginal operates in terms of textuality and sexuality, revealing the generative interactions between these cultural fields.

CHAPTER 2

Virginal Sex, Vaginal Text: The "Folds" of Frankenstein

Gerhard Joseph

In an earlier treatment of *Frankenstein,* I argued that, given the rich eclecticism of its family structures, Mary Shelley's novel might well be read as a child's myth, as the adult lover/scientist's destructive working out of repressed infantile fantasies.[1] As the title of that essay, "Frankenstein's Dream: The Child as Father of the Monster" suggests, the synecdochal moment I took as the key to the whole was the creator's nightmare in his troubled sleep immediately after the forging of his monster, a nightmare filled with multidirectional loathing.

Let me return to that dream as I try first to recapitulate and then to extend the earlier argument. "I thought," says the nauseated Victor Frankenstein,

> I saw Elizabeth [Frankenstein's life-long companion and bride-to-be], in the bloom of health, walking in the streets of Ingolstadt. Delighted and surprised, I embraced her; but as I imprinted the first kiss on her lips, they became livid with the hue of death; her features appeared to change, and I thought I held the corpse of my dead mother in my arms; a shroud enveloped her form, and I saw the grave-worms crawling in the *folds* of the flannel.[2]

The barely disguised Oedipal implications of such a fantasy led to my earlier reading based upon dream theory of a rather classical psychoanalytic sort, since the dominant impression one gets from the completed tale is one of oneiric fragmentation, precisely the "displacement" and "condensation" Freud set up in *The Interpretation of Dreams* and elsewhere as the basic mechanisms of dreaming. What I should now like to add is Lacan's linguistic turn, his notion that interpretation is a matter of "writing rather than of mime," a perspective that seems more relevant than Freud's at the present theoretical moment.[3] For the Lacan to whom the unconscious is structured like a language, Freud's displacement expresses itself *syntactically*—that is, as metonymic juxtaposition. In contrast, condensation expresses itself *semantically*—that is, as metaphoric equivalence.[4] I will exemplify that distinction (indebted to Roman Jakobson's metonomy/metaphor division in his groundbreaking discussion of aphasia) in Victor's dream after an exploration of his tale's wider grammar of desire. For Victor Frankenstein's nightmare is what Lacan would call a linguistic "symptom" of the larger pathological structure in which that nightmare is embedded.

With respect to characterization, the pathology of that structure takes the form of a splitting of personality. The most obvious of such divisions in a novel filled with doubles is of course Frankenstein and his monster, two of the many doppelgangers of nineteenth-century literature, as several readers have pointed out.[5] What the dream intimates on some level of consciousness is the certainty that Frankenstein associates the disgust for his creation with a revulsion he feels toward what can happen to the bodies of both his beloved and his mother, doubles of one another in gendered counterpoint to Frankenstein and *his* double. If Frankenstein's nightmare may thus be taken as a clue, one suspects that the psychic mechanism which forced the splitting of the monster off from the primary self is in some obscure way stimulated by feelings of guilt associated in Frankenstein's mind with his mother and with his beloved Elizabeth, the mother's extension—as the nightmare makes clear—in a second generation.

To associate the words *revulsion* and *guilt* with Frankenstein's feelings for his mother and fiancée seems, on the face of it, absurd when one examines the aura of domestic bliss in which the text envelops the family of Victor Frankenstein. The marriage of his parents is marked by selfless generosity on both sides. Quite a bit older than his wife, the elder Frankenstein had married Caroline Beaufort, the daughter of his best friend, at the latter's death, in a determination to become her "protecting spirit." The language in which the union is couched intimates the "amiableness of domestic affection" that the novel pits against Victor's icy and alienating scientific experiment: husband and wife yoked in "bonds of devoted affection"; his feelings are those of "gratitude and worship," of "reverence for her virtues." Children do come to this most spiritual and benevolent of unions, and their eldest, Victor, becomes for his parents "their plaything and their idol," an innocent bestowed upon them by heaven to be reared according to the principles of "patience, of charity, and of self-control" by which they regulate their own lives (33–34).

Caroline Frankenstein is, in short, one of the earliest of the Angels in the House, the staple of a Victorian woman-worship to come. In her, if we need such proof, we can see how much the emerging Victorian ideal owes to late-eighteenth-century notions of domestic benevolence. One of the acts of generosity by this "guardian angel of the afflicted" is to bring into the family the creature who becomes her mirror image and eventual replacement. Elizabeth Lavenza, a child whom Caroline and her son discover one day during their periodic visits to the poor, is the angelic projection of the mother: her hair is "the brightest of living gold," her face completely "expressive of sensibility and sweetness." When Caroline adopts this "being heaven-sent, and bearing a celestial stamp," as the daughter she has always wanted, she conceives of Elizabeth as a gift for her adored son. "I have a pretty present for my Victor—tomorrow he shall have it," she tells him on the eve before Elizabeth's arrival. When the promised gift does indeed appear the following day, Victor cannot but take his mother's words literally: he thinks of Elizabeth thereafter as a "possession" to be protected and cherished. The "almost reverential attachment" he forms toward "the beautiful and adored companion of all [his] occupations and pleasures" takes the guise of a continuing worship of his "more than sister" (35–36).

Victor's adoration, split as it were between mother and "more than sister," is intensified and frozen into its lifelong cast shortly thereafter by the death of the mother, which is in its oblique way caused by the *quasi*-sister. Elizabeth catches scarlet fever and, although the entire family tries to dissuade her, Caroline insists upon attending the sickbed. Though Elizabeth recovers, the mother catches the fever and dies. Just before her death, however, she joins the hands of Elizabeth and Victor and urges upon them a future union, insisting furthermore that Elizabeth literally replace her as maternal comforter within the family: "Elizabeth, my love, you must supply my place to my younger children" (43).

Such a concentration upon the incestuous skein of the opening chapters reveals one of the completed work's latent subjects: the price in the form of psychic fragmentation to be paid for the high-minded search for purity, goodness, or scientific truth that seeks to leave bodily limitation behind. The determinedly spiritual connections among husband and wife, mother and son, lover and beloved, indicate a passion for a purity so fine that it intimates the perfection of the human race's prelapsarian infancy. A gnostic attempt to transcend the corruptions of the body is of course an ancient and persistent Western impulse, but *Frankenstein* gives it a characteristically nineteenth-century form, what Norman Holland has called "a dominant—perhaps *the* dominant—mode in Victorian fantasy": the wish to see parents, and by extension one's beloved, as a child would wish to see them, as virginal or nonsexual creatures.[6] One has only to recall the many lovers in the century's fiction and poetry who think of each other as cousins or even brother and sister to sense the truth of Holland's assertion. The all-but-incestuous implications of such unions will tend to encourage excessively spiritual alliances which skirt the taboo of sexual contact between consanguineous partners.

That Mary Shelley was at least partially conscious of the consanguineity of her lovers *as* a problem is indicated by a significant change in kinship that she made between the two versions of the novel. In the 1818 manuscript, Elizabeth is Victor's cousin, the daughter of his father's "tenderly loved" dead sister, whom Caroline, desiring "to bind as closely as possible the ties of domestic love," selects as Victor's future bride. It is only in the 1831 version that Elizabeth is distanced into a foundling that Caroline adopts, though Victor still habitually refers to her as his "cousin."[7] And to round the matter out, Ellen Moers has noted how "excessively fond" Robert Walton, Victor Frankenstein's primary foil, seems to be of *his* sister in the letters that frame Victor's narrative.[8]

But the passion for an Edenic purity puts an unbearable strain upon the human psyche. The consequence is a monstrous dualism in which the aspirant toward perfection breaks up into warring elements, joined to one another none knows how. On the one hand, we see the gross body whose tainted corporeality magnifies itself toward grotesque proportions in the form of the monster; on the other, a soul which strains heavenward in its drive to elude corporeal corruption, that is, the scientific passion to unlock the secrets of the universe which drives Victor Frankenstein away from the domestic hearth of home, family, and sexual union with his beloved Elizabeth.

For Frankenstein's unwillingness to subdue the sexual other through the senses is the veiled impulse behind his feverish experimentation, a flight from the senses into a redoubt of spiritualized benevolence on the one hand and the abstractions of science on the other. Because Frankenstein had been given the "possession" by an angelic mother of her angelic double, he can allow himself to conceive of Elizabeth in only the most virginal or "sisterly" of terms and to seek instead the scientific penetration of a feminized nature as a substitute for the veiled incest.

In confirmation of the foregoing pattern, let me now return to the dream sequence with which I began, applying to it Lacan's linguistic transformation of Freud by which displacement stages itself syntactically as metonymy and condensation semantically as metaphor. For the phallic threat that Victor dreams to the virginity of his mother is metonymically displaced upon the contiguous more-than-sister Elizabeth—or is it vice versa? And in the "folds" of the mother's flannel through which the worms crawl in the dream (folds that both refer to and veil the underlying maternal folds which the son both wishes to see and to avoid in a primal scopic scene marked by the father's absence), we can read Freud's condensation that for Lacan takes the semantic guise of metaphor. The dream sequence thus seems to be a version of and to represent a Kleinian, maternalized reading of the displacement pattern in the *History of the Inconstant Lover.* This story is one of the ghost stories translated from the German into French that Mary Shelley identifies in her Author's Introduction of 1831 as the stimulus to the narrative competition among Shelley, Byron, Dr. Polidori, and herself, a competition that produced *Frankenstein:* "There was the History of the Inconstant Lover, who, when he thought to clasp the bride to whom he had pledged his vows, found himself in the arms of the pale ghost of her whom he had deserted" (7). Missing from such a description is the specifically visual revulsion of the *Frankenstein* dream, a scopophobia Mary Shelley would have met in and may well have absorbed from Polidori's projected tale of female voyeurism chastized, as described in her Introduction: "Poor Polidori had some terrible idea about a skull-headed lady who was so punished for peeping through a key-hole—*what to see I forget: something very shocking and wrong of course* (7; emphasis added). It may just be that the shocking something that Shelley "forgot" in Polidori's story she dimly remembered and transformed into a punishment for the forbidden *male* gaze in her own.

The troped folds of the dream appear a second time in the novel to reinforce their significance. When the monster kills Frankenstein's younger brother, William, he buries a locket with a miniature of the mother that William had borrowed from Elizabeth within the "folds" of the dress of the servant girl Justine (144), still another protegée and double of the mother. That semantic echo of "folds," I would suggest, weaves together Justine's outer garment with the mother's flannel shroud through which the phallic graveworms had earlier crawled. In the monster's ambiguous act that thus replicates Victor's earlier dream, we can see Frankenstein in the guise of his double shrinking from the spectre of female mystery, attacking in the abstract what the male imagination has mythologized as woman's "folded" lack, her notorious "castration": the crime, the original sin of human fleshliness, "had its source in her," in woman, as the monster so monstrously puts it (145).[9]

And that "source" recedes ever backward in an apparently bottomless *mise en abyme,* the Freudian lack-as-woman that the contemporary androcritical imagination, in Elaine Showalter's phrase, stages as Derridean "trace" or Lacanian *objet petit a,* "a book in the book, an origin in the origin, a center in the center," beyond the inmost bound of readerly desire.[10] The verbal "folds" of the mother and of Justine have their extension in and are the semantic correlative of what one might call the tale's larger vaginalized narrative structure—and I so label it at the risk of echoing Morris Zapp's hilarious lecture on "invagination" in David Lodge's *Small World.* For the deeply nested center, the ultimate "source" of meaning, seems ever to recede before the reader as he (or should I say merely "I"?) gazes ever inward, following Mary

Shelley's introduction concerning the ghost-story competition, as it enfolds Walton's letters to his sister, as they enfold Frankenstein's narrative, as it enfolds the monster's narrative, as it enfolds the tale of Safie and her father . . . . Such Chinese-box scopic regressivity serves to implicate the reader, whom I would of course gender male or androcentric, and seems ever to "draw us on," as Goethe mystifies the eternal feminine of heterosexual male desire. (What a gynocentric reader would do with such "folded" regressivity I hesitate to say, though I should think that Ellen Moers's biographical reading of the novel based upon Mary Shelley's "guilt, dread, and flight" surrounding the issue of childbirth provides the best clue.[11])

In calling the novel's structure a *mise en abyme,* and a "vaginal" one at that, *I* momentarily enter into Frankenstein's own dream, provisionally echoing what I take to be his mystification of the feminine lack covered over by a "folded" textuality (from *texere,* "to weave"), what Hélène Cixoux's Medusa laughs to scorn as man's "fawn[ing] around the supreme hold."[12] Such an androcentric gaze upon woman's "folds" feminist theory has indicted in its classical form: Freud's notorious but influential concept of woman's "genital deficiency" covered over by the "weaving" of pubic hair.[13] Mieke Bal has thus defined the endless regressive potential of the *mise en abyme* as a version of the "Lethal Woman" in the Old Testament, for, in demystifying the male feminization of the "trace" in Derridean and the *objet petit a* in Lacanian theory, Bal insists that the *mise en abyme* is never really endless. In that revisionist context, I would certainly now admit that the layering in *Frankenstein* is hardly without end, rippling only through the five distinct structural folds I have itemized above. The feminized *mise en abyme,* as Bal thus says, always *interrupts* the linearity and chronology of the text. We should therefore see it, this "bottomless" fold of textuality frequently troped as woman, as "a general mode of reading" for specific ideological, frequently patriarchal ends.[14]

My commentary has thus aspired to be, first, a self-reflexive and, then, a self-critical instance of such a general mode: the embarrassed readerly gaze at the maternal fold and its displacements that dares express itself only in the coded guise of Victor and the reader's monstrous dream. And I mean "monstrous" in the root sense of that which is looked at or "demonstrated," as a final twist in the novel's dream sequence suggests. For Victor is woken from his dream by the monster who, entering his room and holding up the bed curtain, fixes his eyes on his creator. Thus, to end parabolically, he who has created or "seen" the other as monstrous is, in the ultimate metonymic displacement of this our dream of life, seen as monstrous by it.

CHAPTER 3

The Reader and the Virgin: What Next?

L. J. Swingle

This essay is about some factors in the relationship between reader and text in nineteenth-century British literature. My point of departure, to which point I will return later in order to move off again in a differing direction, is the following passage from Tennyson's *The Idylls of the King:*

> the King
> That morn was married, while in stainless white,
> The fair beginners of a nobler time,
> And glorying in their vows and him, his knights
> Stood round him, and rejoicing in his joy.
> Far shone the fields of May thro' open door,
> The sacred altar blossom'd white with May
> The Sun of May descended on their King.
> ("The Coming of Arthur," 454–61)

I

The particular detail in this passage from Tennyson that I wish to begin with is the phrase, "while in stainless white." This phrase points to a tradition of reader manipulation that Tennyson has chosen to employ in his epic poem. The tradition is what we might call the Virgin's Tale.

What enticement can a writer offer to whet a reader's interest in the literary work being composed? What might persuade a reader to start reading, and then, hopefully, keep on reading to the sweet or bitter end? One such enticement is the Virgin's Tale. It is an enticement with which we are fully familiar in our own time. In one of its cruder forms, it flaunts its snow-white body for us today in bulky supermarket paperbacks, offering the hungry shopper—female as well as male, it looks like—the ultra-soft-core delights of encountering in extended detail the Perils of Pauline, now frequently called Fawn or Amber or Tiffany. The appeal is that of following at close distance the travails of the virgin and witnessing eventually either the preservation of purity or its desecration. Will the virgin "in stainless white"—usually a female, but occasionally a male—escape irreparable staining? It is an old story. Think of Spenser's Red-Cross Knight, pricking doubtfully across the plain.

Why is this subject appealing? It might be argued, invoking the ghost of Shaftesbury, that the appeal is basically to our readerly compassion. We yearn to watch innocence triumph over the dark forces of desecration; and then (yet?) we feel some sort of satisfying, cathartic burst of pity and fear if bloody desecration finally wins out over stainless purity. Alternately, invoking popular recent notions about the sexual twitch at the heart's core, we might suppose the appeal is more that of having our sensual cake without getting fat. We can get our thrills on the blueberry hills of unacceptable sexual fruition vicariously by reading about it. Actually, this very experience of reading itself, so some critics would slyly say, is connected to a vague or maybe profound sexual impulse. One might think, for example, of the language conventionally pounded into the heads of small schoolchildren—how the dynamics of plot development is concerned with things called rising action, climax, falling action. Diagram that, the teacher says.

In any case, whether it be that we yearn to witness the virgin saved or the virgin ravished (or maybe some of us yearn for one thing, some of us for the other, and some of us don't know and wouldn't like to know what we are yearning for), invocation of the tribulations of the virgin has a long literary tradition. A classic case, if we look back a century from Tennyson whetting our appetites with the "stainless white" of his *Idylls,* is Samuel Richardson's *Clarissa.* Terry Eagleton has discussed the intense sexual tension of this work, and his discussion turns, significantly, upon the acts of writing and reading: "Richardson sees well enough that sexuality is mainly a matter of discourse: the sexual power struggle between Clarissa and Lovelace is a primarily rhetorical affair, a matter of strategic textual moves, the gaining of a momentary linguistic advantage, the reluctant concession of a meaning."[1] Everybody in *Clarissa* is busily reading, first, their own and others' experience in the physical world, and then, each other's letters about that experience. We, peering in from outside the novel, read over shoulders; and thereby we obtain the voyeuristic delights of being teased gradually toward the novel's climax without needing to get ourselves physically soiled along with the sweating soldiers in the trenches.

This sort of literary manipulation, which lets the reader sing, as Robert Herrick might not say, in cleanly wantonness, becomes immensely popular, and somewhat vulgarized, in the later eighteenth-century craze for gothic fiction.[2] But then it begins to be employed in subtly interesting ways in literature of the Romantic period.

In *The Eve of St. Agnes* John Keats writes of how "in youth" the brain may become stuffed "with triumphs gay / Of old romance." But he invokes those triumphs of old romance only in order to direct our attention away from them: "These let us wish away, / And turn, sole-thoughted, to one Lady there, / Whose heart had brooded, all that wintry day, / On love, and wing'd St. Agnes' saintly care" (40–44). This "one Lady," as the reference to the saintly care of Agnes emphatically underscores, is a version of the virgin, a tender lamb bounding about on the margins of the wolfish wilds.

Keats is going to give us a new romance for modern times. It is interesting that this new romance is set off against the gay, spring-like romantic triumphs that entertain the stuffy brains of youth. Straightforward youth, one might say, has a propensity for Making It, yearning to do it, like the Beatles song says, in the road. But Keats's tale of Madeline will be a winter's tale: "St. Agnes' Eve—Ah, bitter chill it was!" (1). Its appeal will be to the more contemplative sexual appetites of the aging, experienced sensibility. Thus, as our minds are wishfully directed, "sole-thoughted," to Madeline, Keats's poem makes us think most especially about watching her, not interacting with her. Positioning us at a distance, with Porphyro, the text offers the pleasure of spying upon Madeline: "her vespers done, / Of all its wreathed pearls her hair she frees; /

Unclasps her warmed jewels one by one; / Loosens her fragrant boddice" (226–29). Ours is neither the virgin's nor the joyously participatory perspective here. We are, instead, with Porphyro, voyeurs peering in upon Madeline's "soft and chilly nest" (235).[3]

It seems likely that Keats's game plan here, in connecting us with Porphyro, is to make us look, by way of our vicarious reader's experience with Madeline, into the deep core of our own souls (hence that earlier pun "sole-thoughted"). Readers have differed enthusiastically over whether *The Eve of St. Agnes* is about Porphyro's ravishing of Madeline or about his saving of her.[4] What needs notice is that Keats's manner of writing his poem insures that this issue be raised but that it be left uncertain. Keats provides us with contradictory or ambiguous evidences about Porphyro. This maneuver serves to create something like a vacuum, an open space, concerning Porphyro's yearnings and motivations; and our own souls move in to fill that space. When *we* watch Madeline—"In sort of wakeful swoon, perplex'd she lay" (236)—what sort of thoughts are really going on in the hidden recesses of our souls? We find out by reflecting upon the implications of the way we finally read Porphyro, our stand-in within the poem.

Some of this teasing ambiguity of possible response (though now the teasing takes a much more delicate, or perhaps esoteric, form) is also being cultivated in the seemingly chaste world of Jane Austen's variations on the Virgin's Tale. Consider, most particularly, *Emma*. Readers of the Shaftesburyian, benevolent-compassion school of response would likely be inclined to endorse the famous, cheerful proposition that "The subject of *Emma* is marriage."[5] Virgin-Emma evades a series of traps in the course of the novel and emerges unstained, triumphantly married to her one true knight, Mr. Knightley.

Emma's wedding, however, has "very little white satin" to it, according to Mrs. Elton (vol. 3, chap. 19). The most obvious way to read this detail, to be sure, is as a parting snub, whereby Austen pushes Mrs. Elton with her petty jealousy and crude taste forever out of the high society that gathers around Emma and Mr. Knightley's perfect union. However, calling to mind the powerful traditional associations of the whiteness motif (as with Tennyson's "while in stainless white"), we might sense the vibrations of a more complex maneuver in the move.

Jane Austen was reported to have remarked of Emma that she is a "heroine whom no one but myself will much like."[6] A favored occupation of an earlier generation of critics was to explain why this turns out to be untrue. We *do* like Emma, so the conventional argument goes. Despite her self-love and associated faults, as Lionel Trilling once argued, "Inevitably we are drawn to Emma."[7] But, positing that "drawn to" is, in some sense or other, a term that accurately describes our reaction to Emma, what exactly is that sense? and is it necessarily the same sense for all of us? Trilling's "we" covers a lot of population and looks a little like one of those truths universally acknowledged that Austen elsewhere mocks. The Porphyro or Lovelace in us, or in some of us—if, St. Agnes forbid, such creatures exist in our lower depths—may be drawn to Emma and her tale in a rather different way from that which critics like Trilling have (publicly) in mind.

There is, let us say, a possibly muted sexual undercurrent to Trilling's "drawn to Emma," which reflects something going on in the subtle dynamics of Austen's treatment of the Virgin Tale in *Emma*. Emma is introduced to us, in the famous opening sentence of the novel, as "handsome, clever, and rich, with a comfortable home and happy disposition." The introduction is aggressive: this virgin is not presented to us—à la, say, Keats's Madeline—as a tender little lamb. This is, rather, a version of the happy vestal, untouchable, perched comfortably on a pedestal. What, then, is going on here? This introduction to Emma is the teaser to the text, the speech that accompanies the opening of the novel's curtain and aims to glue us to our seats for the dramatic duration. What relationship does it set up between Emma and our reading selves?

It may be, presumably, that we are attracted to the vision of transcendence that Emma projects; and our yearning is to see this elevation preserved. But it may be, alternately, that we are attracted by a somewhat more exotic sensual delight: that we anticipate the possibility of becoming witness to Emma's fall and degradation. Or, perhaps, it may be both. Whatever be the case, it is quite clear that Austen's version of the Virgin's Tale aims to entice us with prospects of dangerous staining of the virgin's whiteness, just as in conventional melodrama. Early in the action, Austen gives us a nudge by way of a remark from Mr. Knightley: "There is an anxiety, a curiosity in what one feels for Emma. I wonder what will become of her!" (vol. 1, chap. 5). One notes here, by the way, how "anxiety," which suggests warmly solicitous concern for Emma's welfare, immediately metamorphoses into the considerably more distant term "curiosity."

Austen's novel does not reward this anticipation it sets up by offering the grossly fleshy threat (or pleasure) that is provided for us in Richardson's *Clarissa* or Keats's *Eve of St. Agnes*. Emma's ravishment takes the more delicate form of a psychic humiliation. The key moment occurs during the Box Hill excursion, when Mr. Knightley (he, appropriately, of the "curiosity") denounces Emma for her behavior to Miss Bates: "How could you be so insolent . . . Emma, I had not thought it possible." Emma's initial response, simply to blush and attempt "to laugh it off," fails to protect her. Mr. Knightley pursues his attack ("This is not pleasant to you, Emma—and it is very far from pleasant to me; but I must, I will") until, at the chapter's end, we see Emma brought symbolically to her knees: "Never had she felt so agitated, mortified . . . Emma felt the tears running down her cheeks almost all the way home, without being at any trouble to check them, extraordinary as they were" (vol. 3, chap. 7).

If this scene is "not pleasant to you, Emma" and if (is this questionable?) it is "very far from pleasant" to Mr. Knightley, does it offer, nevertheless, some sort of pleasure for us readers? One readily imagines some post-Freudian theorist of reading, caught up in the enthusiasm of the passionate moment, insisting that this Box Hill incident, a dramatic high point of the novel, produces a considerable vicarious pleasure for us readers. Our reading of the novel has succeeded in letting us spy out (at a gracefully safe textual distance) this hidden, soft center of Emma's life. We have watched Emma playfully flaunt her powers and desirability before us; but now here at Box Hill (one need not say more) we have seen her lose control and cry. Following this moment, as is appropriate in a classical dramatic structure wherein the rising action builds to climax, then gradually falls back toward flaccid satiation, the remaining chapters of the novel generously extend the sweet pleasures of Emma's anguish ("this was the spontaneous burst of Emma's feelings: 'Oh God! that I had never seen her!'") before letting us down gently upon the conventional ground of bourgeois pleasure with the marriage theme that Kettle takes to be the novel's primary subject.

A less strenuously sensual ideology of reading would tone down the heavy breathing in this version of our reader's concern with Emma. And yet . . . ? Unless we decide that marriage to Mr. Knightley constitutes merely the last stage in the process of Emma's degeneration, we are likely to feel that Emma has been happily saved by marriage at the novel's conclusion.[8] However, this salvation that is served up to us in the final chapter of *Emma* does get its rich seasoning from what came before it: the agitation and tears; the mortification; our witnessing of the process by which a high vestal, handsome, clever, rich, and of happy disposition, has been reduced to anguish. Austen, whose imagination gives her access to fine ingredients and whose skill lets her blend them wonderfully, has not dished up a serving of cheap sexual thrills in *Emma*. But her basic recipe is the same as that which produces the gothic romances for which she felt such whimsically contemptuous affection.

This maneuvering of the reader's complex attraction to the virgin in such widely differing literary works of the Romantic period as Austen's *Emma* and Keats's *The Eve of St. Agnes* carries over powerfully into the strategies of Victorian literature. We might think, for example, about what a Jamesean "realist" literary perspective used to consider, with irritation, a clumsy convention of Victorian novels: their obsessive tendency to cozy up the reader through direct address. Anthony Trollope begins *Can You Forgive Her?* with the sentence: "Whether or no, she, whom you are to forgive, if you can, did or did not belong to the Upper Ten Thousand of this our English world, I am not prepared to say with any strength of affirmation" (chap. 1). Literary moves like this are clearly more than a merely hack writer's tic. They fling out a web (consider the aggressive pressure exerted by Trollope's "she, whom *you* are to forgive, *if you can*") that immediately entangles the reader in moral issues that will subsequently arise from the intricacies of plot. With this in mind, we should think, further, about how much Victorian fiction focuses our attention upon some variation of the perils of Pauline. It is suggestively significant, for example, that Trollope's novel is not about whether, if we can, we are to forgive a *him*.

Victorian fiction is fond of taking us readers by the mind's lapel, coyly making clear to us that it knows we reader-voyeurs are out there and peering in. Victorian fiction is also much concerned that we readers should watch what happens especially to women, and particularly to variations of the young, virginal Romantic Emma or Madeline. Victorian fiction gives us Trollope's Lily Dale: "Lilian Dale, dear Lily Dale—for my reader must know that she is to be very dear, and that my story will be nothing to him if he do not love Lily Dale" (*The Small House at Allington,* chap. 2). It gives us Thackeray's Amelia Sedley, who could "not only sing like a lark . . . but she had such a kindly, smiling, tender, gentle, generous heart of her own, as won the love of everybody who came near her" (*Vanity Fair,* chap. 1). It gives us Dickens's Louisa Gradgrind: "She was a child now, of fifteen or sixteen; but at no distant day would seem to become a woman all at once. Her father thought so as he looked at her. She was pretty" (*Hard Times,* bk. I, chap. 3). It gives us Eliot's Dorothea Brooke: "Miss Brooke had that kind of beauty which seems to be thrown into relief by poor dress" (*Middlemarch,* bk. I, chap. 1). It gives us Isabel Archer: "The young lady seemed to have a great deal of confidence, both in herself and in others; but this abrupt generosity made her blush" (*The Portrait of a Lady,* vol. I, chap. 2).

Each of the above-quoted passages, gleaned from the ways in which their texts introduce us to these famous Victorian heroines, almost cries out to become the introduction to a critical meditation upon how the text implicates us in the experience of the young heroine's sexual education/fall. Such critical meditation would, like a Miles Davis riff, play off against the beat of the conventional getting-married pattern that provides the apparent driving force propelling Victorian novels toward their endings. Recall the famous first sentence in the concluding chapter of *Jane Eyre:* "Reader, I married him." If we are really good, if, as one might say, our powers of critical penetration are sufficiently acute, our readings of reading should produce intriguing progeny.

II

As my rhetorical fade-out in the previous paragraph will have suggested, I intend to forgo development of such readings of reading. I return, instead, to the "stainless white" passage from Tennyson's *Idylls.* In that passage Tennyson has introduced the Virgin's Tale into a structure of literary manipulation that is dramatically different from the one informing the texts we have just been discussing. I want now to offer some suggestions about the nature and implications of this difference and the significance it holds for understanding the evolution of tensions in nineteenth-century British literary thought.

> the King
> That morn was married, while in stainless white,
> The fair beginners of a nobler time,
> And glorying in their vows and him, his knights
> Stood round him, and rejoicing in his joy.
> Far shone the fields of May thro' open door,
> The sacred altar blossom'd white with May
> The Sun of May descended on their King.
> ("The Coming of Arthur," 454–61)

As this passage indicates, Tennyson's *Idylls* plays delicately upon traditional enticements concerning the sullying of the virgin. The King's marriage ceremony is attended by the circle of his knights dressed "in stainless white." On one level of reading the *Idylls,* then, it seems that we are being drawn into yet another version of the Clarissa/Emma/Madeline story. However, as noted previously, all those earlier stories pursue variations of the getting-married pattern: the individual begins in virgin isolation or purity and moves through the course of the story toward ultimate union—be that union ill, as in the rape of Clarissa, be it a (perhaps) saving and joyous grace, as in the marriage of Emma, or be it an ambiguous sexual-spiritual connection, as in Madeline's escape with or seduction by Porphyro. But Tennyson's poem begins with marriage. It asks that we associate the virgin theme with this marriage union and with the union of the table round that circles it. Then it invites us to witness the tale of the virgin's travails through a series of stories (each, significantly, slightly disconnected with the others) which traces the disintegration of union into fragments, a scattering of separate, isolated individuals. Thus a point of high symbolic significance in the concluding idyll is the spectacle of Sir Bedivere, left alone on the shore and crying out: "Ah! my Lord Arthur, whither shall I go? / Where shall I hide my forehead and my eyes?" ("The Passing of Arthur," 395–96).

Further, whereas invocation of the Virgin's Tale commonly functions to set up considerable tension, teasing the reader into anticipatory curiosity or excitement concerning whether the stainless white will become stained, Tennyson aborts the tension at the outset. Unless our willing suspension of disbelief is working overtime, we already know that the king's marriage and the table round come to ruin. And Tennyson apparently wants us to remember that we know it. In "The Coming of Arthur" he underscores this foreknowledge of ruin. Beyond that, he makes us think of it as having been inevitable. Particularly noticeable in our quotation is the way the king's marriage is emphatically positioned in a time frame: it is "morn" and, repeatedly, it is "May." The thrust of the maneuver is to make us think about these human beings with their "vows" and their blossoming "sacred altar" as creatures caught up in the budding season of an inexorable temporal progression: morn passing gradually into night, May into December. Tennyson's *Idylls,* as the poem traces this process of disintegration and decay, repeatedly invokes a leitmotif of the changing seasons. Thus, to take a single example, "The Last Tournament" begins with the lines: "Dagonet, the fool, whom Gawain in his mood / Had made mock-knight of Arthur's Table Round, / At Camelot, high above *the withering woods,* / Danced *like a wither'd leaf* before the hall" (1–4; emphasis added).

Here in Tennyson's *Idylls,* then, invocation of the Virgin's Tale functions not so much to stimulate excitement and anticipation, but to create a frustration of anticipation. The insistent seasonal references in which the virginal theme is embedded prevent the mind from excited speculation about what *may* happen. May does not lead in any direction but the witherings of autumn and the desolations of December. The reader is confronted thereby with only the bleak impotence of yearnings for arousal in this Tennysonian Virgin's Tale.

Tennyson's *Idylls* comes out of an orientation of thought contrary to that which grounds the literary works we discussed previously. Traditional systems of literary propositions, building up plot forms that range from the Adamic bildungsroman through the conventional Virgin's Tale, tend to share the axiom that time, at some point out there in the future, somehow stops. Most of us in the common muddling course of life entertain this thinking comfortably. There is an end to the story. Now in some sense, to be sure, we know (think we know) this is not quite the case; but we tend to ignore or veil such awareness. We posit some version of apocalypse or of happy ever after or of damnation. And that ends things. This ending of things is very important. It makes what happens before the posited ending seem significant. If things end, then we can believe that particular things that happen make a difference. Something happens and the virgin is saved! or, alternately, ravished!

But what if we were to inquire into what follows this saving or ravishing? Tennyson's *Idylls* prods thought toward this question. The traditional getting-married plot is one of those time-honored mental devices that, by creating an end ("Reader, I married him"), makes things appear to matter. Tennyson's *Idylls* starts with marriage. Then it asks, "Now what?" The poem starts out looking as if it will give an agreeable answer. Well, now the Virgin's Tale. Just as we can generate expectation, excitement, and significance by thinking in such terms about life's events that preceded marriage, so too we can think in those terms about what follows:

> Far shone the fields of May thro' open door.
> ("The Coming of Arthur," 459)

But this door opens, as Tennyson's imagery ironically suggests, only onto the progression of the months. Whether we wish to admit it or not, we know that through the "far" fields of May can be glimpsed, inevitably, the fields of June, and through those and succeeding fields the bare stubble of December.

Here, though, is our ending, is it not? The *Idylls* thus becomes painful and tragic, the tale of the virgin stained. But at least, then, it somehow has meaning, makes sense.

However, Tennyson withholds from us even the sober consolations of this nicely tragic ending. In the last of the *Idylls* Bedivere cries out in his anguish to Arthur, "Where shall I hide my forehead and my eyes?" And, most horribly (for a mind that thinks), Tennyson makes Arthur answer him:

> And slowly answer'd Arthur from the barge:
> "The old order changeth yielding place to new,
> And God fulfills himself in many ways,
> Lest one good custom should corrupt the world.
> Comfort thyself; what comfort is in me?"
> ("The Passing of Arthur," 407–11)

What rises before our eyes is not a conclusion but only another year, a "new" order replacing the old—another series of idylls, another May, wherein the fields will shine far through open door. We have drifted into a revolving world, a realm of mirrors, an endless succession of May (each turning in its turn into the May not of December). Tennyson sends us spinning forever down the ringing grooves of change that repeats its own pattern.

This vision of recurrence recalls the extremely unsettling cry that concludes (or, rather, refuses to conclude) Shelley's *Ode to the West Wind:* "If Winter comes, can Spring be far behind?" But if spring comes, does winter again follow? Do we, then, after all, want spring to come again? The possibility that April is the cruelest month did not spring new-born to the mind of Eliot. The early nineteenth-century Romantics tormented their dreams with that question. So, for example, in Shelley's work we get *Hellas* with its eerie choral lyrics, "Worlds on Worlds are Rolling Ever" (197–238) and "The World's Great Age Begins Anew" (1060–1101). The latter lyric, which concludes the play, ends with the lines, "Cease! drain not to its dregs the urn of bitter prophesy. / The world is weary of the past, / Oh, might it die or rest at last."

In one mood Romantic writers try for optimism. The young Keats, in his poetic Maytime, plays with the notion that the "reading of an *ever*-changing tale" (*Sleep and Poetry,* 91; emphasis added) might be a wonderful experience, a cornucopia. So, fondly, his own youthful poetry tends in the direction of cataloguing, offering a flow of images that, seemingly, might be endlessly extended: "A bush of May flowers with the bees about them; / Ah, sure no tasteful nook would be without them . . . Here are sweet peas, on tip-toe for a flight . . . Linger awhile upon some bending planks" (*I Stood Tip-Toe,* 29–30, 57, 61). The cataloguing goes on and on. "What next?" he eventually asks; and then, simply, he continues: "A tuft of evening primroses, / O'er which the mind may hover till it dozes" (*Tip-Toe,* 107–8).

If one thinks of an ending as a boundary and if a boundary suggests a trap or tyranny, then the prospect of a door opening onto another beginning beyond each ending suggests possibilities of liberty. What next? why, lots of things. So, for example, when Wordsworth writes *The Prelude,* he commences with the conclusion of *Paradise Lost.* Milton had left us with the poignant lines:

> The World was all before them, where to choose
> Their place of rest, and Providence their guide:
> They hand in hand with wand'ring steps and slow,
> Through *Eden* took their solitary way.
> (12.646–49)

Wordsworth, picking up Milton's phrase, "The World was all before them," turns it into a beginning (and, for that matter, the beginning only of a "prelude"):

> Oh there is blessing in this gentle breeze
> That blows from the green fields and from the clouds
> And from the sky: it beats against my cheek,
> And seems half conscious of the joy it gives.
> O welcome Messenger! O welcome Friend!
> A captive greets thee, coming from a house
> Of bondage, from yon City's walls set free,
> A prison where he hath been long immured.
> Now I am free, enfranchis'd and at large,
> May fix my habitation where I will.
> What dwelling shall receive me? In what Vale
> Shall be my harbour? Underneath what grove
> Shall I take up my home, and what sweet stream
> Shall with its murmur lull me to my rest?
> *The earth is all before me:* with a heart
> Joyous, nor scar'd at its own liberty,
> I look about, and should the guide I chuse
> Be nothing better than a wandering cloud,
> I cannot miss my way.
> (1805 version; 1.1–19; emphasis added)

But Wordsworth also has other moods that come upon him when he begins to think about how the earth, all before him, revolves through its seasons. Wordsworth's *The Two April Mornings* invites meditation on whether the human mind can actually find solace in the fact that April keeps coming again, offering endlessly to replace the lost joys of Aprils past. Such revolution of the seasons threatens—as Wordsworth's companion poem *The Fountain* suggests—to drive the mind mad. One thinks of Shelley's Demogorgon, asking Asia, "For what would it avail to bid thee gaze / On the revolving world?" (*Prometheus Unbound,* 2.4. 117–18).

What it might avail—whether it might avail—to gaze on the revolving world is a question that the darker side of Romantic speculation passes on to Victorian thought. From Victorian pondering of that question we get such literary musings as Browning's companion poems *Meeting at Night* and *Parting at Morning*. In *Meeting at Night* Browning condenses the conventional story of movement toward climax between man and woman into a lovely two stanzas:

> The gray sea and the long black land;
> And the yellow half-moon large and low;
> And the startled little waves that leap
> In fiery ringlets from their sleep,
> As I gain the cove with pushing prow,
> And quench its speed i' the slushy sand.
>
> Then a mile of warm sea-scented beach;
> Three fields to cross till a farm appears;
> A tap at the pane, the quick sharp scratch
> And blue spurt of a lighted match,
> And a voice less loud, through its joys and fears,
> Than the two hearts beating each to each!

But having set up this highly sexualized accentuation of a conventional literary climax, Browning now adds to it *Parting at Morning*, a one-quatrain poem that in its abruptness seems designed to undercut the sufficiency of the previous poem's satisfactions:

> Round the cape of a sudden came the sea,
> And the sun looked over the mountain's rim:
> And straight was a path of gold for him,
> And the need of a world of men for me.

The two poems leave us with the disturbing sense that human value may shift like the tides, or change places like sun and moon—endlessly revolving back and forth to no apparent end.

A similar bleak sense hovers about the shadows cast by the heroic rhetoric of Tennyson's poem *Ulysses*. *Ulysses* plays off against the mind's conventional vision of the victorious hero as the one who achieves the ending. Winning, the hero puts a stop to the sound and fury. Ulysses in particular seems a hero whose epic journey ought to endorse the venerable and pleasing notion that you can both look homeward, angel, and actually get home again. But Tennyson, brooding on hints from Dante concerning the hero's damnation, builds up in Ulysses a different portrait. Ulysses exhibits a consciousness that has developed an almost drug-like obsession with the revolving world: "all experience is an arch wherethrough / Gleams that untraveled world whose margin fades / Forever and forever when I move. / How dull it is to pause, to make an end" (19–22). The modern poem, accordingly, begins where the ancient epic ended: asking, after union (or, in this case, re-union), What next? The poem will not be about getting married, which would be "to make an end." Instead, it will be about breaking the union: Ulysses, disgusted at finding himself "matched with an aged wife" (3), is intent upon setting out again in pursuit of "something more . . . new things" (27–28).

Tennyson's Ulysses wants to arouse his mariners with his stirring words: "Strong in will / To strive, to seek, to find, and not to yield" (69–70). The power of the rhetoric is marvelous. But has Ulysses become one of the sirens? His vision of the margin fading forever and forever as he chases the horizon of the revolving world leaves the mind with nothing to value, finally, but the chase itself. No given thing is *the* thing; it is, instead, once touched and held, only a hindrance. It is not Penelope but only "*an* aged wife" and the hero must be heroic enough to leave her behind. There are an infinity of Penelopes, "new things," to be gotten through out there beyond the horizon.

Climax, the attractions (or terrors) of marriage, the terrors (or attractions) of ravishment—the thrills and chills that make up the power of the Virgin's Tale—all begin to fade for a mind that has started to think, "What next?" Multiple climaxes may seem desirable, but endless climax loses its savor. Back in the Romantic period, Wordsworth celebrates "infinitude" as "Our destiny, our nature, and our home." He urges upon us a Ulysses-like vision of "Effort, and expectation, and desire, / *And something evermore about to be*" (1805 *Prelude,* 6.538–42; emphasis added). The rhetoric sounds splendid. But later Victorian meditations disturbingly reveal that there is a worm in this apple of infinitude that Wordsworth so grandly offers. A mind that is ever looking forward toward "something . . . about to be" is a mind that will never quite value any given thing it can get its eye or hand on.

An uneasy sense that value is somehow fading away gives a sober coloring even to a good deal of apparently cheerful maneuverings in Victorian literary art. One of the games Victorian novelists are fond of playing with (or upon) the reader, for example, is that of offering getting-married endings, but presenting them as a sort of joke. In *Framley Parsonage,* for example, Trollope gives his final chapter the title, "How They Were All Married, Had Two Children, and Lived Happy Ever After." This chapter opens with an apparently whimsical address to the "Dear, affectionate, sympathetic readers" of Trollope's novel: "we have four couples of sighing lovers with whom to deal in this our last chapter, and I, as leader of the chorus, disdain to press you further with doubts as to the happiness of any of that quadrille. They were all made happy" (chap. 48). It is conventional among critics, I think, to propose that such maneuvering reflects simply the novelist's impatience with an overworked literary convention and a yearning to break out into new territory.[9] But something darker is operating here as well.

Trollope's invocation to his readers as "Dear, affectionate, sympathetic" calls to mind rhetoric he is fond of employing to characterize his more endangered, lamb-like virgins. So, for example, as noted previously, he describes Lily Dale of *The Small House at Allington* as "Lilian Dale, dear Lily Dale—for my reader must know that she is to be very dear, and that my story will be nothing to him if he do not love Lily Dale." If the reader "do not love Lily Dale"—yearning to see her saved, yearning to see her ravished, yearning for something concerning her, one way or the other or both—then "my story will be nothing to him."

The power of yearning is derived from and depends upon a virginal trait, a whiteness of thought that has not yet gotten stained by the question, "What next?" Lily Dale's salvation or ravishing matters in a world where there are high stakes like the possibility of living "happy ever after" or, alternately, of living "in endless shame and degradation." If stories are to be told, and not be merely nothing, then the reader's own virginity must be preserved. Let the reader believe. Let us believe (or persuade ourselves to forget that we do not believe) in a world of Lily Dale and of Penelope. Let us not envision a world of the aged wife and that terrible question, What next?

As Trollope says, then, in the concluding chapter of *Framley Parsonage,* he does not wish to play Lovelace to our Clarissa: "I, as leader of the chorus, disdain to press you further with doubts." Yet Reader, this leaves us, does it not, thinking about doubts?

CHAPTER 4

White Narratology: Gender and Reference in Wilkie Collins's The Woman in White

Diane Elam

Thackeray's description of Becky Sharp in *Vanity Fair* appears to explain what a Victorian woman in white would represent: "She was dressed in white, with bare shoulders as white as snow—the picture of youth, unprotected innocence, and humble virgin simplicity."[1] Thackeray, however, was never one to let the double meaning of appearances go unremarked, and it seems not unimportant that this description of Becky comes at a time when she is at her most artful, trying to woo Jos Sedley. The orphaned Becky, as the narrative reminds us, has no parents who can arrange a marriage for her; she must replace their delicacy and expertise in such matters with her own artfulness and self-conscious behavior. In other words, Becky is faced with the task of appearing to be the quintessential Victorian, innocent virgin—the woman in white—at the same time that she must be anything but innocent and youthful. If the woman in white is a blank or virginal space, Becky's task is both to be that space and to represent that space, to bring it forward and give it value within culture. To reinscribe the meaning of Thackeray's figure, then, we could say that while the woman in white is supposed to represent the virginal, innocent, young woman, within the space of the narrative she stands for the constructed, even deceptive, nature of such a representation.

Here Thackeray's contradictory figure presents a basic problem of reading: what does the woman in white represent? Does the woman in white present a Victorian idealization of woman, or does she represent the ways in which the idealized image is recreated as a *representation* of the ideal woman—the sign of the ideal woman and not the ideal woman herself? One way to answer this question would be to argue that by rendering this image transparent, by revealing Becky's artful construction of her own self-image, Thackeray's novel tries to tell the "truth" about this potentially deceptive figure of woman.

Yet if Thackeray's text can be read as presenting the "truth" about the woman in white—the angel in the house may be the devil in disguise—then Wilkie Collins's novel, appropriately entitled *The Woman in White,* extends the problem. Rather than settle for an easy distinction between appearance and reality (certainly the resolution for which Thackeray's text calls), *The Woman in White* more closely examines the relationships among the figures of woman, referentiality, and truth. In Collins's text, the figure of the woman in white first of all genders the problem of referentiality and truth. This is not simply because the body of the woman in white is figured as a blank page, as virginal space, to be inscribed by the pen of the authorial and authorizing male, after the contours of a by-now-familiar critical and sexual analogy. More interestingly, the woman in white appears as the figure of reference itself, haunting the representational claims of the realist novel and thus upsetting its pretension to present the truth. The paradox of the representation of the essence of woman as one of virginal whiteness is that the representation of woman appears as a gap in representation itself. The virginal sexuality and textuality of woman thus poses a fundamental problem: to what does *woman* refer? That is to say, the figure of the woman in white leads us to question whether or not we can get at the truth of this representation: whether it is possible to represent truthfully or to know the truth about representation.

Collins's text sets up these questions by first claiming, in the tradition of the realist novel, "to present the truth always in its most direct and most intelligible aspect."[2] To fulfill this claim, the novel tries to reveal first the truth *about* the woman in white, and second the truth that *is* the woman in white. We could phrase this another way and say that the text attempts to address two referential problems: (1) In its attempt to present the truth about the woman in white, it sets up a textual or epistemological problem that concerns finding the true identity and origin of the woman in white; (2) In its attempt to present the truth that is the woman in white, the text outlines a sexual or ontological problem that centers around discovering the essence and material signification of the woman in white.

This double look at referentiality is focused by the rather simple mystery that Collins's text is quick to establish: who is the woman in white? What is the narrative reference for the figure cited in the title? In the first two chapters, the woman in white is conspicuously absent, but in the third chapter the figure dramatically acquires a reference in the form of an "extraordinary apparition."[3] Walking home to London one evening, Walter Hartright is "brought to a stop by the touch of a hand laid lightly and suddenly on [his] shoulder from behind." Turning around, he observes:

> There, in the middle of the broad, bright high-road—there, as if it had that moment sprung out of the earth or dropped from the heaven—stood the figure of a solitary Woman, dressed from head to foot in white garments, her face bent in grave inquiry on mine, her hand pointing to the dark cloud over London, as I faced her . . . . All I could discern distinctly by the moonlight was a colourless, youthful face, meagre and sharp to look at about the cheeks and chin; large, grave, wistfully attentive eyes; nervous, uncertain lips; and light hair of a pale, brownish-yellow hue. (33–34)

Walter's description concentrates significantly on facial features and includes references to coloring (the face, like the dress, defines itself through its lack of color), age, cheeks, chin, eyes, lips, hair, and the emotional condition these features betray. In contrast, the description of the body is almost absent:

> Her figure was slight, and rather above average height—her gait and actions free from the slightest approach to extravagance. This was all that I could observe of her in the dim light and under the perplexingly strange circumstances of our meeting. What sort of a woman she was, and how she came to be out alone in the high-road, an hour after midnight, I altogether failed to guess. (34)

Beyond the most general parameters, her physical form remains undefined. Her slight body is a slighted body. This woman in white is primarily viewed as a face above a white dress—a figure without proper name, history, or body. On the one hand, this is little different from the trope that Thackeray gives us in *Vanity Fair:* what else was the Victorian idealization of woman but a figure denied both a sexual body and an identity? Yet on the other hand, there is something decidedly strange about this virginal figure appearing in the middle of the road in the middle of the night. Not a woman in white but rather a woman of the night would be more appropriate in this setting.

The narrative does little if anything to resolve this problem of referentiality. Although Walter tries to "lift the veil that hung between this woman and me" (38), the woman in white refuses to be unveiled, to reveal the secret of her identity. When questioned about her sudden appearance on the road, the woman in white will do no more than point to a place at the junction of the road to London and the road to Hampstead, where there was "a gap in the hedge" (35). She remains a mysterious figure of absence who originates from an absence, a gap at the junction of the limbs of the crossroads, a virgin figure yet to be assigned a reference.

Not without irony, the character whose narrative function it is to assign a reference to the woman in white, to uncover the truth about her, is Walter. But he will not undertake the pursuit of this virgin figure on his own. He begins his detective work by enlisting a female partner, another virgin by the name of Marian Halcombe.[4] Yet as Walter and Marian begin to unveil the first woman in white to be someone named Anne Catherick, another virginal figure punctuates and punctures the narrative:

> There stood Miss Fairlie, a white figure, alone in the moonlight; in her attitude, in the turn of her head, in her complexion, in the shape of her face, the living image, at that distance and under those circumstances, of the woman in white! (71)

First described by Walter as having something "strangely inconsistent and unaccountably out of place . . . something wanting" in her presence (62), Laura Fairlie's continued "presence" proves to Walter that that "something wanting" was his recognition of the "ominous likeness" between Laura Fairlie and the woman he met on the road. The likeness causes Walter to conclude that the first woman in white was indeed the Anne Catherick of Mrs. Fairlie's letter, and the mystery now is the striking resemblance between the two women in white.

At this point, it may be tempting to conclude that the mystery surrounding the woman in white has been solved, that the questions of referentiality and truth, which the narrative has raised, are really not so complex after all. First, the narrative seems to reveal the epistemological truth *about* the woman in white by solving the mystery surrounding the identity of Anne Catherick. Unraveling the complexities of Anne's story, the narrative seems to live up to its epistemological promise. It discovers that her "origin," hence the reason for her resemblance to Laura, is the fact that they are half-sisters, sharing the same father; and it discovers her ultimate end (she dies as the result of heart disease). Secondly, the narrative seems to reveal the ontological truth that *is* the woman in white and is signified by Laura's "truthful, innocent blue eyes" (61). This is a spiritual order of being, not the perfection of the body but the metaphysical truth that is the beauty of the soul:

> Lovely eyes in colour, lovely eyes in form—large and tender and quietly thoughtful—but beautiful above all things in the clear truthfulness of look that dwells in their inmost depths, and shines through all their changes of expression with the light of a purer and a better world. (60)

Laura's truth (beauty) is not in her physical perfection; in this passage, and from his perspective as an artist, Walter continues to dwell at length on her physical blemishes. Laura's truth instead is manifested in her ability as a woman to give "life, light, and form to our shadowy conceptions of beauty, [to fill] a void in our spiritual nature that has remained unknown to us till she appeared" (61). In this way, the woman in white illuminates the text by revealing the previously unseen void in the soul and filling that darkened space with the light of her truth.

If Laura's essence reveals a spiritual order of being, her relationships to property—and relationships with her through her property—reveal a material order of being. The order she gives to property relations results in a properly formed social order. The first of these relationships involves Laura's marriage to Sir Percival Glyde. Sir Percival, although pretending devotion, actually desires to marry Laura so that he may further legitimize both his social and economic position by acquiring a connection with Laura's property—her wealth, her family, as well as her self. Laura's combination of these two types of cultural property—her material wealth and her social standing—are, for Sir Percival, her "priceless value." However, this marriage of propriation proves unstable: it is an improper relationship which is not allowed to stand. Laura's truth instead effects a change from an old to a new social order, legitimizes a new genealogical order in preference to the impotent tradition Sir Percival represents. The change to the new order takes place with Laura's relationship to Walter, who unlike Sir Percival does not desire Laura's real estate; he wants to possess her self as the property that is truth. When Laura, although no longer a woman of property per se, finds herself free to remarry upon Sir Percival's death, Walter is eager to take possession of his truth, his priceless Laura, and heralds the occasion of his marriage by pronouncing, "she was mine at last!" (413). Having possessed his wife properly and without property, Walter goes on to find his investment in truth multiplying, as Laura bears him a son who, in fact, does inherit the family property. This relationship to Laura's self plus her property effects a social healing, by creating a new, invigorated social order. In short, Laura's spiritual truth fills the void in the soul, while her material truth manifests a social-economic equilibrium.

The double revelation of truth—the epistemological truth about woman, revealed through Anne's history, and the ontological truth that is woman, revealed through Laura's second marriage—seems a neat solution to the problematic relationship between figure and reference. According to this analysis, the narrative solves the problem through the double closure of death (Anne's) and marriage (Laura's). In the end, we have no women in white at all—one virgin dies, the other marries and bears a son, and both figures have been assigned a decidable reference.

However perfect the circle such an analysis draws, it does so by eliding a number of textual problems along the way. First of all, the division between the truth about Anne and the truth that is Laura ignores the problematic confusion of identity that occurs later in the text. When Anne dies under the assumed identity of Laura and Laura is placed in an asylum under the assumed identity of Anne, the text forces the issue of metaphoric replacement—is one woman in white really just as good as another? What is at stake in an exchange of identities carried out under the guise of the figure of the woman in white? Second, and even more to the point, has the truth that *is* woman and *about* woman actually been revealed? To answer these questions, we need to take a closer look at the ways in which issues of identity, essence, and property trouble the narrative's quest for "truth."

The epistemological and ontological "truths" constructed around each woman in white, around Laura and Anne, are only made possible by ignoring the textual interstices where the narrative refuses to disclose vestiges of essentiality, identity, and property. Such a process of selection, which creates the illusions of truth, replicates male phallic desire and attempts to possess woman as truth by narrating, by inscribing, by confining her figure as presence. If caught within such narrative violence, woman would be contained by the ordering obsession of mid-Victorian society; her potentially disruptive appearance would be viewed no differently from the misplaced book in the library, the stray flower-blossom on the carpet, or the missing knife at the dinner table, all of which Sir Percival's "mania for order and regularity" must correct (219).

The figural play inscribed by the infinite supplementarity of the woman in white works against such balance. The doubled w's, the doubled whites, the doubled women, disrupt the singular narrative closure of the text. Not simply a question of pairs, the "white" infinitely doubles "woman"; the entitled figure of the woman in white, seemingly single, already has inscribed within her a doubleness, a like and unlike (an Anne and Laura) that redoubles as it is deployed throughout the narrative in substitutive ploys. That is to say, whiteness is more than simply a fabric draped on the female body to represent the virginal origin (and a fortiori meaning) of its gender. The woman in white is a figure that is both the (a)sexual, virginal representation of the body of woman and a rhetorical trope which figures the impossibility of literal, descriptive reference.

In illustrating how this figural supplementarity works on the most basic level, we can note that, as women in white, Laura and Anne defy the narrative closure and the illusions of truth with which they were made complicitous. With regard to Anne, the novel purports to tell her true "story"; the truth about this woman in white is discovered after the various narrators piece together the facts and unveil the mystery of her origin, her motives for her actions, and finally her death. This summary, however, leaves crucial points unresolved. To begin with, the narrative is quite concerned with whether Anne had a secret that she herself neither purposely nor accidentally revealed. There remains the possibility that she kept secret the knowledge of a forgery committed by Sir Percival, the disclosure of which would have had serious effects upon the events of the narrative. Interestingly enough, the other prominent woman in white, Laura, believes that Anne does indeed have knowledge of this crime; however, both Anne's mother and Walter contend that it was merely Anne's mental instability that caused her to believe in the "reality" of her secret. As Walter summarizes:

> It was perfectly in character with Anne's mental affliction that she should assume an absolute knowledge of the secret on no better grounds than vague suspicion, derived from hints which her mother had incautiously let drop in her presence. (472)

Anne has died before the narrative reveals this accusation, and her direct confirmation or denial is impossible at this point. Only Mrs. Catherick and Walter remain to assert that Anne was either lying or mentally incapable of perceiving "reality." What, then, is the status of the secret of the absent woman in white? On this count, Anne begins to resemble Nietzsche's paradoxical umbrella, as discussed by Jacques Derrida in *Spurs: Nietzsche's Styles*. In his interrogation of Nietzsche's stray phrase, "I have forgotten my umbrella," Derrida concludes that "[i]ts secret is rather the possibility that indeed it might have no secret, that it might only be pretending to be simulating some hidden truth within its folds."[5] Anne, like the umbrella or like Nietzsche (or like Collins for that matter), refuses to give up the possibility that she may not have had any secret at all, that she may not have known Sir Percival's secret—her "secret" may only be an absence, a blank, that her whiteness figures.

Yet the problem of Anne's secret does not end here with certainty about its uncertainty. Just as Sir Percival relied on Anne's mental condition to confine her to an asylum, Mrs. Catherick appeals to Anne's "mental affliction" to explain why Anne thought she knew Sir Percival's secret. But who's to say that Anne is mad? Who judges sanity? Sir Percival certainly is no quintessence of reason, yet no character within the narrative overtly questions his sanity. Laura, on the other hand, easily finds herself diagnosed as mentally ill, converted into a madwoman, on the basis of her likeness to Anne.[6] Anne, like Laura, hovers in the half-light of reason and madness. As Sir Percival says, "she's just mad enough to be shut up and just sane enough to ruin me when she's at large" (331). Woman needs to be put in her place, kept shut up under the guise of reason. But Anne is the excessive mad woman out of the attic, who hides in the gaps in the text. She is the woman unconstrained by society, unconstrained by narrative, who runs amuck and upsets the principle of reason upon which the narrative tries to ground itself. On the loose, woman represents what Nietzsche, in *The Gay Science,* called, "[t]he greatest danger that always hovered over humanity and still hovers over it . . . the eruption of madness."[7] Signified in this way, woman calls up a phenomenological uncertainty, the overturning of narrative logic and of the associations between figure and reference. The fear of woman's madness, Anne's interpretative hovering between reason and insanity, points to the Nietzschean disruption: the confirmation of the arbitrary character of judgments. Whether or not she's mad, whether or not she knows, we'll never know. The bar between madness/reason refuses any decidable placement; there is always an uncertainty at stake in the grounds of reason and madness.

Yet such an emphasis on the possibility of woman's madness is not to say that the figure of the woman in white reveals another kind of truth: the truth of the power of woman's real uncertainty. Just as the text complicates the question of woman's dissimulating power of madness, it also complicates the relationship between the fantastic and the real. The figure of Anne as the woman in white hovers on the double edge of the fantastic and the real, discursively functioning as the supplemental point of continual slippage.[8] The uncanniness of her figure remains, her possible return poised against the narrative action. As Walter remarks:

> I say again the woman in white is a living influence in our three lives. The End is appointed—the End is drawing us on—and Anne Catherick, dead in her grave, points the way to it still! (448–49)

Driven by the prospect of an end even more final than Anne's death, Walter desires to reach the point where all meaning hidden within the interstices of the narrative will reveal itself—where the secret of Sir Percival's past, where the secret of Laura's real identity, where the secret of the woman in white, will all be known. Only then will Laura and Walter, in their blissful state of revelation and total knowledge, live happily ever after (452). Following Anne's direction and attempting to trace out the pattern of secrets through her past, Walter does indeed discover the secreted knowledge which he had been seeking. He therefore concludes that the woman in white will return no more:

> So the ghostly figure which has haunted these pages as it haunted my life, goes down into the impenetrable gloom. Like a shadow she first came to me in the loneliness of the night. Like a shadow she passes away in the loneliness of the dead. (552)

Walter's remarks highlight the narrative's drive to settle the difference between the real and the fantastic by killing off the body of the woman in white. This is not an unheard of move, as Sarah Kofman observes when she writes that "to make a dead body of woman is to try one last time to overcome her enigmatic and ungraspable character, to fix in a definitive and immovable position instability and mobility themselves."[9]

The figure of the woman in white, however, refuses to be put to rest as comfortably as Walter would like. She continues to haunt the text as the figure standing before us in the title, the figure that refuses to have a decidable reference, that refuses to represent the truth. The woman in white infinitely reinscribes herself through a supplementary, metonymic series—an infinite vanishing point within a textual *mise en abyme* which is neither purely "real" nor purely fantastic.[10] Like the woman with long tusk teeth at the top of the stairs, who Collins himself believed lay waiting for him each night so that she could take a bite out of his shoulder, the woman in white's uncanny figure reflects the inevitable return of the repressed, the inner compulsion to repeat. She will never really die; the narrative always will be in a state of semi-mourning over her uncanny figure. Seen in this way, the question of repetition cannot be isolated from the question of figurative language itself.[11] The uncanny, as the woman in white, is the figuration of figural language, is the entitled figure figuring her own figurality. Functioning (figuring) in this way, the woman in white has a decentering effect on the narrative, which never can place and center the possibly mad woman in white, despite the phallogocentric impulse of narrative desire. Anne, as a woman in white, refuses to be placed as property, as essence, as a single identity prescribed by reason's principle. And her secret remains unrevealed: The secret of figural language is that it might not have a secret, that it might not hide any meaning at all.

Like Anne, Laura also refuses any fixed narrative placement, and her supplementary inscription continually disrupts the illusions of truth that the text attempts to construct. Laura's refusal to be commodified and captured within the relationship of property repeatedly unbalances the equipoisal structure of the "universe of commodities."[12] The economy of male desire tries doubly to inscribe Laura (as representation) into a narrative projection of commodification. First, Sir Percival is interested in marrying her as the sign of wealth so that he can acquire her (as) property and pay off his debts. Secondly, Walter's motives, though hidden in metaphysics, are much the same. But in each case, the narrative attempt to treat Laura as commodified sign (of commodification) fails; as supplementary mark, she denies the closure of proper placement. The claims to Laura are false claims; her figure refuses to be controlled and possessed as a commodity.

Obviously, when Sir Percival dies and Laura remarries, his claim is no longer valid; however, he did not properly possess her in the first place. The narrative uncertainty explores the problem that a man never knows if he possesses a woman. Extending the analysis of the economy of desire from the bank to the boudoir, Sir Percival repeatedly reveals his desire to possess Laura through his sexual mastery. Laura tells Marian that:

> he locked the door, pushed me down into a chair, and stood over me with his hands on my shoulders. "Ever since that morning when you made your audacious confession to me at Limmeridge," he said, "I have wanted to find out the man, and I found him in your face tonight. Your drawing-master was the man, and his name is Hartright. You shall repent it, and he shall repent it, to the last hour of your lives. Now go to bed and dream of him if you like, with the marks of my horsewhip on his shoulders." (264)

Driven by his need for the certainty of sexual possession and his resulting jealousy of Walter, Sir Percival tries to gain control of Laura through his brutal threats. Yet the questions always remain:

is she all his? can the narrative give away all of the woman? "If men think they have or possess women in sexual mastery," Gayatri Spivak argues,

> they should be reminded that, by this logic, women can destroy the proper roles of master and slave. Men cannot know when they are properly in possession of them as masters (knowing them carnally in their pleasure) and when in their possession as slaves (duped by their self-citation in a fake orgasm). Woman makes propriation—the establishment of a thing in its appropriate property—undecidable.[13]

Sir Percival Glyde cannot possess Laura simply by appending his name to hers and then threatening other sexual rivals. The appendation of the proper name, instead of indicating possession, undermines decidability and propriety. His name "glydes" off her because Laura, like Anne, can always escape possession by inserting the uncertainty of her blank, her whiteness, her unrevealed secret.

Laura's proper(ty) relationship with Walter is even more problematic. Walter certainly assumes that Laura is his: he marries her, appends his name, and lays claim to her as his sign of truth. We have already examined the problems with the proper name as a mark of possession, but what about Walter's claim for Laura as the purveyor of truth? Woman as truth is taken more as an a priori fact than as a proposition in need of proof. There is, however, room to challenge such an equation. More precisely, Laura as the woman in white, is set up as an illusion of unification, as "the visionary nursling of your own fancy" with "the light of a purer and a better world" (60–61). She is not the light of aletheia; the promised truth still remains outside the boundaries of the text. Even though woman is not truth but rather an illusion of truth and unification, she continues to seduce as the model of truth. Walter is seduced by Laura's veiled deceit, by what he believes is her truth. Yet Laura Fairlie is not the truth; she is the fair-lie that is woman. She is the just untruth and the white lie, veiling her lie in fairness, hiding herself in whiteness. Laura is fairly placed, laid in the white spaces of the narrative, and as such disrupts any claims for truth. Walter cannot possess Laura as the truth which she is not; but he also cannot possess her as the fair lie. Woman will not be possessed at all. She refuses possession and commodification because she refuses presence. She will not lie still and be confined within the phallogocentric space of narrative.

Thus the double movement within the narrative is still the search for the truth about woman and the search for the truth that is woman. But this continual resituation of women within the blanks of the text suggests that women will always elude while alluding to representation within realist narrative. The doubling of woman by her whiteness in effect creates the indeterminacy of her position, an indeterminacy which leads us to question the situation and representation of identity. The double play between Laura and Anne breaks apart the boundary which signifies their separate identities as characters; their physical similarity demonstrates that one woman in white can be substituted for another under the dual guises of death and madness. Such substitution raises the problematic question of what signifies identity. Is identity ascertained through facticity or through knowledge? The narrative attempts to equate identity with knowable truth, conceiving both as totalities with definable boundaries and ascertainable interior spaces. But this attempt ends up referring back to the untruth of truth that is inscribed within the figure of woman. Although Laura's and Anne's identity is finally "confirmed" through a comparison of dates (facts), their subjectivity is actually relationally constituted (not based on the facts as such at all). The possibility of slippage remains, as does the narrative palimpsest on the tombstone: Anne's name inscribed over Laura's erased name. The fair lie is the lie of identity, which claims that a totalizing truth, based on absolutes, both exists and is discoverable.

Refuting the claims for totality, the text further problematizes identity by focusing on the undecidability of gender.[14] To cite a few of the more noticeable examples: Marian, as described by Walter, has a quintessentially feminine body, but a decidedly masculine face; Mr. Fairlie is repeatedly referenced according to his feminine traits, as are Walter and Count Fosco. In each of these instances, "woman" refuses to be confined within the reference of a single figure of woman. The entire question of figurality is again reopened and reclosed, as "woman" refuses, through her supplementarity, to be appropriated by a single figure in the text. Put another way, as Derrida would have it: "Although there is no truth in itself of the sexual difference in itself, of either man or woman in itself, all of ontology nonetheless, with its inspection, appropriation, identification and verification of identity, has resulted in concealing, even as it presupposes it, this undecidability . . . . Man and woman change places. They exchange masks *ad infinitum.*"[15] Ignoring traditionally constructed boundaries between characters or figures, the feminine refutes the decidability of identity and instead unveils the untruth of decidable sexual difference.[16]

Just as the "feminine" is not confined to the figure of woman, neither is her signifying whiteness. Her endless but not totalizing garment of white spreads throughout the narrative.[17] The woman and any identity associated with her figure dissolve into: Mrs. Catherick's white tomb (105, 290, 409); Laura's white bed (199); the black and white spaniel (210); the dogs' white teeth (225); the white fog (260); the white despair of Walter's face (264); the white cloud of mist (265); the white field of the blind (322); the white outline of Madame Fosco's face (328); the awful whiteness of Sir Percival (387, 533); Anne's ghastly white face (400); the white sea birds (558); and Fosco's white mice, which run a pattern in and out of the entire narrative. The woman in white exceeds any single figure, any trope of metaphor *or* metonymy. The abyssal structure of the woman in white is the paradoxical abyss of endless metaphorical and metonymical replacement.[18] Her figure—as trope and as body—remains indistinguishable, blurred throughout the text. She is always more and less: three halves and never a one—dividing, multiplying, infusing the text, "only ever add[ing] up to a plural," as Lacan would say.[19] Assuming her metaphoricity by erasing herself, she ensures that she never will be in view as one.

As such, "the woman in white" is not *the* woman, in the sense in which Lacan asserts that "there is no such thing as *The* woman," where the definite article stands for the universal.[20] The entitled figure, "the woman in white," stands before the narrative as an absence, a blank, denying the possibility of the universal, of the all, of visible presence. Any attempt to arrest the slippage between figure and reference, any attempt to confer the uniqueness of the proper name on "the woman in white" fails. Woman escapes the logic of the name, the universality of the "the." "The woman in white" is instead anasemic. The capitals which privilege the title fall away into the narrative spaces of whiteness, and the figure of woman refuses the proper name, as she refuses placement and proper(ty).[21] She inserts herself instead as the possible absence, stepping out of the gap in the hedge.

Unable to assign a decidable referential value to the woman in white, Collins instead performs a strange reversal: the virginal woman, as the figure of pure referentiality—reference without the "color" of content—paradoxically "rapes" the narrative, bursting through a hole in the hedge to derail the opening narrative. The impassable diectic gesture invokes the insurmountable bar of reference: woman is she to whom realist representation, the authorization of the realist novel, can assign no identity. Yet she is this figure of absence precisely because she is the figure of reference itself, a figure to which no meaning can be assigned. Woman, in this sense, cannot be known (assigned a reference), but neither can she "be" within the space of the realist narrative of description, because her whiteness refers to nothing other than itself. Her sexuality appears only as the absence of sexuality, as virginal whiteness. The "virgin rapist" disrupts the possibility of narrative closure by insisting that literal, descriptive reference is itself a figure, a trope. That which grounds the possibility of descriptive realism can only be seen as a swerve away from the real or the decidable into the binding, recurrent, uncertainty of the woman in white. Thus when the narrative poses the questions, "What does it all mean? What has really happened?" (94), the woman in white prevents narrative closure by veiling the answers. She leaves the narrative, which she refused to enter, with the conundrum that the secret of the woman in white may be that the answer to any such question is: "You heard the words—but you don't know what they meant" (253).

PART 2

Virgin Poeisis

CHAPTER 5

Representation and Repristination: Virginity in The Ring and the Book

Herbert F. Tucker

I

Virginity defies representation; representation defiles virginity. We like to imagine virginity—our own, our children's—as a mode of pure and original being that is the most natural thing in the world. Yet we no sooner come to define the term, and yield its patent up to representation, than it disappears in the folds of the double negative. Innocence, immaculateness, inviolacy, and a dozen other locutions fill our dictionaries with testimony to the difficulty of affirming what is everybody's birthright. Once virginity gets into language, or vice versa, it is flawed by definition. We cherish it in images of presence, but are reduced to talking behind its back. What makes it as hard for language to conceive virginity as for a virgin to conceive, I submit, is the difficulty of untangling a natural fact from its cultural construction. This difficulty becomes especially urgent where the differentials of language are tasked to constitute an integral essence. For virginity belongs among those ideals that culture posits in compensation for its own belated derivativeness, ideals whose allure is due to their supposed immunity from the very forces of acculturation that establish them. Our communal codes of representation may prize virginity only at the cost of violating that supposedly presocial nature or presymbolic order in whose name we hold it dear.

Virginity is thus riddled with economic and political determinants, and nowhere more than in common parlance. It is the apparent disposition of virginity to be disposed of, yet it invites the terms of possession only to confound them. You can lose your virginity or, with a crucial difference, you can give it away; yet if you do neither for a sufficiently long time you risk wearing it out by disuse and outliving it in any but a clinical sense. You can keep your own virginity or take somebody else's, but you can never have them both. The one maidenhead Don Juan cannot acquire is his own; nor may he transfer title to any of the thousand he has collected. The reciprocal embarrassment of virginity and language is most clearly preserved in English with the double entendre of *knowledge*. To "know" virginity is to undo it, in a vanishing act whose carnal sense rehearses the conceptual conversion of virginity from a physical presence into an intellectual representation. Virgin forests are hypothetical topoi where trees fall silently through philosophers' minds. The reconnaissance of a virgin land entails, as its explorers acknowledge with virtually postcoital tristesse, a recognition that its *terra* is *incognita* no more. The knowledge even of one's own virginity seems to entail a partial loss of innocence, as it transgresses the frontier of pure being that is virginity's metaphysical correlative. In some abstract sense we all experience virginity, yet to speak of an experienced virgin is to flirt with oxymoron if not slander.

Nor are such difficulties confined to language. Nonlinguistic media amply attest to the representational paradoxes posed by virginity, which at least in the West have assumed spectacular proportions. For a millennium the imagination of virginity in Christian culture has devoted itself to pictorial and plastic representations of a Virgin who, being also a mother, is more than virginal—is indeed, to the eye of reason, the precise opposite of virginal. Virginity and maternity, while biologically continuous, are logically incompatible, since the latter actualizes a potential that the former must shelter in latency. Yet in Christian art we unerringly hail the Madonna by the Child beside her, or by some pregnant mark of the Child that shall be. It is as if the iconographic traditions of Christianity solve the problem of representing virginity through emphasizing its very insolubility in human terms. Mary of Nazareth becomes the orthodox representative of virginity only by special canonical dispensation. Since virginity defies representation, Christian art seems to say, let us make of Mary a miraculous figure whose representation defies her virginity; and let the mystique of her self-contained regard perennially call to mind the limits of representation that she makes manifest.[1]

The extraordinary case of the Blessed Virgin thus constitutes an exception that proves the rule of virginity's unrepresentability. By contrast, as we have seen in considering the embarrassments virginity occasions in ordinary language, an ordinary man or woman apparently may embody virginity but may not know it. Something quite like this is what W. B. Yeats famously declared, not about virginity but about truth.[2] Now truth, it is generally acknowledged, forms the leading topic of Robert Browning's epic *The Ring and the Book,* and virginity its leading trope.[3] Images of virginity structure both the historical action of Browning's epic—a mythos of draconian oppression, virginal distress, and heroic rescue—and its hermeneutic activity of getting at the truth about that historical-mythical action. I propose in what follows to explore the mutual figuration of virginity and truth in *The Ring and the Book,* looking first at the outermost ring of the text, where the poet defends his methods; and then at its heart, where the two maiden principals Caponsacchi and Pompilia declare their mutual devotion. Poet and protagonists alike repeatedly express in images of virginity their cognate fidelities to the love of truth and the truth of love; and the paradoxes entailed by the imagination of virginity enforce a recognition of the inevitably constructed nature of the faiths they espouse.

II

Browning's recuperation of his principals' truth entails a preliminary disclosure of his own hermeneutic operations, which entails in turn a commitment to the admittedly partial version of the truth that those operations have produced. Browning is less interested in the truth than in the truth about the truth, which is that it is absolutely contingent on the processes of its manufacture, processes themselves subject to the motives and circumstances of the laboring mind. "The patent truth-extracting process" (1.1114), as Browning calls it, always involves "The instinctive theorizing whence a fact / Looks to the eye as the eye likes the look" (1.863–

64).[4] This recognition does not disable the search for truth in *The Ring and the Book* but necessitates it. And the finding of truth—from the mutual discovery of Pompilia and Caponsacchi, to the legal findings of the court and the Pope, to the poet's *trouvaille* of an old yellow book on a Florence bookstall—partakes of the complexities of invention, where the creative will discerns in lucky circumstance the form of its seeking. *The Ring and the Book* engages the complexities of invention in such detail, and at such length, as to reground the search for the truth in the truth of the search. If the truth did not exist, we would have to invent it; and, since it does not exist outside the cultural representations that constitute our modernity, invent it we must. On this act of invention Browning stakes his epic claim for the renovation of heroism in a skeptical and sophisticated age.

The parallel between truth and virginity that runs through the poem furnishes an exemplary case on which to test this epic claim. I have noted how in common parlance we may lose our virginity but never find it. Yet for Browning, tireless customizer of common parlance that he was, the only virginity worth having is the virginity we can find. Whatever we think about virginity as a biological given in the realm of nature, our thinking may take place only within a system of institutional power relations that is mediated by the languages of state and church, of poetry and art. Virginity means as it is constructed, and the constructed character of the virgin keeps it open to appropriation for a diversity of purposes. It is Browning's purpose in *The Ring and the Book* to expose that construction to view and challenge unthinking socialization; to rescue virginity from the dragon clutches of custom and restore, in the fallen present, a quantum of culturally originative power; to "write a book," as he says on its last page, that "shall mean, beyond the facts, / Suffice the eye, and save the soul beside" (12.862–64).

Browning emphasizes the constructed character of virginity from the very beginning of the poem, in the wonderfully, typically devious way he introduces the ring as a symbol of his epic project:

> Do you see this Ring? 'Tis Rome-work, made to match
> (By Castellani's imitative craft)
> Etrurian circlets found, some happy morn,
> After a dropping April; found alive

Spark-like 'mid unearthed slope-side figtree-roots
That roof old tombs at Chiusi: soft, you see,
Yet crisp as jewel-cutting. There's one trick,
(Craftsmen instruct me) one approved device
And but one, fits such slivers of pure gold
As this was,—such mere oozings from the mine,
Virgin as oval tawny pendent tear
At beehive-edge when ripened combs o'erflow,—
To bear the file's tooth and the hammer's tap:
Since hammer needs must widen out the round,
And file emboss it fine with lily-flowers,
Ere the stuff grow a ring-thing right to wear.
That trick is, the artificer melts up wax
With honey, so to speak; he mingles gold
With gold's alloy, and, duly tempering both,
Effects a manageable mass, then works.
But his work ended, once the thing a ring,
Oh, there's repristination! Just a spirt
O' the proper fiery acid o'er its face,
And forth the alloy unfastened flies in fume;
While, self-sufficient now, the shape remains,
The rondure brave, the lilied loveliness,
Gold as it was, is, shall be evermore:
Prime nature with an added artistry—
No carat lost, and you have gained a ring.
(1.1–30)

Out of the "gold" of "pure crude fact" (1.35) that he has mined from an old yellow book, together with the "alloy" of his imaginative apprehension of such fact, the poet-"artificer" has shaped a perfect round whose claim to authenticity has a distinctly virginal ring of truth. Yet these virginal qualities arise not despite the "added artistry" of the poet-jeweler's "imitative craft," but because of it. The chastely "self-sufficient" shape of the ring, and the emblematic lilies that betoken its purity, result from the labors of hammer and file. And the halo-like sheen of its surface comes from an acid wash, which has effaced the alloy whose presence made those prior acts of shaping and adornment "manageable" in the first place.

Browning's word for this last act of self-concealing craft is "repristination"—a term whose dialectical relation to its near anagram "representation" informs the entire poem.[5] The intricate play of "fancy" with "fact" in *The Ring and the Book,* and of imagination with historical reenactment, is anticipated by the figuration of virginity on which this passage turns. "Repristination" is a "trick," Browning cheerfully concedes, which ingeniously devises an effect of ingenuousness. Effacing his own creative authority, the artist presents a palpable illusion of the prior authority of facts, their ability to represent themselves and stand on their own as "self-sufficient": "The untempered gold, the fact untampered with" (1.365).

But haven't the facts of Browning's Roman murder story been tampered with? "Don't you deal in poetry, make-believe, / And the white lies it sounds like?" The poet answers this blunt objection with an equally blunt equivocation: "Yes and no!" (1.454-55). Of course the facts have been tampered with, if only through those processes of selection and arrangement that Browning insists are necessary in order to let facts speak their simple truth. But when he says, in defense of such molestation, that "Fancy with fact is but one fact the more" (1.464), he insists further that his tampering with the facts is essentially continuous with those evidentiary operations that make facts facts to begin with. For the documentary raw materials in the old yellow book have come to him as data already heavily processed: affidavits, arguments, rebuttals—special pleadings all, stamped over and over with traces of rhetorical fancy footwork. What Browning calls the "pure crude fact" that supports his book is, as a matter of fact, a bookful of previous interpretations. His epic essay in the interpretive construction of fact foregrounds the stubborn fact of construction itself. His dizzying initial figuration of fact as gold, book as ring, in effect revives the etymological sense of "fact" as performance: a *factum* is a deed or product, something made out and made over if not indeed made up.

In the beginning was the derivative. So runs the first law of repristination. Its bearing on the question of virginity emerges in the first epic simile of the poem, where Browning calls the "slivers of pure gold" from which the ring is formed "Virgin as oval tawny pendent tear / At beehive edge when ripened combs o'erflow." Pure gold is "virgin." But "virgin *as* . . ."? How virgin is that, exactly? Is virginity a quality absolutely inherent, or is it, as Browning's somewhat decadent simile implies, a relative concept capable of measurement in a jeweler's carats or of comparison in a poet's tropes? The comparative form, with its suggestion that something can be more or less virgin, infects the very essence of the concept. It is as if Browning were bidding defiance to virginity's defiance of representation, and thereby to the absolutism that it stands for.

The arts of standing-for, the arts of representation, exert throughout *The Ring and the Book* an inexorably relativizing force, which this privileged simile is designed to make us appreciate. For whether we mine the honeycomb that is its vehicle or stand back to consider the gold that is its tenor, we encounter a tangle of cross-references that give virginal literality the lie.[6] When virgin gold oozes from the mine like honey from "ripened combs," the adjective *ripened* constitutes a trope within a trope, which problematizes the virginal nature of the tenor. What ripens by biological process is fruit, but only after fertilization has deflowered a once-virginal body and made it a fruiting body instead. Lest we miss this point, the adjective *oval* reminds us that, where ripening is at issue, it is not the flower (or chicken) that comes first, but the fertilized egg. After all, the only flowers on the scene are the lilies that the jeweler's file has embossed on the finished product. That "lily-flowers" thus appear at the end of a process which begins with rhetorically "ripened" raw materials puts in a nutshell the dialectic of repristination. Moreover, what "ripens" here is not literal fruit but honey, the metaphorical fruit of the coordinated labor of a hive of bees. The ambiguous position of these naturally social worker insects—dear to epic similists from Homer and Virgil to Milton, and dear in part by reason of just this ambiguity—defines the space of interaction between nature and culture that it is Browning's epic task to explore.

In *The Ring and the Book* the thematic relation between nature and culture is epitomized in the rhetorical relation between literal and figurative meaning on which Browning's introduction lays such stress. As the passage unfolds, we learn that the simile likening gold to honey forms part of a much more extended comparison likening the poet's sources to gold, and his poem to an elaborated and repristinated ring. The ring itself, we discover, is "a figure, a symbol, say;/ A thing's sign" (1.31–32). The same structure of trope-within-trope that informs the ripening of the bees' problematically virginal honey, inside the simile, also informs the setting of that simile within the governing analogy between goldsmith and poet. This point is reinforced by the else-impertinent flourish of Browning's casual transition, "the artificer melts up wax / With honey, so to speak." This little insertion within the larger conceit suspends disclosure of the jeweler's "trick" or trade secret, in a way that seems capricious if not perverse; yet it epitomizes, in passing, the rhetorical trickery that the larger conceit simultaneously elucidates and exemplifies.

Honey is to wax as soft gold is to firm alloy, as shapeless documentary fact is to crafted poetic truth, and also as the literal tenor of a metaphor is to the figurative vehicle that represents it. Browning thus begins his epic by turning the reader loose *in medias res et media verba,* into a wilderness of similitudes.[7] From this analogical labyrinth the poem offers no escape into the virginal simplicity of natural, literal truth; it offers instead a guide to living maturely in a cultural and rhetorical world. For the entire complex of opening similes ultimately refers to the poetic act that has produced both it and the enormous text that it precedes. The common denominator among Browning's elaborate correspondences is the work of building forms and making meanings. By analogically describing the book it occurs in, and moreover by repeatedly foregrounding the very act of analogical description in which it engages, the passage seems to be about itself. But the purpose of Browning's concentric self-referentiality is to center attention on his larger subject, the verbal and imaginative processes that generate meaning to begin with. "The thing signified" in *The Ring and the Book* is neither a ring nor a book, except as either signifies in turn the effort that has shaped it. "Figure," "symbol," "sign": even this slippery appositive ring of not quite synonymous keys to interpretation suggests that, if a master key is to be found, it must be one of the reader's forging. The poet's introductory rhetoric about rhetoric thus proposes in brief what his epic will dramatize: a vision of facts as compromised results rather than virginal givens; a vision of history as the product of past interpretive performances, multiplied—or rhetorically amplified—by the comparable interpretive performances of poet and reader in the historiographical present.

III

One of Browning's principal means of enforcing this hermeneutic parallel between past history and present historiography is to show how thoroughly enmeshed with interpretive contingency the events of the past were for their original actors. This situation obtains even for Caponsacchi and Pompilia, the characters who are closest to the core action of the poem, and whose relationship occupies its moral and textual focus. As Book 6 begins Caponsacchi has just received the news of Guido's murderous assault; the victimized Pompilia in Book 7 has mere hours to live. Both thus speak under the pressure of circumstances that condense their monologues into sustained acts of autobiographical self-discovery. The selves they discover are in one sense uncommonly free from conditions, but in another sense fraught with them. A rhetoric of virginity gives Caponsacchi and Pompilia a way to assert their unconditional mutual commitment in the face of a culture whose hostility to such free love they know all too well; yet it is in this very culture that they find the imaginative wherewithal to resist the conditions it imposes. Browning's lovers thus invent a paradoxically conditional virginity which, like that of his ring, reveals historically persistent discrepancies within the Western moral imagination that his epic explores.[8]

Because all that Caponsacchi and Pompilia most care about lies in the inalterable past, neither of them speaks with a view to influencing events, as do Guido and the lawyers in the flanking books; each occupies instead, with the pope and the poet, a largely retrospective vantage. Each retrospect draws lyrical urgency from a need to authenticate and organize a checkered and recently shattered life. For both Caponsacchi and Pompilia the organizing principle that validates their past lives, and mends them into continuity with the present, is the authenticity of self that they have experienced most vitally in relation to each other. Their separate monologues constitute mutually confirmatory accounts of mutually confirmatory lives; and these accounts dovetail so well because a mutual idealization has transformed Caponsacchi and Pompilia into what, as they now see it, they always truly were. Books 6 and 7 thus compose the collaborative autobiography of two lives "who, apart, / Know themselves into one, are found at length / Married" (7.1833–35).[9]

As this fine, late formulation of Pompilia's suggests, the match between the poem's two most harmonious minds owes much to their joint espousal of virginity. A shared mythology of virginity provides Browning's heroic lovers with a plot model for understanding what they have done; a shared rhetoric of virginity provides them with a psychology for understanding who they are. This mythology and rhetoric come naturally to Caponsacchi and Pompilia because the culture they inhabit has made them readily available. As we shall see, Browning takes care to demonstrate how deeply embedded in contemporary culture their self-actualization is: how "circumstances make or mar / Virginity" (7.756–57). But if Browning demystifies his protagonists' claim to virginal autonomy, he does not therefore invalidate it. Consistently with the overall strategy of the poem, and with his own characteristic mixture of skepticism and faith, he shifts the burden of mystery onto the processes of imaginative self-invention that for him constitute the poetry of culture. Through Caponsacchi and Pompilia he illuminates the historically conditioned making of a true, a credible life.

Both lovers are concerned to establish for themselves an innocence that entails each other's innocence as well. "But, all the same, I know / I too am taintless," the priest insists, "and I bare my breast" (6.196–97). For Pompilia, "Others may want and wish, I wish nor want / One point o' the circle plainer, where I stand / Traced round about with white to front the world" (7.1644–46). If such virginal exposure seems candid to the point of aggressiveness, that is because Browning's protagonists realize that the only way to "have done with being judged" (6.1860) is to reckon with local gossip about their relationship and to expose the corruptions of rumor. The same after-the-fact vantage that clears both speakers of rhetorical suspicion also obliges them to contradict a prevalent bad story. Both are, like Browning's readers by the middle of the poem, going over ground they have covered before—Caponsacchi for the same tribunal six months previously, Pompilia for her confessor a few hours ago—and in retracing their lives again, the couple's joint *apologia pro vitis suis* exhibits a markedly reconstructive agenda.

Caponsacchi and Pompilia make a case for their innocence by

imagining their own virginity, as a matter at once of outward record and of inward integrity. They undertake the creative task of rebutting scandal by associating the world's misprision with a corruption that is at once physical and textual. Caponsacchi regards Guido's forgery of the love letters not just as evidence-planting or psychological terrorism, but as a bodily affront to his person: "Touching us with such pustules of the soul / That she and I might take the taint, be shown / To the world and shuddered over, speckled so" (6.1801–06). Pompilia has a yet livelier sense of the way a pristine truth gets perverted with "every fresh transmission" (12.16). Before Pompilia ever spoke with Caponsacchi, she admits, his innocent name had been sullied "Like any bye-word . . . Born with a meaning, changed by mouth and mouth" (7.1331–32). Yet, despite such communicative disorders, she celebrates in a triumph of explicitly textual imagery her champion's hermeneutic power to divine the maiden truth of womanhood:

> a sense
> That reads, as only such can read, the mark
> God sets on woman, signifying so
> She should—shall peradventure—be divine;
> Yet 'ware, the while, how weakness mars the print
> And makes confusion, leaves the thing men see,
> —Not this man,—who from his own soul, re-writes
> The obliterated charter,—love and strength
> Mending what's marred.
>
> (7.1498–1506)

From its point of entry into the semiotic domain, virginity is "marked" (albeit divinely), and to that extent is maculate even before weak reading can "mar" it. Correcting this original stigma is the repristinative task of a reader strong enough to re-mark and emend it.[10] Caponsacchi can issue a revised and corrected edition of the text "Pompilia" because he possesses a virgin fair copy in the purity of "his own soul." The marriage of true minds admits no textual impediment: discerning an ever-fixed mark, it freely alters foul papers when it alteration finds, because in such mutuality of love the distinction between strong reading and "re-writing" ceases to signify. Editorial emendation being what it is, one wants to say that only an illiterate would choose to exalt love's repristinative power in editorial terms.[11] And yet the faith Pompilia places in

Caponsacchi's recension comes remarkably close to the imaginative credo of the poet, who claims in Book 1 to have made the marred print of an old yellow book "whirl into a white" (1.1362), and to have restored its "obliterated charter" by vindicating a virginity that is not the object of interpretation but its result.[12]

Virginal sexuality and textuality converge, in this surprising passage, on the issue of surprise itself, of change. Virginity gets established much the way a text does: through emendation, or through processes of psychological transformation that assume the force of religious conversion. Here as elsewhere, *The Ring and the Book* represents virginity not as a stable condition but as a conviction dynamically effected and reaffirmed. The joint editorial efforts of Caponsacchi and Pompilia to emend their life stories carry conviction because those stories pivot on parallel episodes of conversion. Exchanging old roles for new ones, they hail their later, reborn selves as virginal. In so doing they reconceive virginity, and bring it into line with Browning's epic vision of representation.[13]

A dense verse paragraph at the center of Caponsacchi's monologue (6.937–73) narrates his ecstatic conversion to authentic selfhood in enraptured terms that curiously commingle imagery of virginity and of violation. "I put forth no thought," he explains in recounting the effect of Pompilia's distress call, but rather "By the invasion I lay passive to, / In rushed new things, the old were rapt away" (6.945–48). Forgoing "thought" and conventional "wisdom" (6.956), he has been penetrated instead by a virtually carnal self-knowledge that lies beyond the philosophy of Aquinas or Plato (6.960–61), and below the conscious will. Describing this spasm of transformation tasks Caponsacchi's language to the limit, but at length he relies on an extraordinary virginal simile drawn from the Book of Revelation:

> Into another state, under new rule
> I knew myself was passing swift and sure;
> Whereof the initiatory pang approached,
> Felicitous annoy, as bitter-sweet
> As when the virgin-band, the victors chaste,
> Feel at the end the earthly garments drop,
> And rise with something of a rosy shame
> Into immortal nakedness: so I

Lay, and let come the proper throe would thrill
Into the ecstasy and outthrob pain.
(6.964–73)

The man who once took holy orders, only to inherit the trifling part of a flirtatious *cavaliere-servente,* now imagines entering a "new rule" involving ordeal by orgasm and a rite of ecstatic defrocking.[14] "I knew myself was passing": because Caponsacchi's virginal self is not a fixed entity but a transitive act of dying into new life, his knowledge of that self is a function of its capacity for change. At once active and passive, subjective and objective, masculine and feminine, Caponsacchi's apocalyptic chastity enacts the Browningesque victory of the laboring spirit over a world of "things" and "states." And these "states" include the state of virginity: the language of priestly initiation represents virginity instead as the deed a "victor chaste" may perform, the vocational "end" a life may prove.

In a comparable passage (7.1200–1259), Pompilia too undergoes initiation into virginity—or in her case into Virginity, since for her the initiatory rite is a consecration of her pregnancy, in typological fulfillment of the pattern set by her autobiographical model, the Virgin Mary.[15] Burdened by the death-in-life that is her marriage, Pompilia awakens from despair to a world of potentiality:

what, first thing at daybreak, pierced the sleep
With a summons to me? Up I sprang alive,
Light in me, light without me, everywhere
Change! A broad yellow sun-beam was let fall
From heaven to earth,—a sudden drawbridge lay,
Along which marched a myriad merry motes,
Mocking the flies that crossed them and recrossed
In rival dance, companions new-born too.
(7.1222–29)

Pompilia never directly answers her opening rhetorical question, but the ensuing descriptive rhetoric answers for her. She receives the "summons" of pregnancy as a new Annunciation, accompanied by the golden beam from heaven that she has seen all her life in paintings of Gabriel's greeting to Mary, and conveyed by angelically winged messengers: first the houseflies, and then "the blessed building-sparrow" (6.1235), a homely yet iconographically apt type of the Holy Spirit as descending dove.[16] Victorian conventions for the representation of pregnancy are notoriously polite, but the delicacy with which Pompilia safeguards the fruit of her womb from verbal profanation illustrates the importance of her preserving the "new-born" sense of self that comes with it: "I too have something I must care about"; "I have my purpose and my motive too" (7.1238–45). The unnamed "something" that charges Pompilia with sudden purpose is both the new life she bears within her body and the concomitant repristination of spirit that makes her own life new as well. In this virginal rapture she has, like the initiate Caponsacchi, a purpose that also has her: she owns—confesses and possesses—an authority beyond the will, "Something that's trulier me than this myself" (7.1439).

IV

The self-authenticating "something" that galvanizes Pompilia's new life and Caponsacchi's *vita nuova* does not arrive from afar, but derives from images of virginity that their culture makes commonly accessible. For both protagonists, to be sure, initiation into virginal selfhood coincides with a decision to resist the institutions of marriage and church to which they formerly swore allegiance. Yet they do not repudiate these allegiances so much as they redefine them, in a fresh acknowledgment of what it means to be a spouse or to be a Christian. Pompilia and Caponsacchi thus fight culture with culture, finding within the complex traditions of late seventeenth-century Catholicism a myth of virginity on which to base an internal resistance. Their psychosocial internalization of this ambient myth gets expressed in the inside/outside rhetoric of their initiation episodes: Pompilia's "Light in me, light without me," and Caponsacchi's "Alike abolished—the imprisonment / Of the outside air, the inside weight o' the world" (6.949–50). The continuity imagined here between interior and exterior realms of experience (which the topological continuity of a ring's "inside" with its "outside" may prefigure in Browning's initial metaphor) reflects Caponsacchi's and Pompilia's absorption in their new-found roles as virgin mother and virgin knight. The sudden totality of this absorption, or ideological saturation, also explains why they regard their self-repristination in miraculous rather than analytic terms. Instinct with the mystique of a "something" that seems beyond them because it is too intimate to name, they trope as a supernatural calling their saving appeal to models of virginity which—as the reader sees even if they cannot—form part of the cultural air they breathe.[17]

Browning most conspicuously underscores the cultural determination of his principals' ideals and behavior by recourse to the motif of the virgin and dragon. At least since W. C. DeVane demonstrated the consistency of this motif in Browning's work, students of *The Ring and the Book* have shown, with a like consistency, how it serves to support and unify a heterodox and centrifugal narrative experiment.[18] Studies along these lines have firmly established the mythic centrality of the relationship between Perseus-Joseph-St. George-Caponsacchi-Browning and Andromeda-Mary-Princess Sabra-Pompilia-Elizabeth. An account of this relationship remains invaluable in understanding the poem; it runs the risk, however, of making structural motifs do the work of psychological motivation. While received accounts of the virgin-and-dragon mythos show that Caponsacchi and Pompilia fulfill traditional patterns, they neglect to show how Browning makes this process imaginatively compelling. We overlook a major epic achievement if we fail to appreciate how psychological and cultural factors combine in *The Ring and the Book* to produce realistic character in historical action.[19] Browning's social psychology is particularly impressive as it extends to his protagonists' developing conviction of their virginal autonomy. Without disrespect yet also without mystification, he makes their virginity at once a credible and an empowering fiction, by showing how they assemble it from those most conspicuously cultural of poetic materials, works of visual art.[20]

Caponsacchi epitomizes the mediated character of this constructed virginity in a memory of his first, wordless encounter with Pompilia:

> I saw enter, stand, and seat herself
> A lady, young, tall, beautiful, strange and sad.
> It was as when, in our cathedral once,
> As I got yawningly through matin-song,
> I saw *facchini* bear a burden up,
> Base it on the high-altar, break away
> A board or two, and leave the thing inside
> Lofty and lone: and lo, when next I looked,

There was the Rafael! I was still one stare,
When—"Nay, I'll make her give you back your gaze"—
Said Canon Conti.

(6.398–408)

Caponsacchi describes this preliminary stage in the "revelation of Pompilia" (6.1866) by draping her in a twofold veil. First he departs from the literal narrative into an epic simile, and then within the simile he compares Pompilia not to the Virgin Mary but to a famous artist's rendition of the Virgin Mary: where he might have said "There was the Madonna!" he says instead "There was the Rafael!" Furthermore, the uniformly overlapping verb tenses of the passage make this last, epiphanic phrase temporally ambiguous. Which episode from Caponsacchi's life does it describe, the revelation of the painting or of Pompilia? Because there is no clear indication where the epic simile ends and the episode resumes, the epiphany of "the Rafael" hovers between the earlier scene in the cathedral and the later one at the theater. The aesthete-priest's "one stare" in effect fuses the two scenes, and merges literal with figurative modes of narration. The typological identification that Caponsacchi here sets up between Pompilia and the Blessed Virgin will govern the rest of his life story. Yet he frames this fulfilling typology, here as with subsequent references to the Rafael Madonna (6.672, 914), in the double mediations of rhetoric and painting. The priest's cultured simile thus deviates into the literal truth about his devotion to Pompilia, which is also for Browning the literal truth about virginity: that it is a cultural artifact, a precipitate that crystallizes, with however fine a suddenness, out of the conditions of an historically contexted life.[21]

For Pompilia, likewise, the conception of virginity is bound up with its cultural representations. Her illiteracy and comparative inexperience keep her especially sensitive to representations of maidenhood in visual and oral media. These representations span a range of popular forms: statuary ("the poor Virgin" in clay on the street corner [7.77–80]), tapestry (the figure of Daphne in a wall hanging [7.193–96]), and primitive forms like parable (7.820–43) and ballad (7.1389–1403). During the carriage ride toward Rome (6.1271–73), it is Pompilia and not Caponsacchi who unerringly proposes for vesper service the complementary virginal benedictions of Mary (Luke 1:26–33) and Sarah (Tobit

3:11–15)—texts she presumably knows not from the gospels or apocrypha, but from a Catholic girl's upbringing within the public domain. Although Pompilia indeed comes to regard Caponsacchi as her St. George or "soldier-saint" (7.1786), she owes that identification in part to Canon Conti's earlier mention of an altar piece by Vasari in the church of the Pieve (7.1323–28).

The close correspondence between this altar piece and the Rafael Madonna that elicits Caponsacchi's homage suggests how, in their mutual devotion, Browning's lovers worship at the same public if neglected shrine. Amid the baroque decadence of a Counter-Reformation culture that pays little more than aesthetic lip service to its traditional images of virginity, Caponsacchi and Pompilia jointly discover a heroic ideal worth living out in earnest. They do not create this virginal heroism ex nihilo; they locate it in themselves, and recognize it in each other, because it is there for the finding in the culture that surrounds them.[22] Ecclesiastical and marital institutions of that culture have appropriated virginity, to be sure, in the respectively oppressive forms of an art dwindled into fetishism and a patriarchal will to power over natural functions. It is nevertheless within this institutional matrix that Caponsacchi and Pompilia locate their virginity, and from this institutional inertia that they rescue it, by an act of invention that itself forms a major part of their heroism.[23] They find in the history that has produced them the means of making a repristinative history of their own: "the first things made new," as the Pope puts it, by "repetition of the miracle, / The divine instance of self-sacrifice, / That never ends and aye begins for man" (10.1654–57).[24]

V

Caponsacchi's and Pompilia's joint invention of virginity effects a miraculous repetition that brings history forth from the mythologized past into the living present. In this they resemble the historicist poet who "Creates, no, but resuscitates, perhaps" (1.719). Book 1, Browning's verse essay in the poetics of historicist representation and repristination, fully recognizes that the author of a Victorian epic must figure as a latecomer to the carnival of history: neither a dusty antiquarian nor a fire-breathing Promethean but something in between, a revivalist.

Man's breath were vain to light a virgin wick,—
Half-burned-out, all but quite-quenched wicks o' the lamp
Stationed for temple service on this earth,
These indeed let him breathe on and relume!
For such man's feat is, in the due degree,
—Mimic creation, galvanism for life,
But still a glory portioned in the scale.

(1.735–41)

These images of light and breath resume the terms that inspired Romantic illuminists fashioned from biblical accounts of creation; while the burden of this double tradition does not snuff out Victorian options for epic, it certainly constrains them. Browning tropes as "virgin" a lamp wick that, like the lily-flowered ring with which the poem commences, is an artifact to begin with. Yet even so artificial an origin needs further trimming before it can light the Victorian poet's way. He finds his occasion for inspiration only once the wick has passed through a history of prior use as well as manufacture. Evidently none but used goods, picked up at second hand like the old yellow book, are good enough for the work of repristination. And yet, within a secondary epic world where pristine *things* are literally use-less, a kind of pristine *act* nevertheless remains indispensable. For the poet assumes a traditionally virginal role in this passage: tending a hallowed fire that others, differently privileged, have struck before him, he performs the service of a male vestal in the temple of history.[25] "Man's breath" enacts "man's feat" by taking a virgin's part. And taking a virgin's part—which Browning, Caponsacchi, and Pompilia all do in various ways—means positing an arbitrary, belated origin amid the continuum of life's "odds and ends" (1.53).

In the terms of epic tradition, we might say that Browning generalizes the *in medias res* condition of narrative openings to the human condition, which looks before and after, and makes its future out of what remnants come to hand. Among poetic genres epic has traditionally held an early or virginal position by reason both of certain preliterate vestiges—invocation, formulaic epithet, bardic stance—and of the epic claim to tell a—if not *the*—culturally originary tale. Radically transmuting such conventions and claims, Browning stakes a modern counterclaim. Origins are where we find them, and they are everywhere; they are, indeed, as ubiquitous as the cultural and rhetorical structures that our every act reinstitutes in confirmatory or revisionary ways.[26]

The Ring and the Book renders at epic length, through a plot that turns on a collaboratively invented virginity, Browning's historicist vision of the production of conditional truth by inevitably cultural means. The publication of the poem in serial installments, its sequence of competing interpretations of the Franceschini case, the way each interpretation gets improvised and revised under the pressure of circumstance, all conspire in a bifocally late-Baroque and mid-Victorian image of the modern mind in labor with the only truth it can know: the truth it has invented, within historical limits and by rhetorical means that the poem conscientiously acknowledges. In the massive representation of representation that is *The Ring and the Book,* I have been arguing, the ring and the book and every other thing ultimately signify the working that has gone to shape them for apprehension and use. This is why the closing lines of the poem revert to the jeweler's craft, by which "rough ore" may be "rounded to a ring," and to the poet's craft, which may "mean beyond the facts" by signifying those operations that produce facts for consumption in book form (12.862–65).

In such an epic world of contingent repristination, things are always consequences betokening their history, and meanings are ultimately the results of signifying acts. *The Ring and the Book* accordingly blocks all recourse to an unmediated virginal *Ding an sich*. Nor does its crucial and imaginatively calisthenic first page ever uphold a *Ring an sich* for objective appreciation. What Browning calls "the ring-thing" is no thing, but instead "A thing's sign"; and "the thing signified" by it is no thing either, but instead a process: the process of poetic or figurative representation. "Do you see this Ring?" The literalist reader's incredulous response—"Well, no, not really"—plays an important, but importantly preliminary, part in the interpretation it incites.[27] For to read the poem at all is to *see* the ring indeed, not in itself but in its constructed significance. This Browningesque kind of seeing foreshadows a dialectic that the monologues of Caponsacchi and Pompilia fulfill: pristine or virginal presence is negated, and figurative representation is repristinated in its place.

If Browning makes the ring or the book no thing, that does not mean he makes them nothing. Our evolving recognition of the special kind of reality the "ring-thing" assumes across three dozen lines, and then a dozen epic books, illustrates and affirms the constructive power of representation. In his first epic venture *Sordello* (1840), Browning endorsed the craft of the "Makers-see," artists who neither retail their own high vision nor produce perfect objects but "Impart the gift of seeing" to their audience (3.868, 929).[28] In *The Ring and the Book* he gives us, through the invisibly elaborate ring, a vision of our own making; and he gives us, through a repristination of the old yellow book, an epic argument that representation—however belated or partial or sullied—is the ground of our every original act. The invented virginity of the figured text is the only kind we can call our own.

CHAPTER 6

Becoming the Poet: The Feminine Poet-Speaker in the Work of Elizabeth Barrett Browning

Dolores DeLuise with Michael Timko

In her early poetry, including *Sonnets from the Portuguese,* Elizabeth Barrett Browning subscribed without reservation to the notion of the poet as a male genius.[1] The flexible identity of this male poet-genius becomes particularized in the *Sonnets* as the female poet-speaker's courter, "*the* poet," Robert Browning. Subsequently, the male poet as hero, genius, and lover develops knowledge of female sexuality, disappears from her work, and is replaced by the female poet-genius, Aurora Leigh, in the text of a woman's experience. The inexperienced, virginal poet speaker is the male poet-genius; and as this figure gains insight and autonomy, the virgin text gives way to the text of experience. By the time Aurora Leigh usurps the role of the poet-genius, Barrett Browning is comfortable with the idea of the poet as an experienced woman having feminized the figure through her earlier poetry.[2]

Up to and including the *Sonnets,* Barrett Browning held the common nineteenth-century critical attitude that creativity of imagination was linked with the idea of the creative genius, embodied in the figure of a poet-hero. She also believed that poetry was the "perfection which the imagination suggests," consistent with Coleridge's belief that the end of poetry was pleasure. Additionally, following Wordsworth's assertion that truth is poetry's telos, she felt that poetry, "dignified, serious, sacred and pure," presented such "truth."[3]

In an 1842 review for the *Athenaeum,* for example, she describes Chaucer: "His senses are open and delicate, like a young child's—his sensibilities capacious of supersensual relations, like an experienced thinker's."[4] In effect, she combines both views of the poet so that Chaucer can be at once the creative child and the truthful thinker. She continues:

> And because his imagination is neither too "high fantastical" to refuse proudly the gravitation of the earth, nor too "light of love" to lose it carelessly, he can create as well as dream, and work with clay as well as cloud; and when his men and women stand close by the actual ones, your stop-watch shall reckon no difference in the beating of their hearts.[5]

Like Chaucer, Robert Browning was creative (his "men and women" were like Chaucer's) but not so creative in a "high fantastical" manner as to render his characters unrealistic. As a critic, Barrett Browning asserts that a poet like Browning was successful in balancing the best qualities of both the Baconian and Aristotelian points of view, Coleridge and Wordsworth in one.

She puts forth this theory most strikingly in her letters to Robert Browning, and indeed, supplies him with the very terminology he would paraphrase in his later essay on Shelley. She assesses his ability thus: "You have in your vision two worlds—or to use the language of the schools of the day, you are both subjective and objective in the habits of your mind."[6] Browning recycles her evaluations of himself in his "Preface" when describing objective and subjective poets.[7] His "phrase" of "modern classification" recalls Barrett Browning's "language of the schools of the day." She goes on:

> You can deal both with abstract thought and with human passion in the most passionate sense. Thus, you have an immense grasp in Art; and no one at all accustomed to consider the usual forms of it, could help regarding with reverence and gladness the gradual expansion of your powers. (1:9)

Regarding her own poetry, however, she is predisposed to worship a male mentor because of her belief that the poet is a male creative genius.[8] Barrett Browning's "secret profession of faith" maintains the superiority of men's intellect: "Let us say & do what we please & can . . . there *is* a natural inferiority of mind in women—of the intellect" (1:113). The superior male intellect makes a superior poet. "You are 'masculine' to the height," she tells Browning, "and I, as a woman, have studied some of your gestures of language & intonation wistfully, as a thing beyond me far!" (1:9). She particularly admires his "high faint notes of the mystics" and "dramatic impersonations"; when these are "thrown into harmony," works such as *Pippa Passes* result (1:22). That poem, she feels, is "most exquisite & altogether original," and she expresses the desire to have "been visited with the vision of 'Pippa'" before Browning (1:24). The vision with which she was visited, *Sonnets from the Portuguese,* took its theme from her admiration of Browning's *Pippa,* just as her translation of *Prometheus Bound* was prompted by the influence of Hugh Stuart Boyd's scholarship, both cases illustrating her attachment to the notion of a male poet-genius who had crossed the boundary from her work to her life.

Sonnet 4, for instance, subtly reflects the weight of Browning's style of expression which Barrett Browning so admired. The poet fashions the listener, the courting poet-hero, into a "most gracious singer of high poems" whose "calling" is to "some palace floor."[9] The persona of the poet speaker reveals herself in a sudden shift of landscape as she defines herself as a house whose "casement [is] broken in," a place which has "bats & owlets builders in the roof." "Hush!—" she tells the listener, "call no echo up in further proof / Of desolation!—" The dramatizations of speaker as run-down house and listener as court poet, along with the interplay between the characters insinuated by the admonition of the speaker to "hush . . . call no echo up," suggest the techniques of the dramatic monologue.[10] The use of the house as metaphor, furthermore, is strikingly similar to Browning's use of a house as a metaphor for Luca in *Pippa.*[11] The house, like Luca, is "mute" (1.20) and "silent as death" (1.24), paralleling Barrett Browning's self-description. It has "rough white wood shutters" and "rusty iron bars" (1.23); it is "deserted" (1.107), and as neglected as the house in Sonnet 4.

Before attaching herself to a male mentor, Barrett Browning's personal, libidinal preoccupation with the figure of the poet is clearly revealed in her poetry. In "A Vision of Poets" (1844), she both sexualizes and feminizes the nature of the poet's work, the challenges of that work, and the poet's reward.

"A Vision of Poets" begins as a poet wanders through a wood and meets a lady to discover that her work is "to crown all poets to their worth."[12] She commands the poet to drink from four pools, which, with their attendant emblems, are richly suggestive of the sexual nature of the poet's work. The first is near a dead tree stricken by lightening, "a monumental tree, alone" (133). He drinks from this pool with its phallic guardian. The next pool is set near some "straight flags," whose blade-shaped leaves contrast with some lilies nearby, suggesting both male and female sexuality (144). The third pool is "whitely smeared" by a "slow slime," and he drinks from this pool for "world's love" (154–58). The last pool from which the poet drinks is populated by snakes, toads, and clinging bats, and strikes a chill into the hearts of all who venture there. He falls backward into a dream state "with Life and Death at each extreme" (190), and is wakened as the lady's "slow kiss" crowns his forehead (199). The virgin poet begins his rite of initiation into a type of sexual experience that becomes explicitly female.

Together they enter a cathedral presided over by a chief angel. Poets, male with the exception of Sappho, from all nations and ages enter, and all have a bleeding wound in place of a heart. The chief angel poses to the poets a long and complicated question about their work and worth; they all agree to the premise that suffering is the price poets have to pay for their art. A Christ-like, woman-like suffering accompanies the poet's crown: "all the crowns of earth must wound / With prickings of the thorns He found" (547–48).[13] Likewise, the questions asked of the poets by the chief angel are framed in terms of a woman's life: is the lack of suffering like the lack of conscience? Should their words, as acts which change the world, "leave their own souls in eclipse?" (529–31). And finally, the angel wants their response to the assertion that they have to be like Christ in his suffering. The poets' unified answer is what a woman's answer was expected to be: "Content. . . . An affirmation full of pain / And patience" (558; 561–62). The poet learns that knowledge of female sexuality is essential for his work.

The vision recedes and "The lady's kiss did fall anew" on the poet's brow (776). That same kiss, previously described as a crowning kiss, "now reversed its own law" by piercing "most subtly" his spirit "with the sense of things / Sensual and present" (779–82). It becomes part of his rite of initiation, transforming virginity into experience.[14]

In a concluding section of "A Vision of Poets," the narrator walks in the same wood at a later time, and retraces the poet's footsteps. She learns that the poet has died; at his death, he contemplated a lily, studying it "as deep down as a bee had sucked" (888). He was "content to suffer much" (927). It is the sexual nature of his poetry, and the female part of that sexuality, that he recalls as having been the aspect of his work important enough to stand as an icon of his death.[15] He recollects and confirms the vision in which his work had been defined in sexual and feminine terms.

In the volumes of poems published in 1838 and 1844, Barrett Browning further marginalizes or in some way feminizes the poet, male genius though he is.[16] It is in "Lady Geraldine's Courtship" (1844), however, that Barrett Browning feminizes a particular poet-genius: Robert Browning. In the course of the narrative, most of which is a letter written by the male poet, the disparity of birth—"She was sprung of English nobles, I was born of English peasants" (15)—is contrasted with the disparity between both male and female, poet-genius and nonpoet. The setting for this occurrence, as well as the description of Browning's poetry which follows, is clearly linked with the issues surrounding the work and worth of the poet raised in "A Vision of Poets." The poet, Bertram, relates how Lady Geraldine walked out "among her noble friends . . . within this swarded circle, into which the lime-walk brings us" (106–9). No music enters this enclosed garden except that pure enough for the "lilies round the basin" to hear (112). The "swarded circle," a woman's space, will only be filled with music pure enough for the lilies, strongly reminiscent of those surrounding the second pool from which the poet drank ("A Vision of Poets"). The entrance to that circle is a "lime-walk." In this poem, and as we shall see in *Aurora Leigh* (1855), the lime tree is closely associated with Barrett Browning's ideas of the male poet-genius: the emotive, creative, Baconian Coleridge. By allying herself to the male poet via the figure of the lime tree as access to the feminine space, she familiarizes herself with the notion of woman as creative poet-genius.

In Coleridge's "This Lime-Tree Bower My Prison," the poet regrets his inability to join his friends as they walk into the woods and meadows.[17] The bower serves as a gateway, or vestibule, to the place his friends travelled, as he himself had travelled, and where the "Almighty Spirit . . . makes / Spirits perceive his presence" (42–43). He imagines his friend, "struck with deep joy," standing as he himself had stood "silent with swimming sense" in that place (38–39). The speaker then feels a sudden delight, and becomes as glad as if he himself were there. Looking around his bower, he perceives the beauty of nature which he had not perceived before, and concludes that it is sometimes "well to be bereft of promis'd good" so that the soul may be lifted and one may "contemplate / With lively joy the joys we cannot share" (64–67). Just as the speaker's desire for freedom is resolved as the prison becomes the source of release, so Barrett Browning's poem reconciles the tension between her conception of the poet as male genius and the fact that she is the feminine poet-genius responsible for having written both the poem and the poet.

Bertram reads to Lady Geraldine: Spenser, Petrarch, Wordsworth, Howitt, Tennyson, and Browning. The words used to describe the work of the first five are commonplaces: the "pastoral parts" of Spenser; "the subtle interflowings" of Petrarch; Wordsworth's "solemn-thoughted idyl" (159–62), and so on. To Browning, however, two full lines of distinctive portrayal are dedicated: "Or from Browning some 'Pomegranate,' which, if cut deep down the middle, / Shows a heart within blood-tinctured, of a veined humanity" (163–64).[18] She particularizes Browning as a poet related to those poets in the vision ("A Vision of Poets"), feminizing him as she links him with poets who have wounds dripping blood. Since it is his work, "some 'Pomegranate,'" to which she specifically refers, it seems clear that she is ascribing to Browning the poets' feminized answer to the angel's question: "Content . . . . An affirmation full of pain / And patience."

"Lady Geraldine's Courtship" functions as a model of Barrett Browning's relationship with Robert Browning as poet-genius and lover. Five months after the publication of "Lady Geraldine's

Courtship," Browning, summoned, as it were, by the two lines of poetry devoted to him, indeed entered Barrett Browning's life, becoming her mentor and role model. She writes, shortly after the initiation of their correspondence: "I am inclined to look up to you in many things, & to learn as much of everything you will teach me" (*Letters,* 1:13). Likewise, he occupied the place previously inhabited by the figure of the male poet-genius in her poetry: "I will reverence you both as 'a poet' and as 'the poet'" (1:79). In addition to emulating his dramatic style which she admired in all his work and particularly in *Pippa Passes,* Barrett Browning casts Browning in the role of poet-hero of the *Sonnets from the Portuguese.* She reimagines him in the *Sonnets* as she has already imagined a poet in "Lady Geraldine's Courtship." What Bertram writes of himself and Lady Geraldine, "I was only a poor poet, made for singing at her casement," prefigures Sonnet 4 where the speaker herself is the house whose casement is broken in.

If the narrative strategies and points of view of the speakers, poets, and "ladies" (that is, women being courted by men) of "Lady Geraldine's Courtship," *Sonnets from the Portuguese,* and *Aurora Leigh* are examined, it will become clear that these roles are at first discrete, then overlap, and finally converge in *Aurora Leigh.* In "Lady Geraldine," the speaker is a male poet-genius, the "lady" of the poem is not fully identified with her author, nor is the poem written from Lady Geraldine's point of view.[19] In the *Sonnets,* the poet is a male poet-genius, and the speaker and "lady" are female and closely identified with the author. In *Aurora Leigh,* all these roles become one: the speaker and lady are female and are closely identified with the author, who is the poet-genius. Barrett Browning, who at first cannot conceive of a woman speaker in the role of poet-genius, gradually assigns that role to a female speaker and poet-genius in a number of ways which overlap incrementally, until in *Aurora Leigh* the role is unconditionally given to a woman.

The poet Browning, narrowly defined in his role of "*the* poet" in the *Sonnets from the Portuguese,* possesses many of the qualities of Bertram in "Lady Geraldine"; additionally, the relationship between Lady Geraldine and Bertram complements the relationship between the speaker and the poet-hero in the *Sonnets.* Like Bertram, the latter is both noble and rich in a manner taken to befit a poet. Bertram declares, with a sudden flash of self-knowledge, that he is "worthy as a King" (316); "noble certes," affirms Lady Geraldine, and rich in virtue (Conclusion, 43). In a more explicit manner in the *Sonnets,* the poet-hero is clothed throughout in purple (Sonnets 9, 16, 39, for example). In Sonnet 3, the speaker addresses him as "princely Heart," and claims that he is a "guest for queens to social pageantries," which replicates Bertram's position as a guest in Lady Geraldine's noble household. He is a "liberal / And princely giver" (Sonnet 8); he is "princely & like a king" (Sonnet 16). Likewise, in Sonnet 4, the speaker says: "Thou hast thy calling to some palace floor, / Most gracious singer of high poems."

While Bertram bears this resemblance to the male poet-hero of the *Sonnets,* equally striking is the resemblance between Bertram and the female speaker of the *Sonnets.* They both have a sense of loneliness and separateness which marks the poet-genius. Bertram does not always join in with the socializing which goes on around Lady Geraldine; "oft," he relates in his letter, "I sate apart" (87). The speaker of the *Sonnets* is likewise alienated, weeping "alone . . . aloof" (Sonnet 4). Before she knew the poet-hero, the speaker "sate alone here in the snow" (Sonnet 21).[20] In addition, their self-descriptions are equivalent; Bertram says he is "poor, weak, tost with passion" and dares not love Lady Geraldine to his "grief and [her] dishonor" (318–19), which is comparable to the speaker's assertion that her soul is "all faint and weak" (Sonnet 12), and that she seemed like an "out of tune / Worn viol" with which a good singer "would be wroth / To spoil his song" (Sonnet 33). Corresponding to the thesis of the *Sonnets from the Portuguese,* and to the speaker's representation of herself, Bertram says he is "born to poet-uses, / To love all things set above me, all of good and all of fair" (29–30). The speaker of the *Sonnets* echoes Bertram:

> And thus, I cannot speak
> Of love even, as a good thing of my own!—
> Thy soul hath snatched up mine all faint & weak,
> And placed it by thee on a golden throne:
> And that I love . . . (O soul, I must be meek!)
> Is by thee only, whom I love alone.
>
> (Sonnet 12)

The responses of Bertram and the speaker of the *Sonnets* to an intimidating emotion are arrestingly similar. Bertram, exhausted by an "inward flow of passion" (337) "fell, struck down before" Lady Geraldine (349), recalling the speaker who compares herself to an "acolyte" who might "fall flat, with pale insensate brow" because of an overwhelming emotion (Sonnet 31).

Bertram and the speaker of the *Sonnets* also have the same approach in contending with the issue of seeming versus reality. Lady Geraldine and Bertram consider a statue of Silence portrayed asleep.[21] Lady Geraldine points out the paradox that the Silence has forgotten to say "hush" (116). One of the statue's hands clutches a rose "held slack" in her fingers, "fallen backward in the basin," and Lady Geraldine feels that an "essential meaning growing" may "exceed the special symbol" of the rose (119–21). Illustrating her point, Lady Geraldine says that "our true noblemen will often through right nobleness grow humble, / And assert an inward honour by denying outward show" (123–24). Bertram, on the other hand, points out that even though Silence seems to drop the rose, she yet holds it; he counters her assertion by telling her that "substance . . . wanes" and "symbol . . . exceeds" (130), and "your" nobles "wear their ermine on the outside," or else society brands them "mere ignoble men" (127–28). In this discussion over what is and what seems, Bertram alleges that symbolic representation is paramount in generating meaning. Similarly, in Sonnet 13 the poet-speaker finds herself unequal to the task of bringing "proof / In words . . . of the love hid in me out of reach." She goes on to say she will depend, rather, upon the manifestation or symbol of womanhood, "silence," to "commend my woman-love to thy belief." Like Bertram, she finds that symbolic representation is more forceful than matter, that "substance wanes, symbol exceeds." While the male poet-hero of the *Sonnets* resembles the poet-genius in Barrett Browning's earlier poetry, the female speaker of the *Sonnets* also ascribes to herself the qualities and opinions of the poet-genius.[22]

Gender dictates that, while there is a relationship between the speaker of the *Sonnets* and Bertram, there is also a relationship between the speaker and Lady Geraldine. As the disparity of social status gives way to a redefinition of virtue and nobility in "Lady Geraldine," so this discourse reappears in the *Sonnets* and the letters between Barrett and Browning. It is made clear in "Lady Geraldine" that a poet possesses inherent virtue and a particular kind of wealth. After explicitly stating that she would never marry anyone not noble "ay, and wealthy" (263–64), Lady Geraldine reveals she loves Bertram and would marry him because he is "very rich . . . in virtues—very noble" (Conclusion, 43). This idea thus features in Barrett Browning's poetry and life, and seems to elucidate a puzzling aspect of her relationship with Browning.

Barrett Browning obsessively reiterates expressions of gratitude to Browning in both the letters and the *Sonnets*. In places, it seems to be her principal feeling (for example, see *Letters,* 1:197). While she was six years older than Browning and did have definite doubts about her physical and emotional abilities, the expressions of gratitude in the letters and *Sonnets* seem to continue the discourse begun in such poems as "Lady Geraldine's Courtship" and "A Vision of Poets," where the male poet is a noble and virtuous genius, close to God.[23] The topic of professional gratitude discussed by the two poets in their letters emerges in the *Sonnets,* where what appear to be expressions of personal gratitude prolong the "poetry question," explored in a medium which is what it discusses. With the knowledge that the personal relationship between the two figures is so inextricably enmeshed in poetry, one is able to assess the seeming self-abasement of the speaker of the *Sonnets* in a different light.[24]

Both Lady Geraldine and the speaker of the *Sonnets* share Barrett Browning's "secret profession of faith" that women have an inferior intellectual capacity. Lady Geraldine is an earl's daughter, "proud," "noble," and breathing "perfumed air" (3–4). Bertram asks: "What was *I* that I should love her . . . I was only a poor poet" (16–17). As the disparity of birth is resolved through Bertram's intrinsic nobility and wealth of virtue, the italicized "I's" become reversed. Lady Geraldine asks: "'Dost thou Bertram, truly love me? Is not woman far above me / Found more worthy of thy poet-heart than such a one as *I?*'" (Conclusion, 31–32). It is this question, in which personal feelings are informed by issues of intellectual and spiritual ability, and the capacity to be a poet, that the speaker of the *Sonnets* asks the poet-hero in many different ways. In Sonnet 11, for example, the speaker, paraphrasing Lady Geraldine, says, "O beloved, it is plain / I am not of thy worth nor for thy place"; in Sonnet 8, likewise, she asks what she can give him in return for his gifts. The gifts are "gold / And purple of thine heart, unstained . . . untold," manifestations of the wealth and nobility of the poetic nature. She asks if she is not cold and "ungrateful,"

> that for these most manifold
> High gifts, I render nothing back at all?
> Not so—not cold—but very poor instead!

Her poverty and ingratitude are her lack of worthiness, in Lady Geraldine's terms.

Descending from the earlier poets figured in Barrett Browning's work, the poet-hero of the *Sonnets* also possesses the female qualities of his predecessors; she had already feminized Browning in "Lady Geraldine's Courtship." In Sonnet 24, the speaker commands him: "look on me . . . breathe on me!" ascribing to him the nurturing, feminine qualities of the maternal child-poet, Goethe, who looks on Bettine and breathes on her brow, in the 1838 poem "To Bettine: The Child-Friend of Goethe." In Sonnet 36, the speaker lays out her anxieties about her life with the poet-hero, frankly asking if she gives up everything for him will he be everything to her. In particular, she wants to know if he can fill the close personal place now emptied through death, "filled by dead eyes too tender to know change" (perhaps her brother Edward, but most probably her mother).[25] Asking to be nurtured, she says "open thine heart wide, / And fold within, the wet wings of thy dove," calling to mind again the image of the child-poet-genius Goethe, and his relationship with the child Bettine: "The poet's arms have wound thee."

Not only does Browning resemble the male poet-genius of Barrett Browning's earlier poetry, in the *Sonnets* he usurps his place. In Sonnet 27, the speaker confesses she lived with "Visions . . . instead of men & women," that is, she lived with the fictional characters she read about and likewise created.[26] They were "gentle mates," but soon "their lutes did silent grow." "Then," she tells the poet-hero, "*thou* didst come . . . to *be,* / Beloved, what they *seemed.*" Just as Browning takes the place of the fictional poets from whom he has descended in her imagination, Barrett Browning gives up her fiction of the male poet-genius to become one herself by achieving a kind of parity with the poet-hero of the *Sonnets;* they usurp the place of the poet-genius together.

While the *Sonnets* are filled with references to her unworthiness and the gratitude she feels she ought to express, ultimately there is a progression toward acceptance of the poet-hero's love which endows her with a reciprocal worthiness. In Sonnet 10, fire can burn either a temple or flax; indeed, "an equal light / Leaps in the flame from cedar-raft or weed. / And love is fire." In Sonnet 23 there is a compensatory equality, related to the fire which is love:

> our two souls stand up erect & strong,
> Face to face, silent, drawing nigh & nigher,
> Until their lengthening wings break into fire
> At either curved point.

The silence which was hers alone in Sonnet 13 here gives rise to "our deep dear silence," encompassing the two souls standing face to face. In Sonnet 44, the last in the sequence, the speaker, in a gesture of reciprocity, offers the preceding sonnets to the poet-hero in the spirit in which he had brought her bouquets of flowers. She "withdrew" her thoughts which "unfolded" like flowers from her "heart's ground": "Take them as I used to do / Thy flowers." Personal gratitude replaces professional gratitude to resolve the "poetry question." By offering poems to "*the* poet," she shows that she has proven herself a poet to her own satisfaction, and is ready to see herself as a coequal figure.

The virginal poet, unaware of his own worth and crowned by another—thus initiated into experience—disappears from the work of Barrett Browning after the *Sonnets from the Portuguese.*[27] The figure gives way to Aurora Leigh, the experienced feminine speaker, courted lady as well as the poet-genius and who, knowing her own worth, crowns herself. Her libidinal preoccupation with the figure of the male poet gone, Barrett Browning transfers that interest to the possibilities which present themselves to the self-crowned female poet-genius. Symbolizing this rejection is the figure of the lime tree. In Book 1, Aurora describes her compliance with her aunt's instruction; she was placed by her aunt in a chair with her "back against the window" (1.483–85), excluding "The sight of the great lime-tree on the lawn, / Which seems to have come on purpose from the woods / To bring the house a message"

(1.485–87).[28] Even though she cannot see it, Aurora can yet get a sense of the "message" the lime tree delivers. Having come seemingly of its own volition out of the woods, the solitary tree, like the "monumental tree, alone" of the first pool from which the poet drank ("A Vision of Poets"), conveys the trope of masculine sexuality and masculine genius, one which is very disturbing to Aurora. This point is made emphatic a short time later in Book 1, as she describes the "little chamber" (1.567), the feminine space which is her own room in the house. It was as "green as any privet hedge" (1.568):

> the walls
> Were green, the carpet was pure green, the straight
> Small bed was curtained greenly, and the folds
> Hung green about the window which let in
> The out-door world with all its greenery. (1.570–74)

She is surrounded by the color of the fertility of nature and of inspiration which encompasses everything she can see, extending out from her womb-like woman's space into the world. Her view is dominated, however, by the lime, whose bees interfered with her creative process:

> I had enough there, of the lime, be sure,—
> My morning-dream was often hummed away
> By the bees in it. (1.579–81)

Out of context, this discernment of the lime tree, bordering on resentment, is perplexing. If one remembers, however, the circumstances surrounding the lime in "Lady Geraldine's Courtship" and "This Lime Tree Bower My Prison," it is clear that she has now given up the belief in the male poet as genius. She creates her poet-genius-speaker as a woman, living and working in a fertile feminine environment literally (and literarily) overshadowed by male genius. As Barrett Browning was fused to the male genius in "Lady Geraldine's Courtship" through the lime trees which led to feminine space, in *Aurora Leigh* feminine space is distinct from the lime tree, the vestigial remnant of male genius, and she experiences it as a separate, disruptive entity because she has endowed her feminine poet-speaker with autonomy.

While the hero who courts the speaker of the *Sonnets* is "*the* poet," Romney Leigh, courter of the speaker of *Aurora Leigh*, clearly is not. In a chiasmic movement, the male figure in *Aurora Leigh* is transformed from a male poet-genius and Aurora, the experienced poet, usurps the role of "*the* poet" from Browning himself. As an experienced poet, Aurora appropriates Browning's theories of poetry, just as Browning had been influenced by Barrett Browning when formulating his definition of objective and subjective poets.

Romney, for instance, accuses Aurora of being irresponsible, like a child playing beside a deathbed (2.180); he holds that women, like children, cannot understand certain things. It is Romney, however, who does not understand the implications of childishness. He knows nothing about Goethe's nurturing, childlike genius, nor of Goethe's counterparts, the feminized poets, among them Chaucer and Browning. He does not properly value Aurora's worth as a poet: if she is able to write as well as other women, "what then?" if she is able to write "even a little better . . . still, what then?" "We want the Best in art now, or no art," he tells Aurora (2.147–48). From his point of view, her femininity will prevent her from becoming a poet; he mistakes, however, femininity for virginity. Unaware of her status as an experienced poet-genius, he advises Aurora to "keep to the green wreath" (2.93), the transformed crown here an image of a woman's space, circumscribed by fertility, and advises her furthermore to maintain her virginal status by avoiding anything which would defile "the clean white morning dresses" (2.96). What he is unable to understand is that the inexperience to which he refers is actually the feminine, childlike genius of the poet; he cannot read and understand the woman's text of experience.[29]

Aurora defends herself by saying: "Better far / Pursue a frivolous trade by serious means, / Than a sublime art frivolously" (2.257–59). Her response incorporates Browning's philosophy, embracing ideas to be found in his poetry. In Browning's "The Lost Leader" (1845), for example, those who had made the leader their "pattern to live and to die" (12) were betrayed by him; he had pursued what Aurora calls "a sublime art frivolously." In Browning's "The Last Ride Together" (1855), the two lovers are united one last day: "So, one day more am I deified. / Who knows but the world may end to-night?" (21–22). A poet is not "nearer one whit" to his "own sublime" than those who have no artistic ability: "Sing, riding's a joy! For me, I ride" (75–77). By riding well, or pursuing a "frivolous trade by serious means," the speaker of the poem transcends the sublime work of the poet. Through her symmetrical relationship with the poet Browning, Aurora is transformed into Barrett Browning's autonomous poet-speaker. As God's "truth-teller" (1.859), she has come to parallel Browning's poet in "How It Strikes a Contemporary" (1855):

> We had among us, not so much a spy,
> As a recording chief-inquisitor,
> The town's true master if the town but knew!
> (38–40)

Both *Aurora Leigh* and Browning's closet drama, *In a Balcony* (1852), further illustrate this transformed relationship when they raise issues of feminine autonomy, self-assertion, and the possibility of the love of a woman for a man.[30] These texts, in fact, engage one another in a discourse which can be traced to Barrett Browning's 1844 volume. The unifying symbol of this exchange is the crowning of the poet. Barrett Browning's male, virginal poet was crowned by another and thus initiated into experience; her experienced female poet, who incorporates Browning's ideas of crowns and crowning, crowns herself, and the two poetic doctrines converge.

Within the first thirty lines of *In a Balcony,* Norbert and Constance discuss whether or not they should immediately inform the queen they want to be married. Constance takes offense at the suggestion that they should inform her immediately, shifting the emphasis from that question to herself, invoking a controversy from *Aurora Leigh.* "I am not yours then?" (19) she asks him, and begins in the next line to discuss Norbert as if he were not there:

> I am not his—who change into himself,
> Have passed into his heart and beat its beats,
> Who give my hands to him, my eyes, my hair,
> Give all that was of me away to him.
> (20–23)

This is the very contention surrounding the sketches that Aurora Leigh's friend Vincent Carrington wants her to assess in Book 3. Vincent describes his sketch of Danaë reaching up to Jove, eager to "burn him faster down" (3.124). The sketch, as described by Vincent, is a sensuous, emblematic replication of the pose Aurora had assumed in Book 2 when Romney discovered her crowning herself as a poet with an ivy wreath; here, although Danaë is in the same posture as the self-crowned Aurora, it is actually Jove who is crowning her with himself. Aurora analyzes the picture: "Surely. Self is put away, / And calm with abdication. She is Jove, / And no more Danae" (3.135–37), paraphrasing Constance's objection to changing herself into Norbert. Aurora, the experienced poet-genius, concludes:

> God says, "Sweat
> For foreheads," men say "crowns," and so we are crowned,
> Ay, gashed by some tormenting circle of steel
> Which snaps with a secret spring.
>
> (3.164–68)

Constance likewise culminates her thoughts about relinquishing her own personality to a man with a cynical assessment of Norbert's potential crowning: "Just that the world may cry 'So much for him— / The man predestined to the heap of crowns: / There goes his chance of winning one, at least!'" (36–38).

The lesson of reciprocal love taught in Sonnet 44 reemerges in Book 4 of *Aurora Leigh*. Aurora begins to define the meaning of love in a reciprocal context while hearing Marian Erle's story. When learning that Marian thought Romney loved her, Aurora thinks "this perhaps was love" (4.176). Aurora invests this new conception of love with the idea of a circle, "A perfect round of love / Includes . . . being loved" (4.179–80), which gives rise immediately to the idea of a crown:

> The cataracts of her soul had poured themselves
> And risen self-crowned in rainbow: would she ask
> Who crowned her?—it sufficed that she was crowned.
>
> (4.184–86)

Marian, like Aurora and unlike Danaë, is self-crowned in Aurora's new formulation of the reward of the woman which is now like the reward of the experienced poet. Like the experienced poet, the woman who loves is autonomous and crowns herself.

Whereas the virgin text celebrates crowning as the reward of the male poet-genius, likening him to Christ and to women, the text of experience spoken by the transformed feminine poet-genius posits a cynical rejection of that notion. What was a tribute rewarding "all poets to their worth" ("A Vision of Poets"), wounding poets "with prickings of the thorns" of Christ becomes a "tormenting circle of steel" with no compensatory divinity attached. The crowning celebrated in *Aurora Leigh* is not earned by virtue; it is the kind one gets for oneself, reminiscent of Browning's "There's many a crown for who can reach" ("The Last Ride Together" [1855], 61). In Barrett Browning's text of experience the poet has become an autonomous, mature woman, a poet-equal to "*the* poet," who recognizes that in order to be crowned, she must crown herself.

CHAPTER 7

The Frozen Fountain: Christina Rossetti, the Virgin Model, and Youthful Pre-Raphaelitism

Barbara Garlick

Edmund Gosse's description of Christina Rossetti as the high priestess of Pre-Raphaelitism, while accurate only in retrospect, ironically grants her a position within the movement which her own poems explore and question through negotiating the dogmas laid down by the Brotherhood. Denied membership, Rossetti was nevertheless both acolyte and central icon of virginity for the youthful group, occupying a space where power could be expressed only through negativity, that is, through retaining by rewriting the inviolability of the virginal self and body. Her recognition of the loss of selfhood involved in repressed sensuality gives rise to an interrogative revision of certain images which were used, within their Pre-Raphaelite pictorial space, forcefully to foreground and reinforce prevailing sexual ideologies. In addition, through those images and through her dream poems in particular, she interrogates the technical means—the white ground and the flattened perspective—by which early Pre-Raphaelite paintings also perpetuated the confinement of their subjects, marginalizing the female model as sign, as Griselda Pollock has said, whose signified is masculine creativity.[1]

The "literary organ of the Pre-Raphaelite Brotherhood," *The Germ,* whose four issues were published in 1850, emphasizes in its conception the close association between art and literature which, at least in the eyes of Dante Gabriel Rossetti, was a necessary part of the Brotherhood's beliefs.[2] It also helps to articulate both the repressiveness possible in the two-dimensional space of pictorial representation and the subversion of that two-dimensionality possible in the written word. The first two issues were subtitled "Thoughts towards Nature / In Poetry, Literature, and Art," and the last two dropped *The Germ* as main title and retitled it *Art and Poetry* with the subtitle "Being Thoughts towards Nature / Conducted Principally by Artists."

The engravings by Holman Hunt which accompany the first issue, illustrating an episode in Thomas Woolner's two poems "My Beautiful Lady" and "Of My Lady. In Death," are typical of both the style and the discursive practices characteristic of early Pre-Raphaelitism (figure 7–1). The top engraving illustrates the stanza:

> This is why I thought weeds were beautiful;—
> Because one day I saw my lady pull
>   Some weeds up near a little brook,
>   Which home most carefully she took,
>   Then shut them in a book.

The distinction between words and picture lies in pose and tone: in the engraving the medieval courtliness of the poem is translated into costume, but the lover is also restraining the lady as she leans towards the stream in her attempt to reach the flowers and water-lilies which are just out of reach. In the lower engraving the lover is prostrate on the ground, a spade beside him and robed nuns in procession in the background. It appears to illustrate a line in the penultimate stanza of the second poem: "I dropped, in a dead swoon, / And lay a long time cold upon my face."

In his Preface to the 1901 facsimile reprint, William Rossetti tells us that "These compositions were, I think, nearly the first attempts which Mr Woolner made in verse; any earlier endeavours must have been few and slight," a mildly critical comment which is, however, balanced by the subsequent assertion that Coventry Patmore thought highly of Woolner's verses. Like many of the poems in the four issues, these two have little to recommend them except a few lush descriptive phrases which accord well with the

FIGURE 7–1
WILLIAM HOLMAN HUNT, ILLUSTRATION TO "MY BEAUTIFUL LADY" AND "OF MY LADY. IN DEATH," BY THOMAS WOOLNER. *THE GERM,* NO. 1, JANUARY 1850.

Pre-Raphaelite desire to study nature firsthand, and an earnestness which is summed up by William Rossetti:

> Being little more than lads, these young men were naturally not very deep in either the theory or the practice of art: but they had open eyes and minds, and could discern that some things were good and others bad—that some things they liked, and others they hated. They hated the lack of ideas in art, and the lack of character; the silliness and vacuity which belong to the one, the flimsiness and make-believe which result from the other. They hated those forms of execution which are merely smooth and prettyish, and those which, pretending to mastery, are nothing better than slovenly and slapdash, or what the P.R.B.'s called "sloshy." Still more did they hate the notion that each artist should not obey his own individual impulse, act upon his own perception and study of Nature, and scrutinize and work at his objective material with assiduity before he could attempt to display and interpret it; but that, instead of all this, he should try to be "like somebody else," imitating some extant style and manner, and applying the cut-and-dry rules enunciated by A from the practice of B or C. They determined to do the exact contrary. The temper of these striplings after some years of the current academic training, was the temper of rebels: they meant revolt, and produced revolution. (6)

The frequently asserted iconoclasm of these "lads" and "striplings," their subversion of contemporary art practices of technique and style, obscures, however, the extent to which they valorized contemporary moral and cultural discursive formations, particularly in the area of sexual ideology. In both their visual art and their literary output, they reinforced the patriarchally defined separate spheres of the day by figuring the centrality of the female other and by confining this other within certain literal and metaphorical framing devices.

Such standard methods of restriction appear in their crudest form in Woolner's second poem, "Of My Lady. In Death," in which the lady's death follows immediately after, for no apparent medical reason, her submission to the lover's ardors. Set amidst nature, "within a huge tree's steady shade," the lovers consummate their love, after which the lady's beauty "Sank, sharpened with disease," and "Her gaze, grown large with fate, was cast / Where my mute agonies / Made more sad her sad eyes," after which, three lines later, she dies.

The framing devices foregrounded by Woolner's poems and Hunt's two engravings—the reversion to medieval costume and pose, the physical restraint of the woman, the allusion to the conventual life, the function of woman as sign and site of contradiction and repression[3]—are as characteristic of both early and later Pre-Raphaelitism as the fleshly medievalism and minute depiction of each blade of grass by which they are more generally categorized.[4] The devices are focused on the dangers of active female sexuality and conversely the erotic promise of virginity. In the engravings the courtly lover's stance signifies moral rectitude as he restrains the lady in her yearning after unattainable pleasures and beauty and then laments her death as the nuns, symbol of both visible purity and reproach to the lady's loss of virginity, pass behind him. In the poems forbidden pleasures are clearly associated both with wild nature, "weeds," and the secret delights of books. More importantly, the naturalizing of the lady robs her of participation in the male world of individuality and existential autonomy. In a particularly telling reference she is also assigned a place within a literary tradition which is most particularly associated with Elizabethan and metaphysical expressions of ultimate misogynistic power, "My day-dreams hovered round her brow; / Now o'er its perfect forms / Go softly real worms." Her corporeality, which had determined the progression from sexual knowledge through disease to the disintegration of the flesh in death, also justifies her function as model, muse, and ultimately as two-dimensional commodity, both the face of the marketable paintings and the physical love object. Flattened perspective underwrites ideological impetus.

Millais's illustration to the first of Woolner's poems, "My Beautiful Lady," which was prepared for but not used in the first issue of *The Germ* is more insistently symbolic. It refers to the stanza:

> Or may be that the prickles of some stem
> Will hold a prisoner her long garment's hem;
> To disentangle it I kneel,
> Oft wounding more than I can heal;
> It makes her laugh, my zeal.

The drawing focuses on the moment of freeing the white dress from the rose as the lady looks backward over her shoulder. The setting is Edenic, with a profusion of flowers and a white greyhound pointing out of the frame, but the briar roses both arrest the moment and hint at the fall from Eden, a treatment later used more consistently by Burne-Jones in his two briar rose series.[5] Once again, however, the poem displays more about the lover's attitude than the conventional courtly pose of the drawing; for, in the poem, the seduction which is to come in the second poem is foreshadowed in the tearing of the white dress by the lover in his "zeal." A metaphorical reading of Ruskin's words, which inspired the Brotherhood in his 1843 first volume of *Modern Painters,* is particularly appropriate in this context:

> They [young artists] . . . should go to Nature in all singleness of heart, and walk with her laboriously and trustingly, having no other thoughts but how best to penetrate her meaning, and remember her instruction; rejecting nothing, selecting nothing, and scorning nothing; believing all things to be right and good, and rejoicing always in the truth.[6]

The placing of the female, then, within nature and as subject to its cycles of bloom and decay, coupled with the second of the professed aims of the young Brotherhood, clearly inspired by Ruskin, "to study Nature attentively, so as to know how to express them [genuine ideas]," indicates the central role played by the female figure in the early Pre-Raphaelite aesthetic credo.

Christina Rossetti's position within the group was an ambivalent one. She was a multiple contributor to the first three issues of *The Germ* and was certainly the model for specific drawings and paintings. Moreover, her serious dark face and slight figure reappear as a type in much of the early work, particularly as an avatar of virginity.[7] As type, the face appears in many of Dante Gabriel's early Dante paintings and drawings as both Dante and Beatrice, where it becomes exaggeratedly Italianate, and also in several of Millais's early drawings, such as Mary in the first sketch for "Christ in the House of His Parents"; his 1849 "Garden Scene with Girl Cutting a Rose," where the domed framing line captures the stillest of moments before the acquisition of knowledge that comes with the cutting through of the rose stem (figure 7–2); "St Agnes of Intercession" which was intended for the proposed fifth

FIGURE 7–2
JOHN EVERETT MILLAIS, "GARDEN SCENE WITH GIRL CUTTING A ROSE," 1849. REPRODUCED WITH KIND PERMISSION FROM THE COLLECTION, ART GALLERY OF WESTERN AUSTRALIA.

FIGURE 7–3

JAMES COLLINSON, *ST. ELIZABETH OF HUNGARY,* 1850. REPRODUCED WITH THE KIND PERMISSION OF THE BIRMINGHAM CITY COUNCIL MUSEUM AND ART GALLERY.

issue of *The Germ* to illustrate "a plaintive story by Dante Gabriel Rossetti about a dying girl having her portrait painted by her lover"[8]; an 1853 sepia ink drawing of "Virtue and Vice" in which the Rossetti face is depicted as a forlorn seamstress in a garret being tempted by an exotically dressed woman offering money; and the drawing illustrating Woolner's poem discussed above.

As model Christina Rossetti is also Queen Elizabeth of Hungary in Collinson's painting (figure 7–3). It is enlightening to read her seductive identification with this portrayed role written approximately two years after she had posed for the painting, "When if ever life is sweet, / Save in heart in all a child, / A fair virgin undefiled, / Knelt she at her Saviour's feet." Significantly enough, Rossetti did not include this poem in any of the collections published in her lifetime.

The two most important representations of her though are by her brother: *The Girlhood of Mary Virgin,* of which Holman Hunt said "Miss Christina was exactly the pure and docile-hearted damsel that her brother portrayed God's Virgin pre-elect to be"[9]; and *Ecce Ancilla Domini* or *The Annunciation.* We know that Dante Gabriel used nude models for the first sketches of the latter, and in the finished painting the emphasis on vulnerable virginity with the narrow bed and the loose nightgown is so pronounced as to verge on the erotic.[10] This painting, which Dante Gabriel called "the blessed white eye-sore" and "the blessed white daub," might stand as an exemplar of the process whereby the model as individual is marginalized and removed from the interrogatory site represented by viewer-painting-painter.[11] Rossetti's sonnet "In an Artist's Studio," another poem not published in her lifetime, clearly confronts the denial of individuality to the model, the painting out of the living subject. As Surtees relates, the hair in *Ecce Ancilla Domini* was painted from another model called Miss Love, and the head was painted over many times, so that William Rossetti records that "When first exhibited in 1850 the likeness was more decided than it is now."[12] G. P. Boyce describes how he

> went to Gabriel Rossetti's studio to see his Annunciation picture, which was exhibited at the National Institution . . . . He has been painting on it since, and sent it off (to Dublin) whilst I was there. The Virgin one of, if not the most exquisite conception I have yet seen, her head, golden hair and blue eyes (although

> painted from his sister who is darkish) full of intense thought and awakened and growing religious awe, almost my ideal of a woman's head . . . . The white drapery with which she is clad beautifully treated.[13]

Again the ambiguity of representation is seen in Holman Hunt's painting of Christ knocking at the door of the human soul, *The Light of the World,* for which Rossetti sat because Hunt admired "her gravity and sweetness of expression."[14] It is also recorded that both she and Elizabeth Siddall sat for the colouring in this painting.[15]

More problematical is a painting by Dante Gabriel, for which William Rossetti recalls that his sister sat.[16] It is called *Hesterna Rosa,* yesterday's rose (figure 7–4). This painting, like Hunt's *The Awakening Conscience,* depicts the remorse, or at least fleeting moral awareness of one participant (yesterday's rose of the title) in an orgy. Here the symbolism is even more apparent: the innocent child on the spectator's left playing the lute, juxtaposed with the gross ape on the right.[17] Innocence is lost, fleshly appetites have triumphed, but innocence may still be recalled with regret as the lute plays. William also recalls that both Dante Gabriel and Millais used Rossetti as model in their illustrations of *The Idylls of the King* in the Moxon Tennyson.[18]

As model and type, Rossetti's presence is carefully controlled.[19] The depictions are either confined to biblical themes as in her brother's paintings, Collins's *Convent Thoughts,* and Millais's *Christ in the House of His Parents,* or frozen at the moment before knowledge is gained through fulfilled sexuality, as in the Millais drawing for *The Germ,* his "Garden Scene with Girl Cutting a Rose," and his painting *Lorenzo and Isabella.* Even in *Hesterna Rosa* the Rossetti figure is inhibited in her sensuality, covering her face, looking out of the frame, with a flowery coronet serving to bind her hair rather than loosely sitting on freed hair like the other, more abandoned female figure.

Rossetti had had some art training herself, and her writing against the stifling atmosphere of the Brotherhood develops through a specific subversion and questioning of their pictorial methods.[20] In the first place, her work inscribes a specific exploration of the ambivalent value of whiteness; secondly, it attempts to break through the mirror of two-dimensionality and the even more limit-

FIGURE 7–4
DANTE GABRIEL ROSSETTI, *HESTERNA ROSA*, 1853.
REPRODUCED WITH THE KIND PERMISSION
OF THE TATE GALLERY, LONDON.

ing flat perspective employed by the Pre-Raphaelites, in order to interrogate the traditional use of women within and related to nature. Through these means, she was able to begin to demystify the codes imposed both by the narrow world of the Brotherhood and the wider mid-Victorian social world. Although in many cases subversion was not finally realized until her later poems and prose works, in her early poems the effort is clearly present. In addition she adopted, adapted, and developed pictorial methods through the medium of her verse.

The use of white was an important part of the Pre-Raphaelite painting method:

> The design would be carefully outlined on the canvas, and over this would be painted—only on the portion to be completed at

> that sitting—a film of white pigment, worked off with a dry brush, then tapped with the brush to ensure evenness. The design would be visible through this thin film, and the painting would be done over it, necessarily with meticulous care, with the smallest of brushes and at a very slow rate. This technique satisfied a demand for brilliance of colour and minuteness of observation, and for a time assumed the status of an article of faith within the Pre-Raphaelite circle.[21]

Rossetti demonstrates in her last prose work, *The Face of the Deep,* how thoroughly she had absorbed and resolved in her own thinking the ambiguities of both the method and its moral implications:

> Nevertheless as whiteness may again be defined not as *absence* but rather as *invisibility* of colour, so these white stones may be contemplated as white because of their proper stainlessness, yet equally as coloured in response to that Divine Light which bathes them: even as the hueless diamond blazes with rainbow tints in answer to the sun's glory.

> Nevertheless whiteness is not an absence but rather a compendium of colour. All tints when united in a perfectly balanced harmony resolve themselves into whiteness, and consequently all tints are capable of being re-developed from whiteness. Thus colourless light paints the rainbow . . . . At the first moment *whiteness* does not suggest *colour:* yet all colour being latent in it, we finally discern in its train every lovely hue and gradation of hues.[22]

Rather than a blankness to be painted over and obliterated, then, whiteness for Rossetti, as for Newton, represents the basic condition of all color and complexity. It is the pallor of the face of experience most clearly seen in the Laura of "Goblin Market," and not the automatic sign of precognizant virginity that was adopted by Dante Gabriel in *Ecce Ancilla Domini,* "the ancestor of all the *white* pictures which have since become so numerous—but here there was an ideal motive for the whiteness."[23] Rossetti's intellectually probing analysis may also be seen as a specific refutation of Ruskin's principle of the innocent eye:

> The whole technical power of painting depends on our recovery of what may be called the *innocence of the eye;* that is to say, of a sort of childish perception of these flat stains of colour, merely as

> such, without consciousness of what they signify—as a blind man would see them if suddenly gifted with sight.[24]

Milton's words in the *Areopagitica* are much closer to Rossetti's conception of experience and of her place in the world, and her Newtonian analysis of whiteness and its ambivalence indicates her affinity with the Miltonic attitude that a true virtue necessitates knowledge:

> As therefore the state of man now is; what wisdome can there be to choose, what continence to forbeare, without the knowledge of evill? He that can apprehend and consider vice with all her baits and seeming pleasures, and yet abstain, and yet distinguish, and yet prefer that which is truly better, he is the true wayfaring Christian. I cannot praise a fugitive and cloister'd vertue, unexercis'd & unbreath'd, that never sallies out and sees her adversary, but slinks out of the race, where that immortall garland is to be run for, not without dust and heat. Assuredly we bring not innocence into the world, we bring impurity much rather: that which purifies us is triall, and triall is by what is contrary. That vertue therefore which is but a youngling in the contemplation of evill, and knows not the utmost that vice promises to her followers, and rejects it, is but a blank vertue, not a pure; her whitenesse is but an excrementall whitenesse.[25]

Unfortunate as the pronouns are in this famous passage—and we may recall here the dual female figures of Virtue and Vice in Millais's drawing mentioned above—it is nevertheless clear that Rossetti develops Milton's principle in the early poems through emphasizing autonomous choice. In "Three Nuns," for instance, which, though written in 1849–1850, was one of those many early poems she chose not to include in her published collections, the three speakers have each deliberately chosen the conventual life, and, by implication, the death in life clearly recognized but nonetheless preferred.[26] The first speaker's assertion, "I would be dumb," in the first stanza is negated immediately as the song of a bird recalls youthful beauty and the world of childhood lived in a natural setting full of conventional symbols which she must now reject even while recording them:

> In the thickest of the wood,
>   I remember, long ago

How a stately oak tree stood,
  With a sluggish pool below
Almost shadowed out of sight.
On the waters dark as night,
Water-lilies lay like light.

There, while yet a child, I thought
  I could live as in a dream,
Secret, neither found not sought:
  Till the lilies on the stream,
Pure as virgin purity,
Would seem scarce too pure for me:—
Ah but that can never be![27]

The startling reversal in all three sections of the poem, whereby purity comes after and not before knowledge, is underscored by a consistent use of paradox. In section 2 "was my sin prayer?" is given force by the terminology of commerce: Having engaged in an activity—praying for her lover's wellbeing—which resembles entering the marketplace of sexual exchange, the speaker now feels that "I sacrificed, he never bought. / He nothing gave, he nothing took; / We never bartered look for look." Lizzie's appropriation of the marketplace in the later "Goblin Market" signifies a triumph in the male world of barter and exchange which had not been possible in this earlier poem.[28] In section 3 the bird image which had provoked thoughts of a past life is now used in the opening paradox:

My heart is as a freeborn bird
  Caged in my cruel breast,
That flutters, flutters evermore,
  Nor sings, nor is at rest.
But beats against the prison bars,
  As knowing its own nest
Far off beyond the clouded West.[29]

From here the earthly but dying world is set against the heavenly future world to which the speaker aspires and in which the red and the white roses can bloom together: "Red roses like love visible / Are blowing on their tree, / Or white like virgin purity." Like the previous two speakers this one also has had worldly experience; neatly labeled in the past as "daughter, sister, wife," she now rejects the "foolish riches of this world" and with them the implied loss of individuality involved in such role-playing. As the poem ends it appears to fulfill the opening stanza's "I would be dumb": "So now, when I am faint, because / Hope deferred seems to numb / My heart, I yet can plead; and say / Although my lips are dumb." Closure is avoided, however, in the final line, "The Spirit and the Bride say, Come," which opens out a potentially paradisal world in which paradox is resolved and renunciation is justified because the role is self-chosen, not imposed.

Dolores Rosenblum's reading of this poem as Rossetti's engagement "in a process of translating the language of Romantic longing" is dependent upon an earlier premise that

> Rossetti's lifelong identity crisis is bound up with a language crisis . . . just as there is a split in the poet-subject's identity, so there is a split between her "own" language of ascetic self-denial and the "other" language of romantic passion and romantic self-assertion . . . . Sensing that the language of romantic feeling and romantic individualism is inappropriate to her vision, Rossetti takes up the officially sacred language partly in order to drown out that other language.[30]

Rosenblum's is an exciting and intricately developed argument, but it fails to confront adequately that element of choice which even in these early poems is a distinctive feature of Rossetti's answer to the demands on the virginal self.

Choice also involves the physical subjugation of that most erotic sign of female sexuality, the hair, which in a painting like Millais's *The Bridesmaid* is not only the visual focus, but also the central erotic motif subverting the innocence implied by the title. The decision to veil or bind the hair in Rossetti signifies the willed renunciation of the worldly pleasures it invokes. Just as the third speaker in "Three Nuns" "gave my golden hair," the first speaker also chooses a bridal state which is not dependent on physical beauty:

> When my yellow hair was curled
> Though men saw and called me fair,
> I was weary in the world
>   Full of vanity and care.
> Gold was left behind, curls shorn,

When I came here; that same morn
Made a bride no gems adorn.

In "The Convent Threshold" (1:61–65), the speaker renounces youth with its "golden windy hair afloat" by the most active of gestures: "I turn from you my cheeks and eyes, / My hair which you shall see no more." Once again the action is taken after, not prior to knowledge, "You sinned with me a pleasant sin," and the language of color delineates the "crime":

There's blood between us, love, my love,
There's father's blood, there's brother's blood;
And blood's a bar I cannot pass:
I choose the stairs that mount above,
Stair after golden skyward stair,
To city and to sea of glass.
My lily feet are soiled with mud,
With scarlet mud which tells a tale
Of hope that was, of guilt that was,
Of love that shall not yet avail;

"The Convent Threshold" also continues a sequence of dream poems in which Rossetti develops that depth of field which is so alien to the Pre-Raphaelite flat perspective.[31] Through dream the other world of the subconscious is explored by means of a conscious act of narration: the double dream is doubly introduced, "I tell you what I dreamed last night" (lines 85 and 110). The reiteration not only foregrounds the subject's desired control of that depth of field which is the subconscious by means of her narrated reproduction of it, it also indicates her Scheherazade-like power over the auditor. Furthermore, unlike the figures trapped literally within the frame, the model functioning as sign only, the narrator has woken and moved beyond the two-dimensional, foreshortened space. The first dream in "The Convent Threshold" is purely Miltonic in both language and image, depicting a Satanic figure who, lusting after knowledge, is confined within the dream by the narrator's conscious conclusion:

I saw him, drunk with knowledge, take
From aching brows the aureole crown—
His locks writhed like a cloven snake—
He left his throne to grovel down

And lick the dust of Seraphs' feet:
For what is knowledge duly weighed?
Knowledge is strong, but love is sweet;
Yea all the progress he had made
Was but to learn that all is small
Save love, for love is all in all.

The second dream is an after-death experience like the early "Dream Land" published in the first issue of *The Germ*. Here the narrator conducts a conversation with her lover beside the grave. Eerily, the after-death conversation continues after waking, and we learn that the speaker is now "veiled in Paradise." The act of narration, then, allows the subject-narrator to explore the subconscious. In "Dream-Love" (1:123–24), her question "But who shall tell the dream?" results in three different versions of the dreams of the male figure of Young Love, a daring demonstration of narrative control and power. In "My Dream" (1:39–40) we are alerted in the first lines to the assumption of narrative integrity which is also an assertion of writerly control of the poem: "Hear now a curious dream I dreamed last night, / Each word whereof is weighed and sifted truth." This control is reinforced by subsequent narratorial intrusions: "The rest if I should tell, I fear my friend, / My closest friend would deem the facts untrue; / And therefore it were wisely left untold; / Yet if you will, why, hear it to the end." Again she balances the passivity appropriate to dream experience, where the subject becomes the object-victim of subconscious fears, with that writerly control of the poem: "But who shall tell the tale of all their woes?"; "I know not what it bore of freight or host"; and finally in the concluding tercet, "What can it mean? you ask. I answer not / For meaning, but myself must echo, What? / And tell it as I saw it on the spot."[32]

Dreams, then, reenact the passage between a renounced life and a chosen position which is frequently death in life, in which a speaking position is nevertheless able to be adopted with some integrity. The oxymoron of "the speaking silence of a dream" ("Echo," 1:46) is given flesh in the poems themselves, where the virginal self speaks of lived knowledge:

Yet come to me in dreams, that I may live
  My very life again tho' cold in death:

Come back to me in dreams, that I may give
Pulse for pulse, breath for breath:
Speak low, lean low,
As long ago, my love, how long ago.

The passage through dream frequently entails a questlike progress through the extremes of fire and ice as in "From House to Home" (1:82–88): "The first was like a dream thro' summer heat, / The second like a tedious numbing swoon, / While the half-frozen pulses lagged to beat / Beneath a winter moon." In this difficult poem which depicts a dream within a dream, the ideologically conventional relationship between physical virginity and nature is made clear; it stands within and is given meaning by nature:

My castle stood of white transparent glass
Glittering and frail with many a fretted spire,
But when the summer sunset came to pass
It kindled into fire.

My pleasaunce was an undulating green,
Stately with trees whose shadows slept below,
With glimpses of smooth garden-beds between
Like flame or sky or snow.

Swift squirrels on the pastures took their ease,
With leaping lambs safe from the unfeared knife;
All singing-birds rejoicing in those trees
Fulfilled their careless life.

In this virginal state, overtly seen in the symbols in the first and third stanzas, the lover is angel-like; the shock of his departure resembles a fall from Edenic nature to a realm of ice in which redemptive suffering finally allows the calm of knowledge:

Therefore, O friend, I would not if I might
Rebuild my house of lies, wherein I joyed
One time to dwell: my soul shall walk in white,
Cast down but not destroyed.

Therefore in patience I possess my soul;
Yea, therefore as a flint I set my face,
To pluck down, to build up again the whole—
But in a distant place.

Here again physical virginity, "my house of lies," cannot encompass the full expression of selfhood.

A poem written a year earlier than "From House to Home" allows us to move further through the ambivalences of this passage between the renounced life and the chosen "frozen" realm. In "A Better Resurrection" (1:68), images of nature lying fallow in winter take precedence over an inappropriate edenic profusion, the lush yet flat background against which woman is most frequently perceived and which allows her objectification and consequent commodification:

I have no wit, no words, no tears;
  My heart within me like a stone
Is numbed too much for hopes or fears;
  Look right, look left, I dwell alone;
I lift mine eyes, but dimmed with grief
  No everlasting hills I see;
My life is in the falling leaf:
  O Jesus, quicken me.

My life is like a faded leaf,
  My harvest dwindled to a husk:
Truly my life is void and brief
  And tedious in the barren dusk;
My life is like a frozen thing,
  No bud nor greenness can I see:
Yet rise it shall—the sap of Spring;
  O Jesus, rise in me.

My life is like a broken bowl,
  A broken bowl that cannot hold
One drop of water for my soul
  Or cordial in the searching cold;
Cast in the fire the perished thing,
  Melt and remould it, till it be
A royal cup for Him, my King:
  O Jesus, drink of me.

In the final stanza the artifice of the remolded bowl of life becomes the artifice of poetry which speaks the complexity of the virginal self and the discovery of fulfillment in the single religious life and vocation as poet. In line with her brazen use of the language of profane rather than sacred love, particularly in the final line of each stanza, the bowl becomes a womb-like vessel in which, through singing the praises of Christ, the fountain of creativity may remain fluent. It is the same image of female fertility that Virginia Woolf, an admirer of Rossetti, was to use for Mrs. Ramsay:

> Mrs. Ramsay, who had been sitting loosely, folding her son in her arm, braced herself, and, half turning, seemed to raise herself with an effort, and at once to pour erect into the air a rain of energy, a column of spray, looking at the same time animated and alive as if all her energies were being fused into force, burning and illuminating (quietly though she sat, taking up her stocking again), and into this delicious fecundity, this fountain and spray of life, the fatal sterility of the male plunged itself, like a beak of brass, barren and bare.[33]

The remarkable use to which Rossetti puts the image, to indicate the possibility of retaining the inviolability of the self after lived knowledge through the exercise of poetic creativity, is prefigured in one of her very early poems, "The Dead City" (3:63–71), written when she was only sixteen. It was classed by William as "Juvenilia" in the 1904 edition and not published in her lifetime. In it the speaker, predating Alice by almost twenty years, enters a dream world of lush vegetation, in which "Here and there the sunbeams fell / On pure founts, whose sudden swell / Up from marble basins flew . . . / In the midst a fountain rose / Of pure milk, whose rippling flows / In a silver basin rolled." But the speaker is alone, the "sole living one" in the dead city, which she has, as solitary poet and subject-speaker, recreated through her art and through deliberately entering into the dream world of the imagination.[34] Only ten months later in "A Pause of Thought," published in 1850 in the second issue of *The Germ* (in manuscript it was called "Lines in Memory of Schiller's Der Pilgrim") she laments under the pseudonym "Ellen Alleyn" her lack of poetic fame:

> I looked for that which is not, nor can be,
>   And hope deferred made my heart sick, in truth:
>   But years must pass before a hope of youth
>   Is resigned utterly . . . .
>
> Sometimes I said,—"It is an empty name
>   I long for; to a name why should I give
>   The peace of all the days I have to live?"—
>   Yet gave it all the same.

In this poem, which William relates specifically to the desire for worldly fame in his Preface to the facsimile edition of *The Germ* (21), Rossetti, most obviously alone in her poignant pseudonym, perceives a wide-ranging sense of emptiness, which may relate both to fame and to worldly pleasures more generally, and which certainly echoes the final line of Schiller's poem, "And the There is never Here!" The deliberate vagueness of the object of desire, moreover, bespeaks a generalized dislocation which her poems of the 1850s interrogate and resolve. Dislocation itself leads to a new becoming which, in "Femmes Divines," Luce Irigaray sees as the goal to which woman should aspire.

Irigaray's text, up to this point unspoken, has been an important influence on this discussion. In it she postulates the necessity of a female God, "Mais sans divin qui lui convienne, la femme ne peut accomplir sa subjectivité selon et dans un objectif qui lui correspond. Elle manque d'"idéal' qui lui soit un but et un chemin pour devenir."[35] For without a female god-figure it is impossible for women to conceive of that divinity within by which complete autonomy is realized:

> Nous nous regardons dans le miroir pour *plaire à*. Rarement pour interroger l'état de notre corps, de notre "âme," rarement pour nous et en vue de notre devenir. Le miroir presque toujours nous sert de moyen pour nous réduire à une pure extériorité, et pas n'importe laquelle. Il intervient comme possibilité de constituer des écrans entre l'autre et moi . . . . Le miroir, et d'ailleurs le regard, s'utilisent frequemment comme armes ou instruments non tactiles, étanches. Coupant le tactile, aussi celui du regard . . . . Le miroir devrait assister et non réduire mon incarnation.[36]

For Rossetti that mirror was the paintings by which she and the other models framed and frozen on canvas were confined. If she was only able to conceive of the way out of repression through love for a male godhead, it was nevertheless an autonomous choice realized through her own creativity. This conception is expressed in these early poems specifically not in the spiritually transcendent language of the male psalmist lifting his eyes unto the hills ("A Better Resurrection" and cf. Psalm 121), but, Theresa-like, in the overtly physical language of profane love; in Irigaray's terms: "Aimer Dieu a souvent été le recours des femmes. Elles sont gardiennes de la tradition religieuse. Et seule parmi elles, ou presque, certaines mystiques ont réalisé une oeuvre importante, notamment historique, notamment politique."[37] Ideologically, Rossetti's assertion of the strength of her subjectivity, her chosen speaking position, fractures the two-dimensionality of the limited view of women seen in *The Germ* and the early drawings and paintings of the Brotherhood.

"The frozen fountain" which is emblematic of the passivity of the waiting bride in her later long poem "The Prince's Progress" (composed 1861, 1865) serves to underline how Rossetti's use of a traditional metaphor for poetic fullness, used unproblematically by both Woolner ("Emblems") and her brother Dante Gabriel ("Sonnets for Pictures 4") in *The Germ,* serves also to foreground her own active protection of the virginal self. William's comment in the 1904 *Memoir* is seen in this context to be bitterly inappropriate, "Her temperament and character, naturally warm and free, became 'a fountain sealed.'"[38] Rossetti's new becoming is traumatically enacted in "The Heart Knoweth Its Own Bitterness" (3.265), in which the phrase used by William appears. Written seven years after "A Pause of Thought" and only two months after "A Better Resurrection," this poem again uses the highly charged language of sexual love, which, through deliberate ambiguity, comments on both "This world of perishable stuff" and on the developing relationship of poet with Christ, "I full of Christ and Christ of me":

> You scratch my surface with your pin;
> You stroke me smooth with hushing breath;—
> Nay pierce, nay probe, nay dig within,
> Probe my quick core and sound my depth.
>
> . . .
>
> Your vessels are by much too strait;
> Were I to pour, you could not hold,
> Bear with me: I must bear to wait,
> A fountain sealed thro' heat and cold.

The paradox of the frozen exterior face and the inner world of the virginal yet creative self becomes in the fifties a politically necessary choice for Rossetti in her decisive reaction to Pre-Raphaelitism, "I will not lean on child of man" (line 29). The frozen realm of worldly renunciation after lived knowledge is paradoxically that space in which the poet becomes the powerful agent of her own self-incarnation. In her recognition in the early poems of the ambivalence of the white ground and the foreshortened space, Rossetti announces both her singularity and her intellectual and creative distance from the "lads" and "striplings" and the restrictive "frames" of reference adopted by the Brotherhood.

CHAPTER 8

Like a Virgin: Coventry Patmore's Still Unknown Eros

John Maynard

We know Coventry Patmore now primarily as the Victorian poet feminist criticism loves to hate. And it is no good saying that *The Angel in the House* is really about the spirit of love in a marriage (Patmore's intention), not the Victorian angel homemaker on a pedestal. The poem—soon notorious even in its day—does represent an idealized, normative view of love between the sexes that leaves out most of the problems of personal relations and sex as well as those of social and legal equality. We can judge it more confidently because we find it repressed most of what Patmore had already discovered in his own early, quite experimental poetry.

What early poetry? Even the expert on Victorian poetry may well ask; for possibly this author is the only person now alive who knows the considerable volume of work before *The Angel,* because Patmore suppressed that early poetry too. You have to care enough to go to the bother of digging it out in one or another of a few rare book collections. What one then finds are poems, immature and silly at times perhaps, but consistently raising questions about the dangers and difficulties of sexual experience while they underline its centrality and importance.[1] Most interestingly, there is an early strong emphasis on the *textuality* of sexual experience. Patmore, son of the scapegrace Romantic man of letters implicated in Hazlitt's *Liber Amoris* affair, seems early to have been aware that the way we write about sex is in itself sexual experience. A poem, "Lilian," half humorously tells the tale of a friend's loss of his beloved (Lilian) to a fellow named Winton, a Frenchified scoundrel whose *instrumenta seductionis* are none other than those scrofulous French novels only Barrett Browning, of all Victorian intellectuals, would admit she enjoyed. Sex talk corrupts, sex texts corrupt absolutely. Another poem, "The Woodman's Daughter" (preserved though emasculated in the *Collected Poems*) has two young lovers, perfect in their innocence in nature, brought down by the young man's reading in the poets. She ends crazed, one of those legion of Victorian women characters who, themselves betrayed, have drowned their unwanted love children. The real culprit is clear in the final picture we have of her, obsessively returning to the scene of the crime: "Maud, with her *books* comes day by day, / Fantastically clad, / To read them near the pool" (emphasis added).

The problematic, somewhat playful character of some of these early poems is not due to any unseriousness about sex on Patmore's part. All his life he insisted on rewriting Wordsworth's Intimations Ode, on the basis of his personal experience, to an almost Freudian awareness of sexual feelings as a dominant human motivation from earliest childhood. He seems rather early aware of the play between words about the thing and the thing itself: a conceptualization that Foucault's Introduction to the *History of Sexuality*, and his approach through intellectual history in the volumes he achieved, have most helpfully clarified.[2] Sex is unspeakable—not because of the lurking Mrs. Grundy but because it is a thing of the body. As Lawrence put it, it is *not* sex-in-the-head. Foucault speaks vaguely of a utopian because unreadable area, the play of the body parts. Steven Marcus similarly saw language about sex used too close to the bone as mere pornotopia: losing its semantic force as it becomes merely part of an unwriteable (and certainly unreadable) physical activity.[3] I find it useful to use the term sex for the unspeakable thing, what Lawrence tried to get out of the head by throwing object-like four-letter words at it in *Lady Chatterley's Lover.* By contrast, sexuality can stand for the cultural writing of sex into one or another text: all the explanations, values, meanings, norms by which each society or group tries to regulate its sex experience.

Where do we place virginity? It really is hard even to give it a place in the order of the unspeakable because there it is merely a non-event: the *non-play* of the body parts (and I suspect that never truly happens as long as we are not yet among the angels). It is really a secondary concept, dependent on the textuality of sexuality. Virginity is the absence of some kind of sexuality; what it is (really what it is not) depends on how sexuality itself is defined in any particular culture. As a concept always already bound up with some particular concept of sexuality, virginity always makes us aware by its presence of an absence of some kind of sexuality. In the realm of the "real" it may be a boring nothing (as Kinsey found the churchy young men who confessed to having little or no sex activity each month to be also generally inactive and dull). As a *textual* event it is invariably a very sexy number.

Which is what Patmore set out to explore when the death of his first wife, Emily Andrews, left him, as far as we can tell, a very aroused repristinated virgin, one who then went on to convert to Catholicism, then to make a marriage with a nunlike rich Catholic lady which, as far as we can tell, was a *marriage blanc*. To confirm his enthusiasm for virginity we need only note that his favorite daughter chose the veil and marriage with Christ alone. Later sections of *The Angel in the House* show Patmore heartily discontented with the Charles Kingsleyan vision of happy middle class married sexuality that he had adopted in the first two books of *The Angel*. Faced with the loss of his first wife and an unwanted popularity for *The Angel* that had badly damaged, if not destroyed, his reputation as a serious writer, Patmore wrote the stunning (though quite uneven) series of odes eventually published as *The Unknown Eros*. They are Patmore's most outspoken poems. An Irish friend told me that even in his boyhood the Protestant *Angel* was memorized by boys in a Dublin Catholic school; but about the convert's Catholic poem there was an aura of danger—advanced work only for the future priests to look into back at the rectory. But their interest for us is primarily in the strength of Patmore's exploration of sexuality as a *textual* phenomenon. In that exploration, virginity is given—now for well-thought-out reasons— its customary place as the central jewel in the crown of sexuality.

As Paul Fry has shown, the ode is intrinsically involved in the enterprise of using mere language to try to reach beyond language to summon a god or power from outside the world of language. As in Fry's formulation, Patmore's odes make us especially aware of tension and play between the oratorical and spoken pretensions of the ode—really to language as an oral form of presence and immediacy—and the actual existence of the poem as text, a form of absence and removal from the god invoked.[4] Patmore, who in *The Angel* foolishly compared his poet figure to Petrarch, here follows much more credibly the traditional two levels of love. Book 1 presents love between humans, no longer a lawn poet's garden party of decorous married love but texts about desire provoked by absence. The fine love poem "St. Valentine's Day" (I.i) celebrates the force of desire stimulated when we create the world of language as sex and love absent: February and its existence as a repristinate virginity of nature only slightly written over by its defining opposite, the triumphant sexuality of roses and summer.[5] Desire is strongest as a text of absence, hence the choice of the odd day in the dead moment of the year—in "vestal February"—for love's celebration. As in a romantic poem in which the failure of nature fully to satisfy the poet sharpens his or her sense of power of imagination, Patmore's winter landscape of unfulfillment raises absent powers of love.

The main cycle of odes is then an autobiographical sequence. In "The Day After To-morrow" (I.v), the power of love for happy lovers is admitted to be a function especially of absence. It is a poem about love deferred and the power of absence to awaken passion. But Patmore's primary theme is the much greater power of desire in sexual loss, on which he insists in the great odes on his wife's death. These odes verge at moments on sentimentality but are always redeemed by their unmitigated focus on the force and finality of loss and the independent existence of the text of his aroused feelings, especially aroused by the forced virginity of widowerhood. The well-known poem "The Azalea" (I.vii) creates a text filled with bed, sleep, sensuality, and perfumed flowers only to show how much more powerfully these counters of sexuality function when we realize, with the poet, that the central presence of his wife is irrevocably absent. The nearness of intense sensual fulfillment, imaged in the marital bedroom and bursting azaleas, brings on anxious dreams of destruction against which the poem invokes God for protection. But just when this strategy seems to be working and he feels assured of his wife's presence—"Bless'd in the delicious sphere / By which I knew so well that she was near"—a hole opens up that will not properly close and that we now realize was there all along, which he has been trying desperately to bridge over: "It *was* the azalea's breath, and she was dead!"

The second book of the odes makes a number of stunning attempts to raise this painful personal insight into the dependence of desire on absence to a general and even mythological level. Although the context is Catholic, Patmore follows his own poetic logic more than any sect or mystic tradition.[6] If absence provokes desire, absolute absence provokes absolute desire: Virginity is the high road to sexuality . . . right to sex with God. Sex is deferred by our usual life of sexuality as text; virginity defers that deferral. Patmore's logic leads him to the conclusion that the most powerful sex experience available is that of writing about virginity. And so he does. "Sponsa Dei" (II.v) tells us, with a splendid odic turn at the end, that all those we have desired with a lust beyond mere mortal consummation (Patmore uses the rather charming homely Victorian terms of "Margaret, Maude, or Cecily") are really mirrors of our own self, the virgin lack and gap within, that only union to God can fill:

> A reflex heat
> Flash'd on thy cheek from His immense desire
> Which waits to crown, beyond thy brain's conceit,
> Thy nameless, secret, hopeless longing sweet,
> Not by-and-by, but now,
> Unless deny Him thou!

The great ode, "Deliciae Sapientiae de Amore" (II.ix), is one of the richest sexual celebrations in English poetry, in which we look voyeuristically through the portals of virginity to see the festival of union with God awaiting the pure, a consummation the more ecstatic and sensual as the realization of a desire conserved and deferred to that moment. In this his most ambitious poem celebrating religious virgin sexuality, indeed probably the finest poem of the entire series, Patmore throughout uses a framing device to guard the direct celebration, the sexy language, from too direct, and thus too quickly deconstructive or reductive examination by us. It is tempting to classify "Deliciae Sapientiae de Amore" in Fry's distinction as a hymn of settled faith rather than an ode reaching after some new god or his quality. Its magnificent ease and control of the ode medium at almost a continuous pitch of exalted celebration does suggest some kind of hymn-like ritual. But if it alludes to former religious modes, especially the rites in Revelation, it presents an essentially original concept of celebration; and the eye of the artist is especially keenly focused on his odic task of bringing a special god down to us while he simultaneously finds a way to lift us up.

Even the title performs the complex double act of inviting us in/teasing us as necessarily outsiders, an act that is repeated again and again in the rhetorical structure of the ode. In an allusion back to the epigraph from Proverbs that Patmore inscribed at the front of the entire *Unknown Eros*—"And my delight was with the sons of men" (Proverbs 8:31; Patmore uses the Latin "*Deliciae meae esse cum filiis hominum*")—with its intricate cluster of associations linking God's feminine counterpart, the figure of Wisdom, to his joy in intimacy with man, we are given something intrinsically and immediately attractive, "Deliciae," delights, allurements, of love, but then pushed back by the high requirement for entrance: wisdom. The poem itself begins with a command to love—"Love, light for me / Thy ruddiest blazing torch"—that would suit *Antony and Cleopatra;* and the setting, a palace, not the temple of Revelation, with roses not lilies, is anything but austere and forbidding. Then it withdraws again; he is only a "beggar by the Porch" of the palace of virginity. He places us, with him, in a voyeuristic relation to the sexual festival within: we are free to enjoy by overseeing, or later by overhearing, the celebration within. The position makes the audience, not part of the cult, comfortable with their outsider's relation to this material; hence it also wakens their desire for what is kept at a distance.

Nonetheless, in the course of the poem there is a slow process of entry, allowing us increasing access as we also make an increasing commitment. In the poem's context we pass through a series of definitions and tests of our belonging; as readers we work to follow a difficult and relatively long ode. The first cut warns us away if we have no idea of "the shining wall," the first of a number of direct allusions to Revelation, here to the wall of jasper in the vision of the New Jerusalem. The effect is, of course, to bring us to claim some vision and hope that we belong. We are pleased to hear there is no room for what we may have thought religious virgins were, those who, "most vile," try to exalt merely a spirit of denial, "The charnel spectre drear / Of utterly dishallow'd nothingness." From warning off those who don't belong, the speaker makes a rapid odic shift to bidding in: "Bring . . . anear." Worrying about our qualifications for entrance, we may be surprised to find we are acceptable as virgins because we are true young lovers, or "wedded spouse if virginal of thought." Presumably this last doesn't mean only those who, possibly like Patmore himself in his second marriage, choose virgin marriage; or if we don't find ourselves strictly included, we may take advantage of the latitudinarian spirit toward access to virginity to draw closer in any case.

As if to further encourage us, the speaker turns from the festival itself to try to define for us the state in which we understand virgin desire. He has already shown us the pomps of virginity as attractively warm, a ruddy blazing torch, a festival which is that of love and whose celebrants wear the nuptial roses of summer fulfillment. The Unknown Eros is thus in one form unmasked as virgin love in sexual celebration. The danger is of course that we take this merely for a love feast and Patmore's digression thus reminds us of origins in absence, not ordinary sexual fulfillment. The ode form allows him to jump to a series of rather metaphysical images, as usually handled well by Patmore. The first set is splendid. The consummation of sex in the natural world, projected on the grandest scale, is contrasted to unfulfilled desire's much greater power. Images set in logical opposition serve also to augment the sense of great desire, which is also thus greatly passionate and sensual, in virgin deferral:

> The magnet calls the steel:
> Answers the iron to the magnet's breath;
> What do they feel
> But death!
> The clouds of summer kiss in flame and rain,
> And are not found again;
> But the heavens themselves eternal are with fire
> Of unapproach'd desire.

A second long conceit moves rapidly and wonderfully from an appeal to our own experience (an inclusive gesture) to an arcane and difficult conceit naming our true desire (a hard action for us to follow). We all recall the great yearning that we felt in childhood which left us at first unsatisfied at the mere facts of life and love. Intimations of desire in childhood help define the greater intimations now. The conceit, a hard but rosy, sexy one is of a "star," evidently a planet that looks on his "Mistress," another planet, all his long year without ever touching. His pace, like that of a bridegroom rejoicing on his course, hastens him one time in his long year "Nearer, though never near" his "love" and "home." Patmore's stress on the light of space allows him to make such certainly withheld fulfillment a thing of enticing beauty, stressed in the rhyming words: *gaze, rays*. Throughout her ellipse there is no eclipse in her light, whose source is an ardent secret clothed in night. The approach brings doubling of light (double is repeated, "doubly" "doubled" in two lines). Like human lovers in Patmore, the bridegroom planet feels the "delicious" approach as one of both ecstasy and fear, suffering even in his sphere, in a cute coinage, "praeternuptial" anxiety (more than regular nuptials with hints of preternaturalism if not dangers of celestial pretermission or even pre-emission). The odd, half-fanciful, half-serious image of love writ large continues to augment and inspire our sense of love's force even as it offers a celestial tease, or even *caelestia interrupta,* as an image of desire provoked by deferral. Patmore wittily *and* mystically suggests the secondariness of all desire by reminding us that all this love light burns from a greater source, that mysterious "ardent secret."

Having explored our awareness of the power of desire, as indeed in so many odes before this, we are now welcomed in further by a poet who has clearly assumed singing robes finer than those of a mere beggar at the porch. Now we may "gaze bold" and we should hear. What we see and hear in the celebration is now at a visionary level, a "dainty and unsating Marriage-Feast," of the "Husband of the Heavens" (which has here at least planetary force) and the Lamb. They sing "*Cor Meum et caro mea,*" an allusion to Psalms 84:2 where heart and flesh sing to the living God. Virgin love is seen for a moment fulfilled, indeed taking its fill, in all senses, of God himself, "The 'I am.' " The language and imagery from biblical texts of man in relation to maker (the Virgins and the lamb, Revelation 14:1–5; the marriage supper of the Lamb, Revelation 19:9; God as husband, Isaiah 54:5; the "I am" of

Exodus 3:14), presented as a palimpsest of quotation and allusion, tell us we are on mythic grounds; we find that they are places especially where opposites meet, where dyads dissolve in each other.[7] Even in the planet conceit desire grows on absence, though this is placed in stasis in a way it couldn't be in the real world of Book I. In the mythic Palace, now also revealed as Revelation's temple, there is no gap between desire and fulfillment, yet each is also maintained fully, desire entirely potent, fulfillment ever plenteous. The ode's language revels in opposites reconciled, a "dainty" (thus virginal) but also "unsating" marriage feast (at the festival of virginity!). The singing choir of virgins (as also in Revelation), are both "shining" and "sacrificial." They give up—offer—their "dearest hearts' desires," but, unlike lovers in the earthly world, loss of desire only promotes its increase and fulfillment: desire comes back "to their hearts . . . beatified." Desire begets desire; it is blessed, in that sense fulfilled, and returns even stronger. Patmore plays the fundamental oxymoron, not for irony but ecstasy, again and again: a "nuptial song" for virgins; Mary hailed as "Virgin in Virginity a Spouse!" (Patmore's own rhetorical embroidery on the angel's simpler greeting in Luke), a place where virgins wear roses, not lilies, and indulge rather than hold back.

Patmore's tact and timing are marvelous here. Having offered the full paradoxical mythical spectacle, a vision of a land of hearts' desire all fulfilled for our gaze and ear, he leaves it, as certainly his earthly language would have, before he actually pulls the god down after calling it up. Instead he snatches away the scene of a sexual Revelation and returns us to the desiring ones: the cry of virgin spouse was heard in the human world in Nazareth; it is heard in nunneries, where paradise is still hidden and sought amid absence. The lines, combining winter absence and a sense of intense hidden sexual joy, are splendid, and master whatever hesitations we have as non-religious-virgins, non-Catholics, or even non-religious non-virgins:

> Heard yet in many a cell where brides of Christ
> Lie hid, emparadised,
> And where, although
> By the hour 'tis night,
> There's light
> The Day still lingering in the lap of snow.

Having pulled us away, forced us to focus on cloistered, very interior scenes where most of us normally don't belong, the poem now ends satisfying our readers' hearts' desire by a series of ever more inclusive invitations again to "Gaze and be not afraid . . . / Gaze without blame . . . / Gaze without doubt or fear." Repetition breaks down our resistance whereas direct description would tire and repel.

The ending builds a sense of sexual celebration that, if not orgasmic (such an easy literary effect to claim!) at least ends in something of a lyric crescendo. Wedded folk are "highly styled" among Revelation's "Thousands twelve times twelve of undefiled" (14.1). Patmore repeats an entire line from early in the poem, "Young Lover true and love-foreboding Maid," with a similar rhyme on "not afraid"; he repeats words or sounds at beginnings of lines: *gaze* or *there;* he uses alliteration similar to what he had found in Anglo-Saxon poetry ("There where in Courts afar, all unconfused, they crowd") to give both strongly marked meanings and a chant-like effect. Young lovers find their true Hymen in the Palace, with total sexual fulfillment as on earth—"No spark minute of Nature's keen delight" being omitted. In this full noon the lovers already at the festival find their early intimations of something better than earthly love are now fulfilled: "each to the other, well content, sighs oft, / 'Twas this we meant!'" The recall of "Twas" not only brings back the discussion earlier in the poem but the entire experience of Book I.

Finally, Patmore makes his most inclusive gesture: "of pure Virgins none"—other than Mary herself—"Is fairer seen" than—whom? Mary Magdalene of course. Patmore splendidly recaptures old church truths—the sanctification of the Magdalene—as striking new truth: yes, even the prostitutes (whom Victorians called magdalenes) are not only at the rite of virginity but stand fair, sexually attractive, there. The concluding line of this section is almost breathtaking: "Gaze without doubt or fear / Ye to whom generous Love, by any name, is dear." The embrace of that "generous love," really God as love at the center, not only welcomes the reformed magdalenes but even all the names and name-callings at their misplaced generosity. From nuns to prostitutes: we have now come to a virgin love so expansive and inclusive that it welcomes the daintiest and ruddiest of human lovers. To say, but they must now all vow virginity, means little as explanation; in the palace (not mere temple) to which our full and open gaze is now drawn sexual fulfillment is the donné: what isn't there is the stinted life of ungenerous love.

Patmore concludes this extraordinary ode with a shower of images and namings of generous love, a phrase repeated itself for ample measure: virginity is a perpetual fountain; by all names the virgins affect God, and he in return is "Husband of the Heavens." His lovers come in potence; they are all heirs; they are all clad in bridal robes "of ardour virginal." The plenitude above all is the repetition of opposites reconciled or oppositions walked over; names no longer matter; signs, the creations of absence, are canceled out and we are left with language fading to an appearance of presence. Patmore's ode moves from inviting us to gaze to the momentary magic of "For, lo," which is vision achieved at the point where language self-destructs. But he is still careful with his terms: this is an experience of the elect, and we hope we may be among them; they "affect / Nothing but God" (a fine phrase in itself), but this is either "mediate or direct": there is some place for other loves in this most generous love.

Of course it is only an appearance of plenitude, a system for suggesting presence built up from our awareness of distance from our approaching gaze. This fine artistic control and even chasteness necessary to render textual absence—virginity—is a way of celebrating the sexual fullness of union with God, the sex in which danger and loss will not dominate as Patmore found they *did* in ordinary human life. But this sexuality is abandoned in three odes where Patmore forgets the artifice of his sexual eternity. These, the Eros and Psyche odes, attempt to realize in a text the power of virgin union with God. Alas, the system, so weighted with Patmore's attractive desire to represent religion in graspable human form for adult consumption, comes tumbling down to mere sexuality—a dirty text trying to represent that finally unspeakable *S* thing, the more unspeakable as it is with God Almighty Himself (Patmore did not say "Herself," though he does create a feminized Christ). The model of Eros and Psyche as allegory for God and the soul is traditional; Patmore makes it so real that we have merely a Turk-like Victorian gentleman of pleasure and one of his many happily seduced innocents. Where we might expect the great achievement of his vision of a sexual union with deity, we find instead the unexpected triumph of his local patriarchal culture over his cosmopolitan religious and sexual discourse.

The odes as a series redeem this failure of art, this attempt to reach out of sexuality as a text of absence and desire and create a sex in words, by their splendid awareness of the problem. "The Child's Purchase" (II.xvii), a prologue ode to a never-written series on the life of the Virgin that Patmore inserts near the end of *The Unknown Eros* as both admission of failure and apology for the attempt, restores through Mary the distinction between word and flesh. We invoke her, specifically name her rather than try to realize her, because like us, she is nothingness in need, indeed more purely absence desiring as she is purer virgin than we. God's power makes her a nest of incestuous sexual consummations. But the poet's gift is not to make them come alive in his language, only to *name* them—

> To One, thy Husband, Father, Son, and Brother
> Spouse blissful, Daughter, Sister, milk-sweet Mother,—

and to express his own wish to be beyond text and mere sexuality of the text entirely. The odes thus end with a prayer, a finer, less obscurantist invocation of the Virgin than Eliot's rewriting in "Ash Wednesday." The poet addresses Mary in the end only as her human self, mother. That humanity is his humility; following the pain of sexual need he has been led and is led "by unknown ways." The prologue for a work, which we know by its presence in the odes will never be completed, ends speaking of the poet's "many wasted days" and doubting openly its aim. Mary's smiles seem dubious; he spells from them mainly the limits of words: "Humility and greatness grace the task / Which he who does it finds impossible." Patmore descends from the ode that would try to capture sex in the text of virgin absence to the prayer that only tries to name its still-absent hope—a hope necessarily deferred beyond realization in any text. I venture to claim these still-unknown odes in *The Unknown Eros*—though there are a good number of inferior odes among the best—as major art of the period.[8] They are unusual poems on love still suitable for grown-ups; fine, difficult, rich poems on sexuality and its cognate, virginity, that test and define the limits of textual representation of sex and desire.

PART 3

Virgin de Siècle

CHAPTER 9

What Lily Knew: Virginity in the 1890s

Adrienne Auslander Munich

Lily-like, white as snow,
   She hardly knew
She was a woman, so
   Sweetly she grew.
Oscar Wilde, "Requiescat"

Even out of context, no one takes Shakespeare's "Lilies that fester smell far worse than weeds," as a statement about horticulture. In Sonnet 94, this culminating line figures the results of sexual unchastity, and if the lilies, "sweetest things," refer to a specific gender at all, they refer to men: "But if that flower with base infection meet, / The basest weed outbraves his dignity."[1] Conventionally, however, the lily symbolizes the Virgin Mary; Lily, a feminine name, unlike Hyacinth or Narcissus, alludes by custom to Mary's virginity. Although the lilies under consideration here are represented as maidens, it would be useful to keep in mind the sexual ambiguity of the symbol, a symbol that frequently has as its subtext a distaste for loss of virginity by heterosexual means. Deflowered, sweet lilies fall lower than "things rank and foul" of Hamlet's unweeded garden. In examining certain cultural values projected on to the lily as denoting purity and its sexual designation, virginity, I focus on representations of young maidens in texts from 1892–1898, a period of a certain kind of heightened interest in *jeunes filles en fleur.*[2]

"Requiescat," Oscar Wilde's eulogy to his sister, dead at the age of nine, defines pure liliness as a state of absolute not knowing, particularly of not knowing one's own subjectivity.[3] A virgin cannot know herself as virginal, for that would give her the unvirginal knowledge she cannot have to retain her flowery sweetness. Once they know their virginal value, lilies fester. In some uses of virginity at the turn of the nineteenth century, when virginity turns (also in the sense of sours) toward its binary opposite, the horticultural metaphor becomes a way of using inviolability associated with womanly purity and with deepest spiritual mysteries as a reference point for something more ambiguous.[4] Placed within time, the works considered here want to convey that the virgin might turn to living rot. Thus Wilde eulogizes the perfect kind of virgin, a dead one.

Leila (1892, figure 9–1), a painting by Frank Dicksee (1853–1928) portrays an alternative to a lily's embalming: a lily's turn.[5] Dicksee positions the dark-haired, dark-eyed Leila in an odalisque pose, but in place of the more conventional horizontal position, Dicksee positions the bed vertically on the picture plane. Leila gazes directly at the viewer, one leg tucked beneath her languishing body; her red draperies emphasize her awareness of her body's allure. At her side blooms an emblematic white lily in full flower. Leila is a fallen lily, an unvirgin, whose coloring announces her exotic origins. The painting's two flowers, lily and Leila, embody the cultural dynamic of virgin knowing.[6]

Dicksee's *Leila* marks an evolution of the lily from Dante Gabriel Rossetti's annunciation painting, *Ecce Ancilla Domini* (1850, figure 9–2). Dicksee intensifies the intimacy of the Rossetti painting, further literalizing its carnal suggestivity. Rossetti's Virgin cowers rather than invites the mysterious event, the substitute for defloration. Yet, like Leila, she sits up upright on an unmade bed, the placement suggesting the activity which the Annunciation makes immaculate. At the foot of Mary's bed stands an embroidered lily panel, while in place of the lily in the Dicksee painting, a disconcertingly corporeal Gabriel proffers a lily to Rossetti's Virgin in a symbolic acting out of the moment of conception.[7] Gabriel's lily, a sign of the virgin, as the instrument of conception, becomes also phallic. Symbol of both virginity and divine phallic power, the lily can make things happen.

Like the miraculous phallic lily which invisibly inseminates,

FIGURE 9–1
FRANK DICKSEE, *LEILA*. EXHIBITED AT THE ROYAL ACADEMY, 1892. REPRODUCED WITH THE KIND PERMISSION OF THE FINE ARTS SOCIETY LTD.

absolute virginity tells no story about itself but enables the story to be told. The idea of semen itself as a richly metaphoric conceptualization of verbal power, from both Greek and Christian traditions, has the same paradoxically dual sexuality as the lily symbol. In addition to quintessential male power, it can be associated with the perpetual purity of a typically feminine power. Some literary virgins—whose essential virginity is never contested and is therefore impossible to lose—have such seminal property, providing the seed from which events proliferate into a plot. Robert Browning's Pompilia from *The Ring and the Book,* Charles Dicken's Agnes Wickfield from *David Copperfield,* and George Eliot's Romola are typically perpetual Victorian virgins. This kind of virginity, in many ways like woman herself, is the silenced basis for civilization, the gap through which desire becomes articulable. Like the sym-

FIGURE 9–2
DANTE GABRIEL ROSSETTI, *ECCE ANCILLA DOMINI*, 1850.
REPRODUCED WITH THE KIND PERMISSION
OF THE TATE GALLERY, LONDON.

bolic lily, it is seminal to the word. Little Nell, Little Dorritt, and Little Eva are such foundational virgins. Their innocence is impossible to violate, indicated by the verbal marker, *little*. This virginity survives childbearing, as in the Virgin Mary.

In contrast to the absolute purity of perpetual virgins, some virgins in texts at the end of the nineteenth century do not signify the white end of a melodramatic polarity—where depravity threatens innocence. Late nineteenth-century virginity assumes darker colors. Imbued with potential destructiveness, this kind of virginity deflowers itself. Knowing rather than nothing, this kind of virginity is often associated with death. Knowing virgins also demonstrate phallic power, indeed, of a more conventional kind—destructive because "unnatural" in virgins. Rather than salvational, the texts they generate fester.

In addition to *Lily*, virgin names are often flowery or spring-like, such as in the nineteenth-century theater, in which the flower name is associated with the innocent virgin.[8] The convention is mocked in such parodies as W. S. Gilbert's poor "little" Buttercup of *H.M.S. Pinafore* (1879) and Rose Maybud in *Iolanthe* (1885). By the nineties, the virtue of young flowering virgins is not undermined by parody: their floweriness begins to turn in less playful ways.

The signal example of the impure virgin of the 1890s appears in Oscar Wilde's *Salomé* (1892–1893), in which the heroine is a seductive creature, virgin but not virginal. A young girl emerging from dependency on her mother, she yearns to donate her virginity to a man of her choosing. Although Wilde fluctuated in his picture of her, he finally made her young, sexually knowing yet associated with a cosmic but natural whiteness ordinarily denoting unassailable virginity. Wilde blends virginal imagery with a name become synonymous for sensuality, an indication of his challenge to traditional sexual typing.[9]

Like Leila, Salomé is an exotic, an Eastern princess of Judea. She flouts sexual knowledge but knows she should pretend not to have it: "It is strange that the husband of my mother looks at me like that. I know not what it means. Of a truth I know it too well."[10] Born of Herodias, like Gertrude a political pawn married to her brother-in-law who has murdered her husband, Salomé breathes an atmospheric corruption. Herod's court reeks of sensuality, expressed in Wilde's synaesthetic imagery, blending appetites as well as senses. Salomé's dance is the dessert of a meal in which she begins with a fantasy of biting Iokanaan's mouth: "I will bite it with my teeth as one bites a ripe fruit" (83).[11] Merging appetite and desire, Wilde's Salomé invests her virginity as an asset in the sexual-religious economy of the play.

Salomé is impervious to Herod's lust and, indeed, to less incestuous male attention. Instead, she desires the prophet Iokanaan who has spoken against Herod's marriage to her mother. As Herod and Salomé form one forbidden sexual pairing, so Iokanaan and Herodias form another, each couple composed of a young and an older person, a symmetrical sexual coupling. Iokanaan, Salomé's counterpart, is obsessed with Herodias's sexual excess.[12] His diatribes against her indicate an almost single-minded fascination with this older woman's sexual activities. To his sensual imagination, Herodias embodies the moral rot in Judea. Iokanaan plays Biblical variations on the theme of Herodias as whore of Babylon. Although probably a virgin and certainly celibate, his libidinous preoccupation marks his purity. An inverted troubadour, he sings an aubade of his Lady's abominations:

> Where is she who saw the images of men painted on the walls, even the images of the Chaldeans painted with colours, and gave herself up unto the lust of her eyes, and sent ambassadors into the land of Chaldaea? . . . Where is she who gave herself unto the Captains of Assyria, who have baldricks on their loins, and crowns of many colours on their heads? Where is she who hath given herself to the young men of the Egyptians, who are clothed in fine linen and hyacinth, whose shields are of gold, whose helmets are of silver, whose bodies are mighty? Go, bid her rise up from the bed of her abominations, from the bed of her incestuousness, that she may hear the words of him who prepareth the way of the Lord, that she may repent her of her iniquities. Though she will not repent, but will stick fast in her abominations; go, bid her come, for the fan of the Lord is in His hand. (28–29)

Wilde imagines the Lord as Alma-Tadema might have painted him: reclining on a chaise, fanning away the heat of Iokannan's descriptions of Herodias's mighty conquests. While acknowledging her imperviousness to repentance, Iokanaan invokes his Queen with a religious telling of her carnal crimes.

Wilde uses the moon as a leitmotif whose meaning varies according to the character who describes it. Salomé imagines lunar virginity, associating herself with it:

> How good to see the moon! She is like a little piece of money, a little silver flower. She is cold and chaste . . . . I am sure she is a virgin. Yes, she is a virgin. She has never defiled herself. She has never abandoned herself to men, like the other goddesses. (20)

By associating the moon with money, a *little* flower, and virginity, Salomé recognizes the economics of virginity as morally and monetarily valuable. Like money it supports the sexual economy; it is a nothing that fuels sexual exchange. Salomé also desires Iokanaan because he is virginally silver like the moon: "I am sure he is chaste as the moon is." Linking silver with chastity, Wilde uses Salomé to expose the sexual economy of the religious soul under capitalism.[13]

Yet Salomé is aware of the lure of the nonvirgin, even perhaps the attraction of promiscuity. Even before she is ravished by the sight of Iokannan's naked body, she knows of Iokannan's interest in her mother. She identifies the subject of his diatribes as Herodias. Her litanies to whiteness turn virginity into yet another attribute of sexuality, diffused into exotic landscapes of polymorphous eroticism:

> I am amorous of thy body, Iokanaan! Thy body is white like the lilies of a field that the mower hath never mowed. Thy body is white like the snows that lie on the mountains of Judaea, and come down into the valleys. The roses in the garden of the Queen of Arabia are not so white as thy body. Neither the roses of the garden of the Queen of Arabia, the garden of spices of the Queen of Arabia, nor the feet of the dawn when they light on the leaves, nor the breast of the moon when she lies on the breast of the sea . . . . There is nothing in the world so white as thy body. Suffer me to touch thy body. (32–33; original ellipsis)

Knowing of Iokanaan's obsession, Salomé attempts to turn his attention to her virgin body. The Jewish princess (Jews being a fin de siècle sign of forbidden pleasure[14]) attempts to turn the Baptist's repugnance against sexuality to desire for her. Knowledge of Herod's look and Herodias's sexual reputation inspires her, but, until she sees Iokanaan's body, Salomé remains a virgin.

Salomé's dance is the center of her myth. It is unrepresented, unimaginable. In the midst of floods of language, Wilde merely indicates it as a curt stage direction: "*Salomé dances the dance of the seven veils*" (71). There is no description of the dance either in the play or in the Bible. The dance, described by Francoise Meltzer as an "aporia," becomes "the blind spot of writing to its own repression."[15] In its unrepresentability, the dance thus occupies the same cultural position as virginity. It is a gap, a textual space that stimulates male desire. Salomé's sexual status as a virgin, represented by her dance, generates and expresses male desire.

Kissing Iokanaan's severed head she mourns his death in a chant that also mourns her lost virginity:

> Iokanaan. I love only thee . . . I am athirst for thy beauty; I am hungry for thy body; and neither wine nor apples can appease my desire. What shall I do now, Iokanaan? Neither the floods nor the great waters can quench my passion. I was a princess, and thou didst scorn me. I was a virgin, and thou didst take my virginity from me. I was chaste, and thou didst fill my veins with fire . . . . (85)

There is no appeasement for virgin knowing. Wilde's Salomé loses her virginity through desire and dies.

Henry James's *What Maisie Knew,* apparently a story founded on an innocent center of consciousness, resembles Wilde's play in its focus on the type of knowing virginity which impels a similar configuration of intergenerational sexual desire. Wilde depends upon an aestheticized but familiar Biblical story, exotically peopled with Syrians, Jews, Cappadocians, and Nazarenes, whereas James depends upon a familiar *haute bourgeois* Western social world, peopled with countesses and governesses, captains and ordinary knights, such as Sir Claude. Although James leaves the virgin's age deliberately vague, sometimes referring to her as an "infant," his Maisie, or "little May," is an ingénue, around six at the beginning of the story and around thirteen at its end. As in *Salomé,* the young girl is surrounded by moral depravity and becomes a pawn in the acting out of others' desires until she recognizes her own, which ends the story in a kind of blankness. Her mother marries a second husband who pays inappropriate, if not Herodian, attention to the daughter. The father marries the girl's governess, who plays the

part, when convenient, of Maisie's mother. Various other couplings occur, during which the girl's real mother allies herself with as many different sorts of men as does Iokanaan's version of Herodias. The two couples resulting from Maisie's parents' divorce resemble the unholy duos in *Salomé:* one involves an older woman and a young man; the other involves an older man and a young woman. Eventually the young man (Maisie's stepfather) and the young woman (Maisie's stepmother and former governess) come together: "I brought you together," Maisie boasts, as if she were a miniature procuress.

As the first paragraph of the story makes clear, economics plays a large part in the dealings between mates, spouses, governesses, and guardians, so that Maisie, like Salomé, becomes a counter in the sexual economy. As Herod is willing to give Salomé half his kingdom for a dance, so the sexual dance in *What Maisie Knew* also depends upon the value of the virgin, at first "twenty-six hundred pounds."[16] James provides Maisie with a "crafty godmother . . . who had left her something in such a manner that the parents could appropriate only the income." Her monetary value compromises the moral purity of Maisie's escape with Mrs. Wix, who dearly needs the money and is clearly no moral paragon. As in Wilde's play, the background alludes to religious, or here, to moral values. James's overt plan places what he advertises as a foundational virgin at the center of the story to show how her purity cannot be assailed by her surroundings. The innuendo of the title, however, compromises the purity of the virginal center.

In his Preface, James describes Maisie as the foundation of his narrative, a center of virginal lack that limits the story's consciousness while adding to the deliciousness of its challenge. Because of the virgin's limited ability to comprehend what she sees and to articulate what she knows, the author finds telling the story all the more delightful. In its aesthetic style, which masks most emotion and moral sense while invoking morality and emotion, James's preface replicates Wilde's atmosphere in *Salomé.* The pleasure of his task, James suggests, is the limitation of the child's viewpoint from which the story needs to be told and the consequent extra knowledge required of the narrator who regards Maisie with the interest of the impure for the pure. Or, more properly, perhaps, his pleasure derives from narrative projections on to the "pure" that is the delightfulness of the virgin subject. James repeatedly refers to Maisie's "freshness," which, in the context of the story's sexuality, is about virginity, a virginity that is continually being assaulted by knowledge:

> Successfully to resist (to resist, that is, the strain of observation and the assault of experience) what would that be, on the part of so young a person, but to remain fresh, and still fresh, and to have even a freshness to communicate? . . . She wonders, in other words, to the end, to the death—the death of her childhood, properly speaking; after which (with the inevitable shift, sooner or later, of her point of view) her situation will change and become another affair, subject to other measurements and with a new centre altogether. (xi)

As James describes her, Maisie's task is to resist successfully an assault of knowledge; in the same symbolic position as Rossetti's reluctant Virgin, her inevitably unsuccessful resistance is symbolized by a peculiar representation of virginity, one displaying its sign as a contradiction to its own meaning, as in Dicksee's *Leila*. As in Wilde's play, this story culminates in the death of virginity, after which the story cannot continue.[17]

Maisie participates in the sexual square dance from which she supposedly stands aloof. Consequently, her name begins to denote a too-easy familiarity, a sexual looseness and tolerance. Her childishly innocent remarks that are nonetheless on the mark suggest that she knows more than she might be supposed to, her characteristic response being, "Oh, I know." The contrast between her "freshness" in the sense of youthful purity and her "freshness" in the sense of cheeky familiarity forms part of the technique James apparently found challenging and delightful.

In balancing sexual knowledge and moral judgement, Maisie seems finally to be making a moral choice. In fact, to the end she remains outside the moral system and, like Salomé, moves according to her own desires. Her final decision emanates from her "fresh" desire to have Sir Claude all to herself: "she had even a mental picture of the stepfather and the pupil established in a little place in the South while the governess and the stepmother, in a little place in the North . . ." (343).[18] In a train station Maisie and Sir Claude play at running off to Paris together in a situation verging on elopement. At this moment, Maisie understands French. The conductor asks Sir Claude in French if they wish him to take their tickets for the departing train to Paris, and Sir Claude relays the question in French to Maisie:

> Sir Claude turned back to her. "*Veux-tu bien qu'il en prenne?*"
>
> It was the most extraordinary thing in the world: in the intensity of her excitement she not only by illumination understood all their French, but fell into it with an active perfection. She addressed herself straight to the porter. "*Prenny, prenny. Oh prenny.*" (345)

Readers are prepared for taking this flight into French as the language of love. Earlier, Maisie hears a guitarist singing about *amour:* "Maisie knew what 'amour' meant too, and wondered if Mrs. Wix did" (285). Her "prenny" is also "take me," an expression of desire.

With a subject similar to the tantalizing juvenile postcards of the period, James's prose aestheticizes Maisie's coming to flower.[19] It charts Maisie's growing knowledge of how to play a sexual-economic game of musical chairs in a tone that, by retaining the child's apparent innocence as narrator, depends upon the reader sharing with the author a knowledge of depravity. As suggested by Maisie's ensuing thoughts, the answer to Mrs. Wix's question, "Have n't you really and truly *any* moral sense?" (279) is probably, "no":

> She judged that if her whole history, for Mrs. Wix, had been the successive stages of her knowledge, so the very climax of the concatenation would, in the same view, be the stage at which the knowledge should overflow. As she was condemned to know more and more, how could it logically stop before she should know Most? It came to her in fact as they sat there on the sands that she was distinctly on the road to know Everything. She had not had governesses for nothing: what in the world had she ever done but learn and learn and learn? She looked at the pink sky with a placid foreboding that she soon should have learnt All. (281)

The passage mingles the superior knowing of an adult with a girl's perspective.[20] By having a knowing narrator tell about Maisie's way of knowing, "from the breeze" (281), a way of knowing similar to the interchange between the Holy Ghost and the Virgin Mary, James places the reader in the same relation to the text as the culture stands to virginity in general. That is, one can only know it by being not it. Knowing virginity, what the narrator knows about Maisie as well as what Maisie knows, produces the narrative. Since she has already told that she knows what *amour* means, the wonder is whether the other is also in the know. As Maisie wonders about Mrs. Wix, so Mrs. Wix is wondering about Maisie. In the last sentence of the story Mrs. Wix—who has also lost her "virginity" in the course of the story: "I've had to pay with my own innocence" (282)—views Maisie as a lost one and contemplates the enigma of Maisie's knowledge: "She still had room for wonder at what Maisie knew" (362).

James's titillating story borrows a whiff of the kiddie porn that flourished during this time.[21] At the fraught moment when Maisie promises to wait while Sir Claude bids Mrs. Beale adieu, James introduces an odd figure of the Virgin: "I'll sit on that old bench where you see the gold Virgin" (348), Maisie promises. Rather than serving as a religious admonition about chastity and purity, the Virgin appearing at this moment, adds to the sexual tension. James has gilded the lily. Maisie, the virgin with gold, is Virgin of the Gilded Age.

This gilded Virgin is a sign of the times: virgin as cultural marker. The final scenes of *What Maisie Knew* are infused with an atmosphere of nervousness and of fear. Particularly in "girls," the combination of these two emotions produces anxiety, a virginal knowing with dread rather than pleasure, what Sigmund Freud in 1895 called "virginal anxiety."[22] Maisie represents a generalized virginal anxiety, a culturally constructed dread for which the concept of virginity becomes a focal point. At the time of the composition of these literary works, Freud turned his attention to anxiety and its sexual etiology. For him, the anxiety neurosis depended upon being unable to determine if the source of the anxiety is internal or external. At least in the case of virginal anxiety, however, Freud need not have worried about the distinction, for it is irrelevant. All subjects internalize cultural values, experiencing them as internal, even physiological. Freud's "virginal anxiety" is the culture's anxiety about virginity as well as the virgin's mirroring anxiety about her own desires.

If Freud's distinction between inner and outer virginal anxiety is false, he nonetheless usefully describes a freely floating emotion that seems to have neither object nor discernible cause, a characteristic of anxiety neurosis. He traces the feeling to a sexual origin: "where there are grounds for regarding the neurosis as an acquired one, careful enquiry directed to that end reveals that a set of noxae and influences from *sexual life* are the operative aetiological factors" (99). Freud describes a series of characteristics in an anxiety neurosis, such as "waking up at night in a fright," "anxiousness constantly lurking in the background," and "moral over-scrupulousness and doubting mania" (93–96), that could describe the ominous atmosphere and moral questioning in the two literary texts discussed above.

The most obvious example of a "virginal anxiety" turning an entire plot is felt by the governess in "The Turn of the Screw," published serially beginning in February 1898. Like *What Maisie Knew,* the story's atmosphere whispers of irregular sexual behavior, at first embodied by Peter Quint, a licentious valet who has corrupted a former governess, Miss Jessel, and perhaps her young charges, Flora and "little" Miles. Together, the children's names combine some qualities of foundational virgins, the little flower whose purity forms the unassailable center of the plot. As in *Maisie,* however, their purity is the structural question. In keeping with contemporary ideas about the existence and perverse nature of childhood sexuality, these beautiful children's pure faces might mask a knowing virginity.[23]

Both Freud's papers and James's two stories reflect the virginal anxiety of the nineties; each writer supplements rather than explicates the other. Both are signal examples of the nineties' idea of childhood. The narratives also need to be read in the context of the contemporary medical interest in sexual perversion.[24] Twentieth-century Freudian criticism of "The Turn of the Screw" mistakenly considers Freud apart from the atmosphere he describes, as if he were not a part of it. Similarly, to read James's story is to surround oneself with that saturated atmosphere in which the horror of sex as something impure needs to be isolated from certain sacred objects, here Flora and little Miles.[25]

In the story, the possessor of virginal anxiety is most obviously a young woman, "dead these twenty years," who writes the harrowing tale of her first job as a governess. Before she dies she sends the tale to the brother of a subsequent charge, who reports that she could not tell her story without revealing that she was in love.[26] This love with no consummation is the etiology of virginal anxiety; free floating, it attaches itself to everything in the tale.

The twenty-year-old youngest daughter of a poor country parson is dazzled by the urbane charms of her bachelor employer and becomes essentially a slave to an irrational contract with him. She succumbed to the "seduction exercised by the splendid young man," acting as mistress of his large country place and agreeing never to bother him with any details or problems regarding her charges, his niece and nephew.[27] Having the master as object of desire, she sets out to please him, while the prohibition of correspondence increases her fantasies about him and her constant expectation of having him materialize.

Virginal anxiety—attributable to the governess as a cultural marker—is the ectoplasm forming the ghosts and erotically charging all encounters. Did Miss Jessel leave because of her sexual activities? Do the children know? Was little Miles thrown out of school not for saying things as he claims but for the schoolboy activity that dare not speak its name.[28]

Everyone in James's story suffers from virginal anxiety, a fear of "knowing" that one cannot have unless one already knows something. The anxiety may be projected on to children who mirror the sexual desire, but one does not know whether they too are knowing virgins. With a precocious charm, little Miles enchants the governess. She compares their silence before the maid during a solitary dinner together to "some young couple who, on their wedding-journey, at the inn, feel shy in the presence of the waiter" (128). Electric with virginal anxiety, the moment precedes defloration, or, here the death of little Miles, whose "little heart" stops while the governess holds him fast in her arms.[29]

Freud describes anxious expectation itself as controlling the choice of ideas, "always ready to link itself with any suitable ideational content."[30] In a state of virginal expectation, these 1890s texts figure virginal anxiety as a flower. The virgin quivering on the brink expresses what the cultural text already knows. These virgins testify to the difficulty faced in the 1890s of preserving a mythical, and consequently, a powerful boundary. The texts belong to an age questioning the economy where sexual knowledge connotes disrespect, violation, corruption, and where virginity means wholeness and purity. Unless death or eternity intercedes, virginity carries the desire it defends against. Preoccupied with sexuality, these texts of the nineties describe a particular construction of virginity as a way of warding off dangerous desires, while the aestheticism of the writers and artists covers with a languid style an anxiety, also in the sense of anguish, associated with ultimate loss.

As one inheritor of this tradition, Edith Wharton's Lily Bart in *The House of Mirth* (1905), too old, too unmarried, too knowing, must die. Liliness, like virginity, is a concept carrying the seeds of its own doom. When Wilde thought of Salomé's dance as a devout ritual of a martyr to her faith, he imagined her as a lily: "Her body, tall and pale, undulates like a lily."[31] In the only description of the dance that we have, Wilde evokes the gender ambiguity of the lily. Powerful and phallic, the lily is a figure for its own undoing.

CHAPTER 10

Confessing and Editing: The Politics of Purity in Hardy's Tess

Susan David Bernstein

I

In the Preface to the Fifth and Later Editions to *Tess of the d'Urbervilles,* Thomas Hardy elaborately defends his novel against what he construes as a vicious assault. He qualifies these critical assailants as "manipulators of *Tess,*" "professed literary boxers," and "sworn Discouragers," all of whom "pervert plain meanings, and grow personal under the name of practising the great historical method."[1] By writing the four prefaces, Hardy too "grow[s] personal" not just because he retaliates against his critics, but because he fashions himself as writer into a figure resembling his heroine.

Like the country girl who falls upon hard times through no fault of her own, Hardy humbles Tess's creator into "a mere tale-teller" of "plain meanings" who might have "overlooked" and "by pure inadvertence have run foul of when in the least aggressive mood" the cultural values which his detractors uphold. Also "in the least aggressive mood," Tess, of course, is asleep at the threshold of her rape. What is most remarkable about this prefatory regress to the act of literary genesis is a distancing between the narrating voice and the "mere tale-teller," the figure of the writer whose innocence, or "pure inadvertence," and vulnerability suggest not the obliquely voiced authorial "I," but the defiled Tess and the defaced text in which she appears. Tess, text, and "tale-teller" converge in this cover story to a narrative that tries to uncover "a true sequence of things"—as the first preface states—about a fallen woman whose plight resembles, in some sense, that of the disparaged writer. Repeating the ambiguous act of confession at the center of the novel, where Tess does and does not confess a transgression that she does and does not commit but pays for nonetheless, this prefatory narration reveals a violated desire that accrues around the textual acts of a "mere tale-teller."

If the novel explores the meaning of "A Pure Woman," the subtitle Hardy appends as the underlying "truth" of his heroine, the prefaces wobble around the notion of a purity of meaning, the metaphysics of a virgin text whose fundamental sense precedes its material and interpretive violations. The novel performs a panegyric for the quintessential, experienced virgin; the prefaces bemoan an equally absurd proposition—the purity of the unread text. Both ideals promote what Jacques Derrida calls "white mythology," the linguistic imperialism of Western culture that privileges the white man's pristine language: "a proper origin [as] the virginity of a history of beginnings."[2] The narrator in the novel and the narrator in the prefaces insist on a pure Tess, a pure text—a kind of absolute coincidence between perception and meaning, between language and truth, between sexual or textual body and essence. This site of unadulterated meaning, this "original figure" untainted by the violence of inscriptions, depends upon overlooking or dismembering the metaphorical status of an "original figure," the *Tess* that constitutes "A Pure Woman."

Hardy tries to wrest both Tess and his text from meanings that devolve from a particular reading of their bodies. Nevertheless, this essential intactness, that would transcend material corruptions, can only assume significance through a history of the heroine's sexual morphology or through the history of the novel's textual morphology. According to Hardy's prefatory accounts, his novel endeavors to heal the original rupture of *Tess of the d'Urbervilles*'s body from this pure meaning. Yet this breach, rather than mended by the ink discharged through the palimpsestic prefaces, is widened by these supplementary acts of inscription. Tess's confession in the novel itself formally signals the paradox of the ideal of the experienced virgin Hardy espouses through his heroine's representation; her disclosure of sexual experience, of her rape, is pure and unsullied, that is, a blank space.

Before returning to the prefaces, I want to consider briefly the description of Tess's rape which poses a corollary to Derrida's white mythology. At this moment in the narrative, on the threshold of sexual rupture, Tess and text collapse into a continuity of body and meaning, white mythology's "purity of sensory language."[3] Here is the narrative's rendition of the rape, or more accurately, the preface to the rape:

> Why it was that upon this beautiful feminine tissue, sensitive as gossamer, and practically blank as snow as yet, there should have been traced such a coarse pattern as it was doomed to receive; why so often the coarse appropriates the finer thus, the wrong man the woman, the wrong woman the man, many thousand years of analytical philosophy have failed to explain to our sense of order. (77)

Not only is Tess figured as text, "this beautiful feminine tissue," but she is also "practically blank as snow," so that these metaphors together render Tess a white page about to be stained with "a coarse pattern." This figuration of rape as textual inscription likewise renders writing an act of violence. Like *Tess* and Tess, novel and heroine, pure writing must necessarily appear transparent, invisible, white, and as such, pure representation cannot be read or consumed or appropriated.

Derrida describes a similar scene of primal inscription: "White mythology—metaphysics has erased within itself the fabulous scene that has procured it, the scene that nevertheless remains active and stirring, inscribed in white ink, an invisible design covered over in the palimpsest."[4] The purity of this white ink or the impossibility of "true" representation offsets the violation intrinsic in the act of writing, just as the originary purity of "invisible design" is tainted or obscured through layers of inscription. Hardy's blank representations of Tess's rape and Tess's confession of the rape (both occur in the narrative in gaps between chapters) as well as Hardy's prefatory frame to the novel all establish a palimpsestic text of *Tess* where the original, necessarily unread, novel fades beneath the assaultive reinscriptions of readers. Hardy's approximation of sexual violation as textual inscription exposes a fundamental white mythology of purity that reifies the stakes of virginity as well as the stakes of its violent undoing, rape.

These boundaries of white mythology, therefore, furnish the terms of Hardy's defensive aesthetics, just as Tess's rape operates metaphorically for the disfigurement of the pastoral countryside by mechanical inscriptions of the Industrial Revolution. Hardy underscores this analogy between Tess and landscape: "A field-man is a personality afield; a field-woman is a portion of the field; she has somehow lost her own margin, imbibed the essence of her surrounding, and assimilated herself with it" (93). Here a figure/ground or vehicle/tenor distinction dissolves as Tess, the "field-woman" featured here, "somehow los[es] her own margin" and blends into the scenery. At the same time, both Hardy's prefaces and Tess's confession can be understood as double-marking this site of indeterminacy. His text is both pristine territory and violated representations, both pure tongue of "original sense" and consumed commodity of circulated reinscriptions. Tess's confession, including its variant renditions in serial and volume forms, is pure white textual space, yet its present absence also signifies the violent foreclosure of Tess's own narrative of her sexual undoing. In other words, both Tess and *Tess* are experienced virgins, wrongly read but purely signified texts.

II
PREFACING CONFESSIONS

The prefaces to *Tess of the d'Urbervilles* convey a preoccupation with violent textual dismemberment. This "castration anxiety," preambling the successive book editions of *Tess*, repeats the event of Tess's rape and the remembering of it in the confession scene.[5] Disclosing the loss of her virginity demotes Tess to what the narrator calls "the un-intact state" (283), a fate the novel also shares. The "pure" intentions of the author repeat those of his heroine whose estimate the subtitle announces as "A Pure Woman," and Hardy posits various states of purity and intactness as chief qualifications of himself, his text, and Tess.

As a writer whose acute sensitivity toward rebuke makes criticism almost a physical attack, Hardy navigates his identity with his text into a position analogous to Tess's body. Because Hardy is writing at the end of the century when social interest increases in "the woman question," this attention frames his identification as a maligned writer with the battered body and reputation of his heroine.

The transgression, whose form and substance confession discloses, features a fallen body, whether the object of textual editing, rape, or illicit or botched reproduction. Hardy's prefaces set up a resemblance between his text—dismembered through enforced self-editing and imposed revisions, and later, to add insult to injury, defiled by the interpretive ravishing of critics—and Tess's fallen body, "edited" through the act of rape as well as in the consequent process of reproduction, and abandoned by her husband as purveyor of social mores.

Hardy's prefatory constructions render his text "pure" at the core, although defiled by surface alterations, like Tess's vulnerable body. Structurally, the body of Tess in the text and the body of *Tess* as text represent the always inadequate, incomplete representation of a transgression that remains essentially unnarratable. Those in positions of power, like Angel Clare, supplement and obstruct, curtail and foreclose, her ability to shape her history in language and to control its interpretation. With the publication of *Tess,* Hardy tries to narrow the gap between the less controversial or edited persona he tried to maintain in fiction and in public addresses and his private, unexpurgated views about society, infrequently expressed in essays such as "Candour in English Fiction."[6]

Like his heroine, Hardy is burdened by the nature of this story about the "undomesticated" or extramarital sexuality of a young woman, a subject that society resists and condemns him for writing.[7] His series of prefaces, marking only some of the revisions the novel underwent, are, among other things, protestations over the "domestication" or forced editing of his text.

This resonance between Hardy's novel and Tess's character begins on the title page with the line beneath the title: "A Pure Woman Faithfully Presented by Thomas Hardy." The constancy embedded in the sense behind both "Pure" and "Faithfully" links Tess's womanhood and Hardy's text as the true presentation of this "Pure Woman." The female character and the textual body intertwine in the title and subtitle with the proper name of the author in the byline so that Tess represents Hardy's female body as textuality.

Tess is a "Pure Woman" and Hardy is "faithful" to her, unlike Angel; the pair become idealized lovers.[8] Hardy's book and Tess's body stand in figurative concert, Tess's body working as a synecdoche for the body of Hardy's text. The prefatory narrative of the book's revisions and reproduction as well as its readers' censure also parallel Tess's rape and illicit reproduction.

Beneath the subtitle is the novel's epigraph from "Two Gentlemen of Verona": ". . . Poor wounded name! My bosom as a bed / Shall lodge thee." This epigraph alludes not only to the heroine's name, linguistically wounded from Teresa d'Urbervilles to Tess Durbeyfield (although the narrative and the title confuse in which direction the wound lies), but also to the wounds her body and her reputation suffer.

"Poor wounded name" might, however, also refer to the injuries the sensitive writer felt accrued to his text and to his signature as author. That Hardy bore criticism of his writing almost as bodily insults surfaces in his autobiography. In an entry written on a day commemorating the ultimate Christian martyrdom, Good Friday, April 15, 1892, Hardy responds to a review of *Tess:* "How strange that one may write a book without knowing what one puts into it—or rather, the reader reads into it. Well, if this sort of thing continues no more novel-writing for me. A man must be a fool to deliberately stand up and be shot at."[9] This sense of the menacing reader recurs in Hardy's speculations about the writer who is physically endangered by "that absolute want of principle in the reviewer which gives one a start of fear as to a possible crime he may commit against one's person, such as a stab or a shot in a dark lane for righteousness's sake."[10]

Hardy's dramatic rendition of the writer at risk to readers on whom he is also dependent repeats Tess's vulnerability to crime: while travelling alone at night she is raped by the man who offers to protect her. The juxtaposition of textual body with Hardy's literal body under fire is reinforced in his postscript to his last novel, *Jude the Obscure:* "So much for the unhappy beginning of *Jude*'s career as a book. After these verdicts from the press its next misfortune was to be burnt by a bishop—probably in his despair at not being able to burn me."[11] These associations position Hardy as sacrificial writer who does "perish" as a novelist after the publication of *Jude,* just as Tess and Jude suffer martyrdom.

Implicitly, the epigraph to *Tess* refers to the history of the material body of the manuscript that had been abridged and rearranged in serial form, the "pure" textual body that the book-length version attempts to reconstruct. In Shakespeare's play, Juliet has ripped up a letter from her lover, but then rues her impetuous act and pieces together the letter signed "Love-wounded Proteus." Similarly, compelled to secure its appearance in print after three rejections, Hardy dismembered his manuscript to conform to serial publication for the *Graphic* and to social propriety by expunging "the naughty chapters" on the subjects of Tess's rape and the baptism of her illegitimate and dying baby.[12]

This textual mutilation by the writer parallels Tess's self-imposed disfigurement of her face with clipped eyebrows and bandages, although, contrary to Hardy's objective, with the intention to repel rather than to attract. Hardy likewise clips his *Tess* through textual deletions and bandages the serial version with an explanatory mock marriage. Like Juliet's reconstruction of her lover's letter, Hardy's publication of the book edition tries to restore its material integrity. The once fragmented text and its metaphorized Tess figure as the lover of the writer. Writer, heroine, and text collapse here under "wounded name." But the epigraph is also an epitaph for the "original" unread (and unwritten) text, repeatedly deformed and reformed through Hardy's persistent editing, just as it marks Tess's death ultimately brought about through her defilement.

The opening paragraph to the Explanatory Note to the First Edition introduces this accretion of Tess and text by figuring the novel as a dismembered organic body: "My thanks are tendered to the editors and proprietors of those periodicals for enabling me to piece the trunk and limbs of the novel together, and print it complete, as originally written two years ago." "Complete" and "originally written" recall the poetics of purity enjoined through the subtitle. The text, dismantled through forced editings, corresponds with the novel's heroine, sexually "edited" and subjected to condemnation as a result. However, just as Tess's depiction is riddled by elisions, like the "critical dismembering" of her subjectivity during the rape and confession scenes,[13] so too does the bibliographic history of *Tess* make the location of an "originary" text impossible.

This first edition of the novel, contrary to the author's assertion, is not "complete, as originally written two years ago." The 1912 preface to the Wessex edition will disclose one supposedly inadvertent omission, the episode of the dance at the hay-trusser's just prior to the rape scene. But according to J. T. Laird's meticulous account in *The Shaping of* Tess of the D'Urbervilles, no original version of the novel ever existed intact due to Hardy's obsessive revisions—his continuous regrafting of alterations onto a manuscript itself in the process of being written: "Most of the text of the First Edition represents a conflation of readings from earlier texts—the *Graphic,* the manuscript, and two printed sketches—a number of readings are entirely new, and illustrate Hardy's continued interest in the novel, an interest that was to show itself again in the revisions of the 1892, 1895, 1902, and 1912 editions."[14] An originary pure Tess and *Tess* are impossible referents, not unlike Derrida's white mythology: "a proper origin [as] the virginity of a history of beginnings." Purity in both contexts is intricately bound to signification and authority; in each case the fall from purity heralds loss to a rapist and to readers who "pervert plain meanings."

Hardy's first preface functions as a confession of an "un-intact state" of his *Tess,* an earlier textual dismembering that he now claims to undo by re-membering the "trunk" and "limbs" together. Like the editing history of this text, confession depends on remembering, but it also initiates a kind of dismembering through the retelling of the transgression. Here Hardy presents this first book edition as the resewn parts of an earlier disconnected text.

Taken together, the prefaces disclose three instances or degrees of dismembering in Hardy's *Tess* and as such replicate the violent acts around which the plot is wound, tightening an association between Hardy and Tess, between the writer's and the woman's bodies.[15] The first preface reveals the novel's literal disfiguring as the author announces this book version as the refiguring of his fragmented textual body, the "poor wounded" words that comprise *Tess.*

In the Preface to the Fifth and Later Editions, Hardy insinuates a metaphoric dismembering, the interpretive violations of *Tess* by critics:

> . . . manipulators of *Tess* were of the predetermined sort whom most writers and readers would gladly forget; professed literary boxers, who put on their convictions for the occasion; modern "Hammers of Heretics"; sworn Discouragers, ever on the watch to prevent the tentative half-success from becoming the whole success later on; who pervert plain meanings, and grow personal under the name of practising the great historical method. (3)

By far the lengthiest of the four, this preface constitutes the heart of Hardy's confession. However, his transgressions of impropriety, vulgarity, blasphemy—all chronicled in reviews and cited here—pale "by pure inadvertence" beside those of *Tess*'s assailants whose interpretive violence is encoded in the words Hardy employs: "manipulators," "boxers," "Hammers." So too do Tess's transgressions, equivocally defined as sexual experience and illicit reproduction, as well as the absence before her marriage and the ambiguous presence on the wedding night of her confession of these events, shrivel in proportion to the penance imposed on her. With this defensive reaction, the slippage between author and text, between the injustices to Hardy's textual body and the plight of the violated Tess, gains currency.

The third layer in Hardy's prefatory confession exposes the author's de-authorization, the anticipated literal death of the author that follows the earlier figurative death of textual mastery. The prefaces may try to maintain the writer's authority by defending the purity of his text and its heroine. Yet this defense also becomes an admission of the writer's limited control over the distribution of meanings that "a mere tale-teller, who writes down how the things of the world strike him, without any ulterior intentions whatever, has overlooked, and may by pure inadvertence have run foul of when in the least aggressive mood." This "pure inadvertence" signifies a curtailment of mastery, a limitation that Hardy reasserts and literalizes in the 1895 preface: "some of the critics who provoked the reply [the heated 1892 preface] have 'gone down into silence,' as if to remind one of the infinite unimportance of both their say and mine." As the great leveller here, death dissolves the differences, so hotly described in the previous preface, between writer and reader.

In addition, Hardy's prefaces draw a distinction between the authorial "I" who has deliberate and conscious control, or authority, over the meanings his words generate and the writing subject, "a mere tale-teller," whose text supersedes whatever meaning he may have intended. This figure of the "mere tale-teller" who eventually will have "gone down into silence," even while the possibility of fixing his meanings vanishes, would critically prefigure both Roland Barthes's death of the author and Julia Kristeva's writing subject.[16]

In both the prefatory material and the novel it introduces, transgression accumulates around the ways the textual body and the female sexual body are read. The prefaces etch out a figurative cross-dressing between defamed writer and slandered woman as they defend the purity of text and Tess. Hardy's prefaces admit his novel has been dismantled and reassembled by the author. Though sliced and sullied by editors and critics, these framing words also establish a pristine, originary text. Within the novel, Hardy stresses that Tess is injured not only by Alec's rape of her, but also by the production and circulation of its narrative representations. Accordingly, the rape and its replay, Tess's confession, are construed through metaphors of inscription, but in fact both are foreclosed as narratives from the narrative itself.

III
A BLANK SPACE: DOES TESS CONFESS?

The sensation of Tess's disclosure in the twin confession scene at the center of *Tess* replaces the conventional narrative climax of marital consummation. Uncovering past sexual events—in Tess's case, her rape and the birth of her child—forestalls the uncovering of bodies customary on the wedding night. However, in the book edition Tess's confession remains covered in a sense by the blank space that witnesses it in the text. Is this textual effacement of Tess's words (which do appear, although with an altered sense, in the earlier *Graphic* version) a defacement of Tess as a speaking subject, as an agent who constructs her own story, or does the elision signify protection from rebuke, a vexed attempt at advocacy for the fallen woman who is inevitably punished for the offense of telling a narrative of transgression?

Prior to the wedding night, Tess's attempts to confess her sexual history to Angel are either aborted by circumstances, truncated by Angel's insertion of his fairy-tale version of her past, or repeatedly abandoned by her unsteady resolve to tell a story that her mother advises her not to disclose.[17] In contrast, here Angel initiates the twin confessional scene of the newlyweds. He begins his story by preambling on church doctrine and citations from biblical scripture and Horace. With this veneer of philosophical support, the trappings of an intellectual and cultural legacy that Tess lacks, Angel aligns himself with the moral system of his father and the church as he professes, before he confesses, to admire "spotlessness" and to despise "impurity." His confession breathes through the cleansing air of his own humility and signifies a redemptive fall from pride and self-righteousness (although the taint of Angel's self-righteousness lingers with his disclosure and through his reaction to Tess's confession) to the humble position of human error: "Well, a certain place is paved with good intentions, and having felt all that so strongly, you will see what a terrible remorse it bred in me when, in the midst of my fine aims for other people, I myself fell."[18]

Angel's confession is succinct and contained in its effect, and entirely integrated with his view of himself, past and present. Divided into two paragraphs, the confession begins as paraphrase and ends as direct quotation, textual evidence of his control over this act of disclosure because his words, though somewhat abstract, do convey the secret of a sexual past. Like the quoted words, Angel too was an agent in some sense of his sexual fall. His generalized confession and Tess's unquestioning acceptance contrast markedly to his demands for details about her history. In short, confession of his transgression makes Angel virtuous; its substance causes no disturbance to the text, to the narrative, or to his confessor.

The irony of confession and of the idiom of the sexual fall emerges in this narrative performance of gender difference. Angel introduces both terms *confession* and *fall* into the scene. Yet his transgression, his account of a deliberate, if brief, fall pales in contrast to Tess's disclosure, even though in her case it is a man who transgresses, who commits the "fall" onto Tess's sleeping body. Hardy's point, of course, is that in both cases "The Woman Pays," as the title of the section of the novel following Tess's confession stresses; the woman is ultimately responsible for the moral rectitude of any sexual act. This transgressive woman appears in Angel's confession as "a stranger," as "her"; otherwise she is nameless and voiceless:

> . . . he plunged into eight-and-forty hours' dissipation with a stranger.
>
> "Happily I awoke almost immediately to a sense of my folly," he continued. "I would have no more to say to her, and I came home." (189)

The sexual nature of this illicit encounter, presumably with a prostitute, is encoded in "he plunged" and "dissipation." Whereas Tess is literally asleep when her rapist begins to molest her, Angel is morally asleep: an ironic instance of resemblance offsetting sexual difference.

Although substantively similar, Tess's confession issues a jolt to an entire signifying system that constructs meaning out of various surfaces and imaginary depths. As a model for this standard system of interpretation, Angel's previous readings of Tess as a simple child of nature break down along with Tess's confession of her sexual fall.[19] The confession functions as intrusion on both Tess's private history and on Angel's construction of her as a fresh, untainted dairymaid. Thus Angel's confession acts as purgative, Tess's as pollution.

Before the trauma of Tess's revelation, the interlude between the confessions encourages the promise of resemblance between the two secrets and the way they are received by each confessor. This possibility recapitulates the romantic convention of twin subjectivities, united through love, something the narrative's attention to gender difference finally collapses. When Angel comments that Tess's confession "can hardly be more serious," she replies: "'It cannot—O no, it cannot!' She jumped up joyfully at the hope. 'No, it cannot be more serious, certainly,' she cried, 'because 'tis just the same!'" (190). The perception of similarity is a crucial field on which difference unfolds, for the spectrum and substance of difference and otherness depend upon the possibility of resemblance. Interestingly, the words, "'because 'tis just the same!'" are omitted in the expurgated *Graphic* version, therefore mollifying the harshness of Angel's response to Tess's confession because the likeness of their faults is not underscored.

While Angel maintains some sense of agency over his revelation, Tess's confession is entirely mediated through a description of the room along with the objects, including her body, that it contains. Nowhere do Tess's words appear in direct quotation or even indirectly through paraphrase, although the physical qualities of her voice and tone are included in the detached inventory. The structure of the text subdivides this description that substitutes for Tess's confession so that the temporal slot of her narrative falls precisely into the blank space between the two divisions of the novel, "Phase the Fourth" and "Phase the Fifth." This structural gap connects Tess's confession with the narrative instance of her rape, also a blank passage on the page falling between book phases. The first paragraph of the description, narratively coinciding with the beginning of her confession, focuses on Tess's body:

> Their hands were still joined. The ashes under the grate were lit by the fire vertically, like a torrid waste. Imagination might have beheld a Last Day luridness in this red-coaled glow, which fell on his face and hand, and on hers, peering into the loose hair about her brow, and firing the delicate skin underneath. A large shadow of her shape rose upon the wall and ceiling. She bent forward at which each diamond on her neck gave a sinister wink like a toad's; and pressing her forehead against his temples she entered on her story of her acquaintance of Alec d'Urberville and its results, murmuring the words without flinching, and with her eyelids drooping down. (190)

Although the "red-coaled glow" colors Angel's face and hand, it does much more to Tess's body which, represented in assiduous detail throughout the novel, in this scene seems to figure her confession within the disturbed specular glare of Angel's perspective. This same glow "peers into" and "fires" parts of her head—hair, brow, and skin—while these verbs also highlight the action of confession, the scrutinizing eye of the confessor. Tess's confession forces Angel to re-view Tess as remote from his earlier construction of her. Her own story, uncovering a woman's sexual knowledge, no matter the circumstances from which it arises, therefore doubly "fires" Angel's image of Tess: the elided confession both erases his version of her, while it also introduces a sexualized female body absent from his previous snow white edition.

In addition, the fire glow deforms Tess's body into a monstrous shadow, a morphological equation with the confessed monster of female subjectivity in *Frankenstein*. This rising of "a large shadow of her shape . . . upon the wall and ceiling" that mediates her elided confession in the text configures the confession as this "large shadow" challenging and overwhelming Angel's restricted reading of Tess through the surfaces of her body. Its magnified projection overarching the room is a reproduction, in a sense, of Tess's body, while the confession reproduces an embodied "other" Tess to the image Angel has construed. This production of otherness, of an inassimilable uncanniness, issues from the operations of feminine confession that multiply images and destabilize the process of representation. If the abject is the uncategorizable, neither subject nor object, then Tess's confession, in a way, textualizes abjection, a kind of concentrated otherness. Kristeva defines the abject as "what disturbs identity, system, order. What does not respect borders, positions, rules. The in-between, the ambiguous, the composite."[20] Quite literally the "in-between, the ambiguous," Tess's confession in the text works through these senses of abjection.

Interestingly, Angel's shadow does not mark the wall and ceiling although he sits next to Tess before the fire, and no description of objects in the room, including his body, accompanies his confession. The gaping shadows, produced both materially during Tess's confession and thematically through the implied substance of her transgression, inaugurate a reading crisis, or a fall from meaning, foregrounded by the structure of this confession as literal blank space and through the semiotic upheaval of objects in the room. Tess's "murmuring voice" and "eyelids drooping down" repeat this fall. The confession itself, prefaced in the final paragraph of "Phase the Fourth—The Consequence" and concluded by the initial passage of "Phase the Fifth—The Woman Pays," literally falls into the dividing gap between these larger sections that structure the narrative.

Catherine Belsey defines a literary text's ideological underpinnings through the absence at its center: "The text is divided, split as the Lacanian subject is split, and Macherey compares the 'lack' in the consciousness of the work, its silence, what it cannot say, with the unconsciousness Freud explored."[21] Is the absence of Tess's confession at the center of the novel merely overdetermined by narrative efficiency or Hardy's ambivalent adherence to social propriety, or does it suggest something more about textuality, sexuality, and the politics of confessing women? To begin to answer these questions, it is important to compare two versions of Tess's confession: the description surrounding the blank space of the book version and the earlier *Graphic* renditions.

Although no direct quotation appears in the *Graphic,* more detail of Tess's narrative does. She describes the subterfuge of a mock marriage in her account to Angel:

> the visit with D'Urberville to the supposed Registrar's, her abiding sense of the moral validity of the contract, and her wicked flying in the face of that conviction by wedding again. She murmured the words without flinching, and with her eyes fixed on the fire.[22]

This confession in the *Graphic*—one that alters the transgression from rape in the manuscript to bigamy here—condenses Tess's fuller disclosure to her mother earlier in the serial:

> Then Tess told. "He made love to me, as you said he would do; and he asked me to marry him, also just as you declared he would. I never have liked him; but at last I agreed, knowing you'd be angry if I didn't. He said it must be private, even from you, on account of his mother; and by special license; and foolish I agreed to that likewise, to get rid of his pestering. I drove with him to Melchester, and there in a private room I went through the form of marriage with him as before a registrar. A few weeks after, I found out that it was not the registrar's house we had gone to, as I had supposed, but the house of a friend of his, who had played the part of the registrar. I then came away from Trantridge instantly, though he wished me to stay; and here I am."[23]

It is worth noting the more elaborate confession in direct quotation Tess makes to her mother. If Tess confesses an errant tale, she can also share the blame with her mother. Because both are vulnerable as women, the mother, who implies she too has had her share of "Trouble," does represent a much less risky confessor than a man, whether father or husband. In fact, in both serial and book-length editions, Joan Durbeyfield cautions her daughter not to tell her "Bygone Trouble" to her "Intended," just as the mother has withheld hers from her husband. In the book version, this confession to her mother is likewise collapsed to a vanishing point: "Then Tess went up to her mother, put her face upon Joan's neck, and told" (69). The next paragraph records the mother's reaction; Tess's actual confession, present in direct quotation in the *Graphic,* is twice absent in the book.

The complicated editing history of *Tess* indicates that the confession scenes in the book are a recollection of the earlier manuscript, which was disassembled, the "naughty chapters" excised as separately published sketches, and patched up with the mock marriage for the *Graphic.* The disparity between these dismembered and re-membered forms suggests a paradox. If the serial confessions Tess makes are decidedly more explicit, more textually present through direct quotation and paraphrase, nonetheless, this thematically ungraphic *Graphic* version covers over with the mock marriage explanation the more striking sexual crime of rape implicated in the book form. In the *Graphic,* Tess is both more and less guilty: maybe—but not quite—a fallen woman, since she consents to premarital sex ("at last I agreed") but only under the pretense of a fake marriage, while she also—in a way—commits bigamy by "her wicked flying in the face of that conviction by marrying again."

Is the *Graphic* confession, therefore, a dismembering of the more dangerous rape scene that can only be insinuated, but never explicitly remembered, in the book? Does the mock marriage confession protect both Tess and Hardy from the moral outrage that accrues around representations of fallen women, even while it protects the rapist by not exposing, however obliquely, his violent act? In a way, the shapes of the two confessions reproduce a tension between what can and what should be expressed about female sexuality in literature toward the close of the nineteenth century.[24]

The novel posits the unnarratable in a way the serial does not. Having Tess confess in the *Graphic* also discounts her privilege of privacy or right to remain silent, just as the supplementary details along with the expurgated sections in the serial signify a dismembering of the manuscript, a textual violation Hardy decries in the preface. Conversely, although the blankness of Tess's confession in the book protects her from humiliating specificity, it also denies her the privilege of speech. And yet if Tess is not an agent of her confession in the book version, this disempowerment also coincides with her powerlessness in the transgression that the confession seeks to remember.

Whether advocating for Hardy's Tess, or his *Tess*, or himself, the blank space might also constitute the impossiblity of remembering, or at least indicate the necessarily skewed shape of any reconstruction of a violent act. The blankness, therefore, signifies more potently than words the unnarratable: a woman's account of her rape. The gap in the text resists absorbing, containing, or domesticating the essential dislocation and otherness of rape into narrative contiguity. The victim's version of this violent assault on a woman's body is neither appropriated through the narrator's paraphrase nor mimicked between quotation marks. Hardy, or his narrator, or language, does not confess for Tess, for a character whose unspokenness at this climactic juncture suggests the impossibility or the injustice of representing rape. At the same time, the blank space substituted for the remembering of a fiercely dismembering act perpetrated against a woman's body likewise protects Tess's story itself from linguistic dismemberment by her confessors both within and beyond the narrative. The description which does surround Tess's (non)narrating of her sexual battery reproduces this terrible disturbance of rape and its consequences on the level of language and signification.

Following the gap in the text, the next "Phase" of the novel opens with the frame of the confession's conclusion, again described through the physical properties of Tess's voice rather than the substance of the disclosure: "Her narrative ended; even its reassertions and secondary explanations were done. Tess's voice throughout had hardly risen higher than its opening tone; there had been no exculpatory phrase of any kind, and she had not wept" (190). This summation assumes the dry contours of a brief report on Tess's delivery. However, the signifying consequences of the eclipsed words brought to light, although offstage, spill over onto random objects. "Pervert[ing] plain meanings"—to recall Hardy's prefatory accusation—the confession seems to convert simple objects into freakish distortions:

> But the complexion even of external things seemed to suffer transmutation as her announcement progressed. The fire in the grate looked impish—demoniacally funny, as if it did not care in

> the least about her strait. The fender grinned idly, as if it too did not care. The light from the water-bottle was merely engaged in a chromatic problem. All material objects around announced their irresponsibility with terrible iteration. And yet nothing had changed since the moments when he had been kissing her; or rather, nothing in the substance of things. But the essence of things had changed. (190–91)

This confession of a violent fall induces a fall from language, not only the narrative foreclosure of Tess's story, but also the dislodged coherence between signifiers and referents, the unsettled connection between surface and depth, or "substance of things" and "essence of things." The narration, in fact, approximates something midway between Tess's and Angel's vision, or rather, it is difficult to ascribe the point of view consistently to one character or even to the narrator alone; subjectivity seems to dissolve as a discrete category. Dramatizing Tess's fall, the narration also executes a fall from a stable viewpoint, a momentary, interpretive arrest that linguistically transfers the thematic indeterminacy of Tess's "fall" as an imposed transgression. This collapse in turn operates as a parodic and sinister (in)version of the romantic twinning of subjectivities suggested in the interlude between Angels' confession and Tess's confession.

Because Tess's "eyelids" are "drooping down" with her forehead pressed against Angel's temple as she confesses, she is not positioned to take in visually the scenario of transformed objects. Yet these objects are referenced to her dramatically vexed situation as they appear wretchedly indifferent. That both are associated with announcements suggests the connection between the personified objects and Tess as objectified person: "her announcement progressed," and "material objects around announced their irresponsibility with terrible iteration." Even syntax bestows agency on the objects, while Tess's is elided.

The displacement of her confession onto the appearance of objects in the room also conveys Tess's own subjection as an object, both in the act of rape and in its retelling where she becomes an object under scrutiny. Tess's subjectivity is problematically yet persistently fastened to the status of bodies, hers and the objects surrounding her. By an eerie personification, the narrative enacts an inversion where subjects, Tess and her confession, become objects—not only of Angel's and the narrator's gaze, but also as barrier to Angel's version of Tess—and objects become subjects with affect. Ironically, at the precise moment where female subjectivity might be expected to appear in the narrative, instead the subject is reinscribed as object divorced from a totalizing perspectival category.

The wrenching apart of objects and meaning in this passage does make provisional sense from Angel's perspective. Since Tess already knows the content of her confession, her reaction to its effects is contingent on Angel's response which, at this point, she cannot know. The "transmutation," replicated in the inversion of substance and essence that marks the objects, corresponds to what Tess's "announcement" does to Angel's perceptual apparatus, how he reads or unreads Tess. The confession demotes Angel's earlier edition of Tess as hallucination, just as the objects in the room "suffer" hallucinatory transposition. To her confessor Angel, Tess—like the objects—has become something other; in the immediate aftermath of confession Angel says, "You were one person; now you are another" (191). In fact, Angel defines Tess's transgression not as the sexual fall itself, but as her iterability, her self-multiplication through the paradoxically blank confession, of "another woman in your shape" (192), "a grotesque—prestidigitation" (191).

The crucial transgression that Hardy takes up in the prefaces and in Tess's confession concerns representation as a fall into (mis)meanings. Hardy's prefatory rendition of his original text of immaculate integrity as well as Tess's foreclosed narrative of her rape are predicated on a white mythology of idealized pure language. In other words, Tess's body—"blank as snow" (77)—functions metaphorically for a white mythology of pure narrative; the confession of her body's defilement is also blank as snow, a gap in the text. Hardy's dismembered text and the way Tess's rape is remembered in the narrative both expose the paradoxes of any white mythology, the impossibly perfect correspondence between representation and meaning, between understanding and intention.

For if Hardy wants to get his *Tess* into print, then he must submit it to revisions and deletions different from the original "master" plan, even though the editing history renders a "master" plan of authorial intention dubious at best. Then again, "by pure inadvertency" the text of this "mere tale-teller" capitulates before other meanings, often inhospitable to the author, that are construed by its readers. As blankness, of course, Tess's confession cannot literally be construed or misconstrued, at least not outside the narration. Ironically, the graphic site of purity in the novel is precisely this blank space of confession substituting for a narrative of rape. Even so, its effects splatter onto the scene, witnessing it as the confession precipitates an interpretive arrest, a momentary passage where meaning breaks apart, not unlike the lacuna that figures in for Tess's disclosure. In effect, Hardy offers a correlation between pure textual body and pristine female body; both categories maintain their inviolate status as abstractions, as idealized constructions. The experienced virgin, Hardy suggests, signifies the perfectly (un)read text.

CHAPTER 11

Gender and Sexual Dis-Ease in Dracula

Jeffrey L. Spear

> A close analysis will show that the only emotions which in the long run harm are those arising from sex impulses, and when we have realized this we have put a finger on the actual point of danger.
>
> Abraham Stoker, "The Censorship of Fiction"

> All men are mad in some way or the other.
>
> Abraham Van Helsing

Dracula is a text that proposes and collapses radical dualities. One duality, a context between absolutes, frames the others: if Dracula succeeds, the human race will become vampiric and devour itself. If the living prevail the undead will be restored to humanity and, according to Mina Harker at least, die happy. Within this broad frame that portends an absolute change in human being, other dualities threaten to reverse themselves or collapse into each other. The text itself consists of documents—diaries, letters, ship's logs, bills of lading, newspaper articles, transcriptions of phonograph dictation, cables and even telephone calls—that are declared to be "simple fact" in the Dedication, but which have, excepting a few items, been reduced by the final note to "a mass of type-writing" that cannot prove what it relates.[1] These pseudodocuments record the pursuit of a monstrous, invasive Other who must, nevertheless, be sought out ("Welcome to my house! Enter freely and of your own will!") or be invited in.[2] They relate the pursuit of Vlad the Impaler by men who hideously impale. They describe the vampire's scrupulous adherence to English law and its violation by the living lawyers. Most central to my argument here, these documents posit an absolute distinction between a self-sufficient manliness that threatens to slide into dependency and a pristine, virginal womanhood that is gender without sexuality. But this womanhood's ostensible purity has no power to resist the vampiric possession that inverts those characteristics, producing what Phyllis Roth calls "sudden sexuality": an aggressive, non- (or pre-) genital, oral sexuality that can dissolve sexual gender distinctions, an appetite that overturns the presumed essence of womanhood by making women overtly sexual beings who will suck from children.[3]

The Victorian bourgeoisie, as Michel Foucault points out, defined its sexuality in contrast to that of earlier periods as being "subjected to a regime of repression so intense as to represent a constant danger."[4] It was increasing awareness of this regime that led Stoker's contemporary Havelock Ellis to examine the variousness of sexuality and publish testimonials and analyses with a view toward relieving repressive pressures. But Ellis's work, like the novels of Zola, overtly concerned with sex and sexual disease, was itself subject to a suppression in England, a suppression of which Stoker approved. Homosexuality was likewise becoming a subject of discourse, representation, and suppression.[5] As a man of learning, of society, and of the theater, Stoker was aware of these developments generally and of the events behind the Wilde trial in particular. Not only was he acquainted with Wilde, as a young man he had been a visitor to the home of Sir William and Lady Wilde, and Oscar had been his chief rival for the hand of Florence Balcombe.

More a late Victorian than an early modern, Stoker lamented the passing of the quality of "reticence," the internal restraint that allowed for the decorous treatment of dangerous, presumably sexual, topics in earlier literature. But if those contemporary authors he delicately refuses to name persist in depicting "flagitious" vices, if, as he puts it, "the plague-spot continues to enlarge, a censorship must be."[6] Stoker's "restraint" is D. A. Miller's Foucauldian discipline, the "unseen but all-seeing surveillance" that orders private and particularly sexual life and its conventional representation.[7] By advocating censorship Stoker acknowledges that inner discipline is breaking down and must be given external support. He enlists in the policing force. The paradox of the censor, the overt moral policeman, is that he must have knowledge of what he would proscribe. He must walk the narrow line between ferreting out vice and seeking it out. He must know and not know at the same time. *Dracula* has been aptly called "a refined attempt by the nineteenth-century mind not to recognize itself."[8]

Stoker demonstrated reticence to his own satisfaction and that of his original audience by having his unvampirized characters speak of love and marriage rather than passion and by deflecting expressions of sexual desire into the realm of the vampire where, because orally displaced, they can be allowed representation before being ruthlessly extirpated. *Dracula* is a perfect projective screen for theories of unconscious motivation involving issues of sexuality, gender, and class. The primary variables in much modern *Dracula* criticism are the ideological stance and the version of psychoanalysis employed in order to explain things the surface of the text denies. Among these superficially denied topics is a male fear of female sexuality, or even, if Dracula's women are read as extension of himself, an unacknowledged male desire to be penetrated which is mediated, as Christopher Craft contends, "through the surrogation of the other, 'correct' gender."[9] Dracula himself is not merely self-reliant in opposition to his collaborative opponents; he would reduce all life to an extension of himself and his will. He embodies both the infantile wish for omnipotence, the wish for a world in which there is only a single ego, and the fear that that ego is the object's and not one's own.

The undead are uncanny, but not supernatural so much as subnatural, elemental, mysteriously animating the very dust to which they should have returned. Dracula may influence animals and the elements, but it is the living, Western allies through their transportation and communication technology who are above nature. By way of Van Helsing the aggressively modern English group retains contact with the older, animistic world of folklore and a demotic Catholicism, but in terms of knowledge rather than belief. Such knowledge is operative in Dracula's world, which is archaic culturally as well as psychologically, and its rules bound his freedom though they are of no use in the modern world as such. Dracula is thus the enemy of the text that would expose his presence to a world in which he is perfectly disguised as a superstition.

Before his last attack on Mina Harker he makes sure to destroy the records of his existence only to be frustrated by reproduction, a copy, the issue of long nights of conjugal typing in the Harker bedroom: "I heard the click of the typewriter. They are hard at it" (205).

The battle between Dracula and Van Helsing's forces of light is conducted by men over and through the bodies of two women, Lucy Westenra and Wilhelmina Murry Harker. The two women are themselves initially contrasting types. Lucy is an heiress: idle, flirtatious, slangy, given to reading her own inscrutable reflection as if she were one of the men it mysteriously captivates. She is flattered by the attention of three suitors; duty-bound to tell two of them about the favored one, yet reluctant to let any one of them go and consequently given to thoughts that she must condemn as ignoble and unfair to constant manhood:

> I suppose that we women are such cowards that we think a man will save us from fears, and we marry him. (61)

> My dear Mina, why are men so noble when we women are so little worthy of them . . . . Why can't they let a girl marry three men, or as many as want her, and save all this trouble? But this is heresy, and I must not say it. (62)

Like Laura, the vampire's prey in Sheridan LeFanu's "Carmilla," she is a nineteen-year-old with a history of somnambulism. In Lucy's case sleepwalking suggests a "double consciousness" that moves her to act rebelliously against constraints she verbally accepts. She has cause, as Alan P. Johnson notes, for despite her attraction to Dr. Seward and Quincey Morris she makes the most socially advantageous match only to be neglected by her fiancé in favor of family interests and then disinherited in his favor by her own mother. The text associates her somnambulism with the "white lady," the unfaithful nun said to haunt Whitby Abbey, and as an undead she appears as the "Bloofer Lady" in white.[10]

Mina, by contrast, is somewhat older, a model of deportment and rectitude who has been employed as an assistant school mistress and was once Lucy's tutor. She is without other means of support or family save for Jonathan, her fiancé and later husband, for whose sake she learns stenography, typing, and generally, as Ruskin says in "Of Queen's Gardens," "such knowledge . . . as may enable her to understand, and even to aid, the work of men." Mina, indeed, is Ruskin's queen almost to the letter. Her intellect is not, like Van Helsing's or Dr. Seward's, for invention, but for ordering, arrangement, and decision. Like the Portia whom Ruskin praises, she demonstrates "what women are fancied most to fail in—precision and accuracy of thought."[11] The queen's God-given "love of power" is expressed through service to others rather than self-advancement, hence Mina's seemingly gratuitous disparagements of the New Woman, who was out for herself professionally and, it was feared, sexually as well.[12] As Mrs. Harker, hers is the bosom on which manly men like Quincey Morris can weep, and form attachments without conscious awareness on either side of desire and sexual rivalry: "I felt this big sorrowing man's head resting on me, as though it were that of the baby that some day may lie on my bosom, and I stroked his hair as though he were my own child," she remarks prophetically. Home is wherever she is: "Mrs. Harker gave us a cup of tea, and I can honestly say that—for the first time since I have lived in it, this old house seemed like *home,*" says John Seward (207). Hers is the guiding but not determining function that the men ignore to the peril of all.

When Van Helsing decides to make Mina "our star and our hope" rather than helpmeet and guide she calls it a "bitter pill for me to swallow," and her deference to their "chivalrous care" and her outward obedience take on an ironic tinge: "Manlike they have told me to go to bed and sleep; as if a woman can sleep when those she loves are in danger! I shall lie down and pretend to sleep" (215). The irony suggests an inner split between her social engendering and contrary desires. Just the night before, she had allowed herself to kiss Quincey Morris and he called her "little girl!—the very words he had used to Lucy, and oh, but he proved himself a friend!" (206). Unacknowledged desire together with enforced idleness make Mina more like Lucy—whose place in the narrative structure she is assuming—and hence vulnerable to the vampire whose first visit to her takes place that night (September 30), the night after the men stake and destroy Lucy.

I noted earlier that it has become commonplace to assert that *Dracula* expresses a male fear of female sexuality. However, I believe it more accurate to say that in the text female sexuality, as women themselves have written about it, has been utterly elided, that the female sexuality represented is fantasized, and that the sexuality Dracula releases in the women he attacks is a male projection to which Stoker's "reticence" denies direct expression. In brief, sexual voracity should not be confused with sexual capacity, and all the sexuality expressed in *Dracula* is male.

Only one vampiric attack by Dracula himself is elaborated in the book, the second attack on Mina as recorded by Dr. Seward who gives his own reaction and records Mina's account. The vampire hunters burst into the Harkers' bedroom just as Dracula is forcing Mina to drink from a spurting vein on his breast, an action Dr. Seward compares to "a child forcing a kitten's nose into a saucer of milk to compel it to drink" (249), and that commentators have read as the upward displacement of a forced fellation. Certainly it reinforces the implied equation between blood and seminal fluid established when Lucy's transfusions were said to make her, in ironic fulfillment of her heretical wish, a polyandrist, though as a scene of nursing it would also make Mina Dracula's child. (Dracula himself blurs lines of gender and associated rules of exogamy claiming Mina as at once "flesh of my flesh; blood of my blood; kin of my kin; my bountiful wine press" [255].) The scene has a surplus of potential meaning involving the exchange or interchange of bodily fluids: Dracula's bloody mouth and breast, Mina's wounded throat, her blood-smeared mouth and nightdress, the blood she transfers to Jonathan's "white night robe" as well. But focusing just on the tableau as a spectacle it has the features of mastery, transgression, and even bondage—"with his left hand he held both Mrs. Harker's hands, keeping them away with her arms at full tension"—that together with a declaration of acquiescence on the part of the woman—"strangely enough, I did not want to hinder him"—form a common male fantasy pattern (249, 255).[13]

The vampire women form a more complex story. It is one that I will here read as the displacement of two male fantasies that Ethel Person describes as at least as common as those of domination in her psychoanalytic practice and in pornographic movies: the fantasies of "the omni-available woman" and of lesbian sex, fantasies that represent both male desires and fears.

According to Person, if castration anxiety is derived only from the Oedipal struggle it cannot account for all fears in adult men, particularly fears of genital inferiority and female rejection. Briefly put, the failure to secure the object of childhood desire is recapitulated in adolescence by the general unavailability of sexual partners at a time when male sexual drives are at their strongest and the phallus not fully under control. Compensation for these fears has two aspects. The consequence of fears of inadequacy is a "defensive phallic narcissism" that rejects the mother and identifies with the mythic phallic power of the father and rival males. The fear of female rejection may be compensated for by the fantasy of the "omni-available woman": a woman who is always aroused, always ready, always easy to please; a woman whose desires mirror his desires, who is essentially interchangeable with other women, and who may be treated with "condescension, contempt, or even sadism," relieving the experience of frustration with the mother and resentment of rejecting women. The fantasy effectively obliterates sexual distinction by projecting a male form of sexuality onto women.

At the outset, the social world of *Dracula* has an obvious surplus of young men and only two marriageable women. In accepting Arthur Holmwood, Lucy rejects both Jack Seward and the peripatetic American, Quincey Morris. Seward feels rebuffed, empty inside, that nothing is worth doing and that the only cure is work, a redoubling of his attempts to "master the facts" of the Renfield case, and Morris wants to restore masculine solidarity after his rejection by inviting his rivals out on a drinking spree that will combine weeping into the wine cup with toasting the health of the victor.

True solidarity among the men is not restored by that sacrament but by the Van Helsing transfusions that give them as it were a joint tenancy in Lucy. The blood of each man seems to convey not only something of his relative vigor, but even a hint of personality. Although she was sedated when the operation was performed, Lucy wakes after her fiancé's donation declaring: "Arthur feels very, very close to me. I seem to feel his presence warm about me" (120). The rival suitors become blood brothers who can indulge themselves in otherwise proscribed mutual tears over Lucy's demise. The transformation of Lucy's appearance into the red and white of the harlot and of her "purity" into a "voluptuous wantonness," whose allure all the men feel, is attributed to the vampire. He has taken her blood, but the blood that animates her—as her life ends, as her sexuality emerges, as she rises undead and displays aggressive sexuality—is literally that of the men.

Van Helsing pulls Arthur violently away from Lucy's proffered deathbed embrace just as later he will interpose a crucifix between the undead Lucy and Arthur, who is about to respond to Lucy's last words, "Come, my husband, come," her carnal reversal of Cleopatra's death-bed utterance: "Husband, I come." If the fantasy of sexual gratification with the omni-available woman is repressed and denied, the sadistic underside of the fantasy may be exaggerated with a vengeance. Demonstrating for all time what not to do with an object, Van Helsing encourages his charges to retain in their mind the ideal picture of the virginal Lucy so that they can destroy the sexually assertive woman with the collective patriarchal phallus, the grotesquely oversized stake that Arthur—the official husband, on what would have been the second night of their marriage—pounds, says Dr. Seward, like Thor:

> his untrembling arm rose and fell, driving deeper and deeper the mercy-bearing stake, whilst the blood from the pierced heart welled and spurted up around it. His face was set and high duty seemed to shine through it; the sight of it gave us courage, so that our voices seemed to ring through the little vault. (194)

Both the "stalwart manhood" that had shrunk under the burden of grief (not to speak of blood lost in transfusions) and the dead Lucy's "purity" are thus restored by a punishment meted out, at least as late as the seventeenth century, to women convicted of murdering their husbands.[14] Violation of the "Thing in the coffin" restores the virginal "sweetness and purity" to Lucy's face, a face that in death may be safely kissed before its expression is preserved with garlic in the mouth, the head struck from her body and the body sealed in a tomb whose key Van Helsing formally presents to the husband Arthur Holmwood, Lord Godalming.

The fantasy of lesbian sex in which a heterosexual male either watches or views and then joins a sexual encounter between women is a common feature in the sexual fantasies of heterosexual men and transvestites, and standard fare in pornographic films. It also brings to mind the many paintings by and for the men of Stoker's world of couched, semi-nude women. The women were often depicted as lying together in sleep, thus casting a veil of ostensible innocence over their contact and the desire of men to see it.[15] Person suggests that at its deepest level the fascination with lesbian sex represents a merger fantasy with the mother "reparative to separation anxiety."[16] But this fascination can also provide a heterosexual alternative to the son's identification with the father, stressed in orthodox psychoanalysis, by eliminating Oedipal rivalry in one of two ways: either by constructing a world made up of women with one of whom he identifies (usually the more dominant one who thus bears the phallus he has hidden from the father), or by imagining a world in which he is the sole male.

There are intimations of desire in the relationship between Lucy and Mina if we consider the characters to be male inventions for an implied male readership that is being given a glimpse into the private world of women among themselves. Lucy to Mina: "we have slept together and eaten together and laughed and cried together . . . I love him, I love him. There, that does me good. I wish I were with you, dear, sitting by the fire undressing as we used to sit" (59). Mina's Journal: "Lucy is asleep and breathing softly. She has more color in her cheeks than usual, and looks, oh so sweet. If Mr. Holmwood fell in love with her seeing her only in the drawing-room I wonder what he would say if he saw her now" (91). But there is no direct vamping of one woman by another even though such a scene came ready-made to Stoker in one of his principal sources, Sheridan LeFanu's "Carmilla," which is told from the point of view of the vamped Laura whose premature demise (reported in the vampire papers of LeFanu's Doctor Hessellius) implies an undeath. The fantasy is masked in the experience of Jonathan Harker, the male in *Dracula* whose masculinity is least stable.

The Jonathan Harker who sets out for Transylvania at the beginning of *Dracula* is a fledgling male on another's errand. He has to remind himself as he approaches Dracula's castle that he has passed his exams: "Solicitor's clerk! Mina would not like that. Solicitor . . . I am now a full-blown solicitor!" (20). Once he enters the castle he is engaged in an unequal contest with Dracula who keeps him up all night pumping him for information about England while revealing something of his history but nothing of his plans: "It was by this time close on morning, and we went to bed. (*Mem.* this diary seems horribly like the beginning of the 'Arabian

Nights' for everything has to break off at cock-crow—or like the ghost of Hamlet's father.)" (33). As the one under the threat of death his position has been feminized. It is that of Scheherazade not the Sultan, as later when Dracula attacks his wife he will be in the position of Scheherazade's sister, who sat at the foot of the bed while "the King arose and did away with his bride's maidenhead and the three fell asleep."[17] The reference to the ghost of the elder Hamlet is also significant for a young man caught between the wills of two paternal figures: employer and client.

Realizing he is trapped, frantic to escape, Harker explores forbidden rooms of the castle and comes into a feminine space of dreadful loneliness, a place he thinks safe for writing, memory, and fantasy: "Here I am, sitting at a little oak table where in old times possibly some fair lady sat to pen with much thought and many blushes, her ill-spelt love-letter"; where women's "gentle breasts were sad for their menfolk away in the midst of remorseless wars." He dozes and wakes to find he is in the boudoir of three female vampires, two dark like the count, "the other fair, as fair as can be, with great wavy masses of golden hair and eyes like pale sapphires. I seemed to know her face, and to know it in connection with some dreamy fear, but could not recollect at the moment how or where" (38–39). Jonathan's confusion is understandable for this is an intertextual memory. The appearance of the golden vampire is almost exactly the same as LeFanu's golden-haired, blue-eyed Laura, whose first encounter with Carmilla in childhood the vampire had passed off as a face in a dream that has haunted her ever since.[18] Harker in effect acts out the experience of a male reader of "Carmilla," who identifies himself with the vamped Laura's narrative "I"; but Laura herself has become the vampire, the reader her prey.

The vampire women are friendly, even "coquettish" with each other as the two dark women insist that the golden vampire dine first. The sensuous description of her advances echo Laura's account of her seduction by Carmilla, to which LeFanu directly attributes the

> ardour of a lover: it embarrassed me; it was hateful and yet overpowering; and with gloating eyes she drew me to her, and her hot lips travelled along my cheek in kisses . . . sometimes it was as if warm lips kissed me, and longer and more lovingly as they reached my throat, but there the caress fixed itself.[19]

Jonathan's account is an elaboration of that text, his glance a stereotypical feminine trope of seduction:

> I was afraid to raise my eyelids, but looked out and saw perfectly under the lashes. The fair girl went on her knees and bent over me fairly gloating . . . . Lower and lower went her head as the lips went below the range of my mouth and chin and seemed about to fasten on my throat. There she paused, and I could hear the churning sound of her tongue as it licked her teeth and lips, and could feel the hot breath on my neck . . . I could feel the soft, shivering touch of the lips on the supersensitive skin of my throat, and the hard dents of two sharp teeth, just touching and pausing there. I closed my eyes in a languorous ecstasy and waited—waited with beating heart. (40–41)

Enter father Dracula who rescues Harker from the women, who seem under his command, but hardly under his control since they proceed to taunt him for never loving. He offers them a child that functions as a substitute for Jonathan, who has experienced both pleasure and a terrifying loss of manhood in the double sense of maturity and gender. The fantasy of reunion with the pre-Oedipal mother is also the threat of a horrific reabsorption by that which gave suck. Like a child, Harker is undressed and put to bed by a parental Dracula, who goes hunting the next night in Harker's clothes so that Jonathan is identified by the distraught mother of the devoured child as a monster. Whether the three vampire women had their promised kisses before Harker escaped from the castle we never know, but his exclamation when he is left alone in the castle with them ("Faugh! Mina is a woman and there is nought in common. They are devils of the pit" [55]) is a desperate assertion of his own masculine identity undercut by its echo of the mad Lear, for whom the "face between the forks" became a "sulphurous pit" that is explicitly a pudendum (IV.vi). If he dies trying to escape those women, Harker insists, he will sleep "as a man," but the text implies that he has become something different, that his sexual identity has an unacknowledged link to what he has experienced in Transylvania.

We next hear of Harker when the nuns of Budapest send for Mina, who nurses her mad beloved back to health and marries him while acting deliberately as the perfect mirror of his every need. Jonathan has repressed knowledge of what transpired at Dracula's castle and invites Mina to share his ignorance by offering her the journal to read should she choose, but without telling him unless dire circumstances demand it. Mina takes the book, binds it with her ribbon and seals it unread with her wedding ring as a sign of mutual trust. But Jonathan remains a "wreck of himself," his "essence gone" (145); as he himself puts it, "impotent, in the dark and distrustful" (170). Even partnership and then inheritance of the practice and fortune of his mentor, Mr. Hawkins, do not improve his condition.

A month into their marriage, after the sight of Dracula in London further unnerves Jonathan, Mina breaks her virginal seal on Jonathan's diary, reads it, and makes it her own by typing a transcript. The date is September 23, the day Lucy first rises from the dead. After Van Helsing confirms to Mina the reality of the Transylvanian adventure on the 25th, Jonathan becomes "a new man." When he rejoins his wife and goes out with the nocturnal vampire hunters on the 30th he is described as "full of energy" (201). If Jonathan's restoration includes sexual desire, Dracula's visits to Mina—culminating in the bloody enactment on October 2 of what had only been threatened in Transylvania—may represent the consummation of the Harker marriage: a displaced consummation that stains the nightdress of the man and the woman with the traditional mark of lost virginity and turns Jonathan Harker's hair as white as Dracula's the instant he recognizes what has happened.

After being attacked by Dracula, Mina is restored to her place of honor among the vampire hunters and supplies vital information, at first through insight and meticulous record-keeping, but later, more passively and ominously, through the telepathic contact established with Dracula when she drank his blood. Mina subsides from queenship into a medium through whom the battle of wills and wits between the rival fathers Van Helsing and Dracula can be played out. At her own request, Van Helsing hypnotizes her to track Dracula's movements at long range. "There is poison in my blood," she declares, and looking significantly past her husband to Quincey Morris says: "When you shall be convinced that I am so changed that it is better that I die that I may live. When I am thus dead in the flesh, then you will, without a moment's delay, drive a stake through me and cut off my head" (291). Only after Quincey ("my true friend") and Arthur have sworn does she turn to the husband who would have shared undeath with her to make him swear, reminding him of those times when "brave men have killed their wives and their womenkind to keep them from falling into the hands of the enemy" (292). Jonathan, his assertive manhood restored by masculine solidarity, is then able to imagine the stake of peace in his loving hand.

Mina's last temptation takes place on the eve of Dracula's demise when the three vampire women reappear outside the magic circle Van Helsing has drawn around her and himself in Transylvania. They do not try to vamp Van Helsing, who later admits his attraction to them as he destroys them in their tombs. Their appeal is to her: "Come, sister. Come to us. Come! Come! In fear I turned to my poor Madam Mina, and my heart with gladness leapt like flame; for oh! the terror in her sweet eyes, the repulsion, the horror, told a story to my heart that was all of hope. God be thanked she was not yet of them" (322). Well might Van Helsing fear, for in the economy of this tale Mina is the last living woman. While it is true that the absolute choice is between Mina's humanity and vampirism, Stoker dramatizes the choice as one between the world of men and a community of women. The excerpts we are given of the journal Mina Harker was keeping, one of the few "genuine" documents to survive, is notably silent about this climactic moment.

The decline that Mina foresees because of her tainted blood and soul parallels the progress of a fatal disease. Her cry after Dracula's attack is that of the leper: "Unclean, unclean! I must touch him or kiss him no more" (252). When the blandly sadistic Van Helsing puts the host to her forehead, it burns like white-hot metal, and again her cry is "Unclean! Even the Almighty shuns my polluted flesh" (263). According to his biographer and grand nephew Daniel Farson, Stoker died of the tertiary syphilis for which the "Locomotor Ataxy" and "exhaustion" listed on the death certificate were common euphemisms, though that diagnosis cannot be certain.[20] Even medical literature on syphilis often made it seem the physical manifestation of a moral tendency, and without conjecturing about the Stoker marriage, or even whether or not he was aware of having the disease at the time he wrote *Dracula,* the late-nineteenth century dread of the disease, the public stigmatization of women, particularly prostitutes, in literature and art as bearers of infection, and the less publicized and probably more justified fears on the part of wives of a syphilitic marriage and damaged children form an important frame for consideration of *Dracula*.[21]

Whether or not the scar on Mina's forehead should be read as signifying "the plague-spot," the pustule of disease, the extreme dread of male heterosexual desire manifest in the terrible allure of the female vampire, the violent staking of Lucy and the separation between woman as sexual being and as mother, which is extreme even for the nineteenth century, make particular sense in that light. It underscores the powerful wish behind the note seven years later that ends the novel. The unscarred Mina is no longer even Ruskin's queen but a mere icon of motherhood whose thoughts are related by her husband and the now-resident patriarchal figure of Van Helsing. In the white space between the end of the text proper (Morris's dying words that highlight the fading of the mark on Mina's forehead) and the concluding note, a son has been born bearing the names of all the male vampire hunters but, his parents believe, the particular spirit of Quincey. In some immaculate fashion, seemingly without the trans/sylvanian journeys of coition and parturition, Quincey Morris, the inconvenient, virile, gun-toting rival has been reborn as the Harker son on the anniversary of his and, though unmentioned, Dracula's demise.

Culturally, of course, the figure of Dracula and the fascination with the non- (or pre-) genital, potentially nonbinary sexuality he embodies lives on. Likewise the ideal of motherhood as a male psychic refuge divorced from sexuality refuses to die. As Jessica Benjamin notes in *The Bonds of Love:*

> The idealization of motherhood, which can be found in both anti-feminist and feminist cultural politics, is an attempt to redeem woman's sphere of influence, the power of the apron strings. However, it pursues this end by idealizing woman's desexualization and lack of agency. This attitude toward sexuality preserves the old gender system, so that freedom and desire remain an unchallenged male domain, leaving women to be righteous but de-eroticized, intimate and caring, but pleasureless. And it fails to understand the underlying force of desire that ratifies male power, the adoration that helps create it ever anew.[22]

CHAPTER 12

"The Inner Chambers of All Nameless Sin": The Beetle, *Gothic Female Sexuality, and Oriental Barbarism*

Kelly Hurley

I

In Richard Marsh's 1897 novel *The Beetle,* London is invaded by a supernatural intruder who hails from the mysterious East. This villainess, variously known as "The Woman of Songs," "the Beetle," or simply "the Oriental," is a priestess from the cult of Isis who comes to procure white victims to torment, mutilate, and murder for her Egyptian rituals. While the text refuses to specify the precise nature of the Beetle's atrocities, it clearly points to some gothicized version of rape, inflicted upon male and female bodies alike.

This essay will focus on a narrative strategy that *The Beetle* shares with other fin de siècle gothic fiction: a textual euphemism, elision, or indirection in representing and naming sensational, "perverse" sexualities, despite the text's nonetheless unmistakably sexual and perverse content. *The Beetle* thus retains a certain "virginality," or at least a hypocritical innocence, while its outrageous popular success indicates that it managed successfully to titillate its Victorian readership.[1] Such a strategy is common enough to the late-Victorian gothic: a more familiar example is Bram Stoker's

Dracula (1897), in which the supernatural status of the villain, and the metaphorical relation vampirism holds to sexual aggression, allow the reader simultaneously to overlook and indulge in a more or less pornographic plot. What interests me about the fin de siècle gothic, however, is not so much the well-documented fact that it euphemistically engages issues of sexuality; I will be concerned instead with the particular moments at which textual euphemism occurs in *The Beetle,* and the types of sexual and racial paranoias such euphemism conceals.

Displacement of sexual energies occurs consistently within the text, at the level of plot and character. While the text implicates, or calls into suspicion, the sexualities of all nonsupernatural characters in *The Beetle,* these characters are finally "exonerated" at the expense of the villainess whose monstrous female—and monstrous oriental—body is the ultimate locus of all perversions. *The Beetle*'s conflation of abject female sexuality with oriental barbarism enables the text to maintain a certain "innocence" through a series of slippages. The nonsupernatural plot of *The Beetle,* disrupted by the arrival of the oriental, is comprised of entangled, "comic" configurations of love triangles and misplaced affections. One problematic in particular underlies these configurations: the possibility of aggressive female desire, as both Marjorie Linden and Dora Grayling prove themselves willing to "chase after" the men they desire.[2] Again at the level of the non-supernatural, a certain process of sublimation softens the edge of this aggression. Both Marjorie and Dora love intensely but not sexually, their desire sublimated into admiration of their menfolk's lifework. Marjorie declares that "the first stirring of my pulses was caused by the report of a speech of [Paul Lessingham's] which I read in *The Times.* It was on the Eight Hours' Bill."[3] Dora, the heiress, translates her love for Sydney Atherton into an offer to fund his scientific research. Marjorie and Dora are socially forward but sexually chaste; however, their girlish aggressiveness serves faintly to mirror the oriental's sexual ravenousness, and vice versa. The monstrosity of the gothicized seductress, embodied, in her avatar of the Beetle, as a hungry and emasculating womb equipped with phallic powers of penetration, marks a Victorian horror of female sexual appetite. In other words, the gothic plot of supernatural female sexuality functions as site of displacement for an active non-gothic female sexuality the text simultaneously points to and denies. But in a crucial textual slippage, this appetite is revealed to be the ugly secret not so much of (white) women as of the barbaric oriental. The Beetle's crimes—the sadistic but unspecified perversities to which she subjects her victims—are represented as sexually executed but racially motivated, as if her Egyptian hatred of a white skin only masked a frustrated longing to "possess" a white body herself, in any sense of the word.

II

> "You'll find that your filthy Egyptian tricks won't answer in England."
>
> Arthur Conan Doyle, "Lot No. 249"

In *The Beetle,* conventional methods of criminal investigation prove futile against a foreign intruder whose supernatural, easily metamorphized body is not subject to the usual limitations of time and space. As a supernatural being she defies natural law and eludes scientific definition: she cannot be countered with rational means. Augmenting—or perhaps comprising—her supernatural potency are the dark and primitive natural forces she may call upon both as a woman and as an oriental. Hers is an aggressive and fearsome femininity that explodes cultural roles, and an Eastern mentality that is utterly foreign: alien, inexplicable, inimical to that of her host nation.

Edward Said's *Orientalism* describes how the orient, the source of one of the West's "deepest and most recurring images of the Other," has "helped define Europe (or the West) as its contrasting image, idea, personality, experience."[4] European values of self-restraint, progress, democracy, scientific precision, and rationality contrast with what is perceived as the sensuality, primitiveness, despotism, superstition, and slovenly mentality of the orient. According to Said's model, the East, defined by the West in terms of all those qualities the West rejects for or denies in itself, serves as a kind of "surrogate or even underground self" for the West.[5] In *The Beetle,* the oriental represents a barbaric other, as opposed to the highly civilized Westerner; a sexually perverse other, as opposed to the chaste and cerebral Westerner; and a magical, supernatural other, as opposed to the scientific, technologically proficient Westerner. She indulges in primitive religious and social rituals, pursues strange and illicit sexual desires, and has access to an occult realm of magic either so ancient that the West has forgotten it, or so unfamiliar that the West cannot fit it into its taxonomies of natural occurrences.

In *The Beetle,* the orient itself, described secondhand by horrified or disgusted British tourists, is a site of backwardness and primitive chaos. Texts like Stoker's 1904 *The Jewel of Seven Stars* (another novel of gothicized Egyptian femininity) evince at least a certain admiration for ancient Egypt's extraordinary scientific proficiency, tempered of course by disapproval of the brutishness and quarrelsome childishness of modern Egypt's degenerate peoples. But *The Beetle* does not grant any sort of recognition even to Egypt's former grandeur. While Marsh indulges his fascination with oriental occultism, he depicts a consistently savage Egypt whose ancient history is an inchoate and abject "prehistory." In their practice of magic, in their superstition, in their primitive and animalistic religious rituals, orientals, both ancient and modern, are subhuman. The Beetle originates from an "idolatrous sect" in the very heart of Egypt,

> which was stated to still practise, and to always have practised, in unbroken historical continuity, the debased, unclean, mystic, and bloody rites, of a form of idolatry which had had its birth in a period of the world's story which was so remote, that to all intents and purposes it might be described as prehistoric. (689–90)

Present-day Egypt, in other words, is a living reminder of the West's prehistory, of that state of animality, or liminal humanity, from which the West has managed to evolve.[6]

On one level, these textual stereotypes that construct the oriental as "Other" serve a unifying function for the culture that produces them, a culture which, in the service of a coherent and idealized self-definition, denies those qualities that threaten or undermine its own self-image and projects them onto extracultural groups (or onto marginal groups, like women, within the culture). On a level of more material and more insidious effects, a paranoiac text like *The Beetle* serves to reflect and feed into British suspicion of and contempt for Egyptians during a period of heightened British military activity in Egypt. The perceived inhumanity of the orient becomes a rationale for subjecting it to the humanizing, civilizing process of British colonization.[7] While the novel's primary setting in London means that it cannot be classed strictly as "colonialist literature," it is precisely that setting which masks the British imperialist project informing and underlying the text. *The Beetle* inverts the issue of colonization by presenting the East/West conflict in terms of oriental aggression—an oriental incursion, with white slavery and genocide as its end, into the very heart of London.[8] It then distorts the issue further by representing Egypt as a site not of relatively stable English rule during Lord Cromer's occupation, but of oriental misrule, under which innocent white tourists are kidnapped, tortured, and murdered with impunity. Reversing the territorial actualities, the text transposes the colonized subject into a savage aggressor whose duplicity and desire for mastery swell across the boundaries of the orient into the homeland of civilized England.

As primitiveness inheres in the "debased, unclean, mystic, and bloody" site of the orient, so too does it inhere in the debased, unclean, mystic, and bloody body of woman. In *The Beetle,* the orient is presented as a feminized space: the female body "embodies" the orient. "The sex" was said to occupy the same space of uncontrolled nature (a space hostile to culture) as the orient; women were too much defined by the body, and thus prone to irrationality and hysteria—more primitive than men, in short, just as the oriental is more primitive than the Westerner. The East, in fact, was often characterized within the orientalist discourse as feminine, with its "penetrability" and "supine malleability."[9] Located in the so-called matrix of civilization, the orient is a highly sexualized site, seeming to suggest "not only fecundity but sexual promise (and threat), untiring sensuality, unlimited desire, deep generative energies." For the West, with its more rigid ethos of sexual behavior, "the Orient was a place where one could look for sexual experience unobtainable in Europe"—the sort of experience *The Beetle*'s Paul Lessingham is pursuing when he wanders into the backstreet Egyptian brothel presided over by the Woman of Songs.[10] Not only is the orient a space in which one may pursue the luxury of the body, it is also a space associated—for the Victorian male—with the body itself, with the body's physicality and fertility, with bodily pleasure. The orient is synonymous with sexuality in the same way that *woman* is synonymous with sexuality: to each is attributed the sort of gross physicality, both in terms of generative power and a sexualized identity, that masculinized Western culture disclaims in itself.

While this raw physicality has a certain appeal for the British characters of *The Beetle,* it is presented more consistently as a threat, a devouring and engulfing force. In the novel, the oriental female, or the feminized orient, is far from being characterized by any womanly "penetrability" or "malleability." The orient seduces, certainly, with the lovely body of the Woman of Songs, but she is no cipher or lazily passive object of desire. She is a powerful, aggressive—most "unfeminine"—creature, who seduces only to emasculate and consume her male object of desire. While her unfeminine behavior may partially be attributed to her orientalness (that is, while one may attribute her savagery to her barbaric racial heritage), one must also read her in terms of a Victorian mistrust of femininity and feminine "nature." As inherently more "natural," less civilized (or civilizable) creatures, women share with orientals their irrationality, illogic, superstition, emotionalism, and so forth; they are the natural opponents of Western cultural values. And just as the supernaturally exaggerated representations of the barbaric, primitive oriental found in *The Beetle* offer a rationale for xenophobia and for a continued British colonial presence within Egypt, so do its fearsome depictions of unleashed feminine potency offer a rationale for the continued constriction of female roles, particularly in the context of the strong feminist movements at the turn of the century.[11]

III

> And once again I was conscious of that awful sense of the presence of an evil thing. How much of it was fact, and how much of it was the product of imagination I cannot say; but, looking back, it seems to me that it was as if I had been taken out of the corporeal body to be plunged into the inner chambers of all nameless sin. There was the sound of something flopping off the bed on to the ground, and I knew that the thing was coming at me across the floor. My stomach quaked, my heart melted within me—the very anguish of my terror gave me strength to scream—and scream!
>
> *The Beetle,* 485.

Like Wilkie Collins's *The Woman in White* and *The Moonstone, The Beetle* employs the device of multiple first-person narrators, each of whom provides a different perspective on the events surrounding the oriental intruder. The story is opened by Robert Holt, a starving ex-clerk long out of work, who tells of the terrible adventures that befell him after he broke into a seemingly deserted house in a seedy London neighborhood, desperate for shelter from the rain. In the darkness inside, he is assaulted by a slimy, foul-smelling creature the size of a small animal, and later held prisoner by an evil-looking oriental, of indeterminate size and age, who seems to be the creature's "keeper" and can call it up at will. Holt is mesmerized and "possessed" by this foreigner, who forces him to break into the house of Paul Lessingham, prominent radical politician, and steal a packet of love letters written to Lessingham by his fiancée Marjorie Linden. When Lessingham confronts Holt in the act of burglary, Holt, as ordered by the mesmerist, hisses the words "THE BEETLE!" to send Lessingham into a fit of hysteria.

Part II is narrated by Sydney Atherton, an inventor who is currently hard at work on a new weapon of chemical warfare. Sydney writes of his unsuccessful wooing of his childhood friend Marjorie Linden and his fierce jealousy of his rival Lessingham, and describes visits to his laboratory by both Lessingham and Holt's mysterious oriental captor. Lessingham, nervously hinting at some shady incident in his own past, comes to seek information from Atherton, amateur orientalist: he wishes to discover whether there is a "shred of truth" in the Egyptian belief that a "priest of Isis" could "assume after death the form of a scarabaeus" (509). Atherton scoffs at the legend, but later witnesses exactly such a transmogrification when the oriental comes to enlist his help (unsuccessfully) in her scheme of vengeance against Lessingham.

Marjorie's narrative describes her love affair with Lessingham, the opposition of her father, a conservative politician, to the engagement, and the events leading to her entrapment by the Beetle. Part IV is narrated by Augustus Champnell, a "confidential agent" enlisted by Lessingham to assist in the search for Marjorie. Through him we finally hear the story of what exactly occurred in the Egyptian temple of Isis twenty years ago, when Lessingham was enslaved by the Woman of Songs, broke free of her influence, and strangled her, only to witness the "transmigration" of her corpse into the body of a scarabaeus. Champnell describes the desperate chase after the oriental and her two prisoners, Holt (who finally expires in a seedy London hotel) and Marjorie. The fugitives are providentially halted by a train wreck which destroys the Beetle. Marjorie is pulled from the debris scarcely alive: "even after her physical powers were completely restored—in itself a tedious task—she was for something like three years under medical supervision as a lunatic. But all that skill and money could do was done, and in course of time . . . the results were entirely satisfactory" (713).

We never get the oriental's own story directly; her words and emotions are always filtered by the distaste and revulsion of the characters relating them. Her version of the story is inessential to the novel; what matters is her gothic embodiment as the Beetle, the nameless horror it induces in all who encounter her, and the terrible effect she has on her victims. As a "foreigner" to the culture—foreign in the sense of both her Egyptian and her supernatural origins—she confronts late-Victorian London with a spectre of gross corporeality, and evokes a response of denial and dread. The corporeal body in *The Beetle* is either a thing of terror, or a thing of sickness and fear. In her avatar of the Beetle, the oriental is characterized by that nauseating amorphousness which one encounters so frequently in the monstrous creations of the late-Victorian gothic: she is dreadfully slimy, foul-smelling, and damp, adhering stickily to the body with her numerous legs. Hypnotized and entrapped by the oriental's horrible gothic embodiment, her victims become entrapped in their own agonized bodies. She drives both Holt and Lessingham into an absolute and gibbering hysteria; with her arcane system of tortures, she reduces Marjorie to the wreck of a human being.

In short, the Beetle is abject in at least one sense of the word as Julia Kristeva defines it. In *Powers of Horror,* Kristeva writes that it is not "lack of cleanliness or health that causes abjection, but what disturbs identity, system, order. What does not respect borders, positions, rules. The in-between, the ambiguous, the composite."[12] The Beetle-woman violates categories: she is an oriental in London; a woman disguised as a man; a human being who can transform herself at will into something that is a cross between a beast and an insect. She is ambiguous in bodily identity (both human and animal), in sexual identity (both male and female), in sexual preference (as a woman, she seduces Paul Lessingham; as a man, she assaults Holt; as a woman, she assaults Marjorie Linden). And she arouses in the onlooker a sense of abjection, of nausea—an instinctive, subrational, and immediate sense of dread. One knows that there is something wrong about her but cannot put a finger on it. Holt speaks of "that awful sense of the presence of an evil thing" (485); Marjorie recalls "an altogether indescribable feeling, a feeling which amounted to knowledge, that I was in the presence of the supernatural" (562); for Lessingham, there was "about her something so unnatural, so inhuman" as to fill him "with an indescribable repulsion" (632–33). Her very smell is nauseating: Marjorie comments on "an uncomfortable odour" in the Beetle's house, "suggestive of some evil-smelling animal" (615).

At times the characters' "instinctive" revulsion from the oriental seems indistinguishable from commonplace xenophobia, the habitual British mistrust of racial difference. The oriental's landlady describes her tenant as a "dirty foreigner, who went about in a bed-gown through the public streets" (666). The local policeman has kept an eye on this "queer fish," with his queer habits, ever since "he" appeared in the neighborhood—"He's known amongst us as the Arab," is his simple and self-evident explanation (675). Whether mistrust of "the Arab" is generated by racism or by the abjectness of this particular oriental individual matters little: abjectness adheres to, is the condition of, the orient, and though she may be a particularly loathsome example of the Arab, she is by no means an exception to her race.

Like most "unscrupulous Orientals," the Beetle is savage in her pleasures, and heartless in their execution. She is cruel, and takes a wanton delight in her cruelty. She toys with her victims long after their spirit has been crushed, seeming to delight simply in eliciting their screams of terror and pain. She is secretive, unsociable, untrustworthy, filthy, foul-smelling. She has an oriental envy of the superior white ("What would I not give for a skin as white as that—ah yes!" [456]), which translates into a boundless hatred of that unattainable whiteness, a desire to punish and mutilate white skin. And she harbors a "typically" Eastern (and also, perhaps, feminine) vengefulness, nursing an inveterate grudge against Paul

Lessingham, the man who spurned her, travelling to England more than twenty years later to destroy him. "Plainly, with this gentleman [sic]," remarks Atherton, "hate meant hate—in the solid Oriental sense" (540).

For the oriental, malice is a racial condition, not simply an emotional response. So deeply engrained, so basic is her cruel nature that it distorts and makes hideous her very countenance: she is literally evil incarnate. Her dreadful face is an index to her blighting depravity. As Holt describes her,

> there was not a hair upon his [sic] face or head, but, to make up for it, the skin, which was a saffron yellow, was an amazing mass of wrinkles. The cranium, and, indeed, the whole skull, was so small as to be disagreeably suggestive of something animal. The nose, on the other hand, was abnormally large; so extravagant were its dimensions, and so peculiar its shape, it resembled the beak of some bird of prey . . . . The mouth, with its blubber lips, came immediately underneath the nose, and chin, to all intents and purposes, there was none. This deformity—for the absence of chin amounted to that—it was which gave to the face the appearance of something not human—that, and the eyes. For so marked a feature of the man were his eyes, that, ere long, it seemed to me that he was nothing but eyes. (454)

The creature, in short, is "supernaturally ugly" (454), with the supernatural effect resulting partly from oriental magicianship, the power of the mesmeric, compelling eyes and voice, and partly from the gross physiognomical traits the oriental shares with various animal species. (The Beetle's landlady remarks that her tenant is "more like a hideous baboon than anything else, let alone a man" [666].) The abnormally small skull is a clue to the creature's inherently depraved nature, marking the savagery of the atavistic criminal, or the incomplete moral development of the inferior, less evolved non-caucasian.

But beyond the creature's mesmeric fascination and preternatural ugliness, what largely accounts for the horror she induces is indefinable, for it has to do with her bodily indefinition—her abjectness. When Holt first meets the creature, he cannot ascertain its age, its sex, its nationality (except that it is "foreign") (453–54); he cannot even vouch for its species: "I saw someone in front of me lying in a bed. I could not at once decide if it was a man or a woman. Indeed at first I doubted if it was anything human" (453). He is particularly vexed by the issue of the creature's gender. At first, taking into account his captor's hideousness, Holt states firmly, "I knew it be a man—for this reason, if for no other, that it was impossible such a creature could be feminine" (453). But soon he begins to doubt. His "instinct," as he later tells Marjorie (604), leads him to note that there is something "essentially feminine" in the creature's face (462), and he is further bewildered by "his" manifest desire for Lessingham, and by "his" teasing advances to Holt himself: "Is it not sweet to stand close at my side? You, with your white skin, if I were a woman, would you not take me for a wife?" (486). These doubts are then again quelled by the animalistic countenance, the aggressively unfeminine behavior of his captor: "after all, I told myself that it was impossible that I could have been such a simpleton as to have been mistaken on such a question as gender" (462).

Perhaps the reader is meant all along to guess the femininity of the oriental and label Holt, as invited, a "simpleton"; but it is more likely that the text intended to shock the Victorian reader with what would have been an unexpected depiction of male homoerotic desire, establishing the general idea of sexual perversion which is to pervade the novel and associating sexual perversity specifically with the oriental. The oriental, whatever its gender, is certainly blatantly sexual in its interests. "He" forces Holt to strip and gloats over his naked white skin with a "satyr's smile" and "devouring . . . glances" (456). After a night spent in a deep trance, Holt finds himself being uncovered and closely examined and "prodded" in his nakedness by his satyrlike host: "Fingers were pressed into my cheeks, they were thrust into my mouth, they touched my staring eyes . . . and—horror of horrors!—the blubber lips were pressed to mine—the soul of something evil entered me in the guise of a kiss" (458).

The reader witnesses this early scene under the impression that it takes place between two men. Later, although the text "relieves" the reader of the fear that what he or she witnessed was a depiction of male homoerotic desire by firmly establishing the oriental's femininity, it provides the reader with a further uncomfortably homoerotic situation—the oriental's sadistic, quasisexual attacks on Marjorie. Certainly the text problematizes the whole issue of sexuality within these first pages. The simple, seemingly basic question of gender identity is thrown into confusion by the arrival of the Beetle.

She is able to cross the boundary between one gendered identity and another, she can cross the boundary separating the human and animal species, and even in her avatar of the Beetle she resists enclosure within the boundary of a definite species classification. After the train wreck which Marjorie barely survives and which squashes the Beetle to death, all that remains of the latter are some "huge blotches" on the seat—"stains of some sort," which "were damp, and gave out a most unpleasant smell" (711). Various experts opine that the stains are comprised of human blood, paint, wild cat blood, or finally, "a deposit of some sort of viscid matter, probably the excretion of some variety of lizard" (712). Whatever the Beetle was resists scientific analysis and classification: it can fit into no taxonomy of natural history. The usually matter-of-fact Champnell has the last word on the subject: "experience has taught me that there are indeed more things in heaven and earth than are dreamed of in our philosophy, and I am quite prepared to believe that the so-called Beetle, which others saw, but I never, was—or is, for it cannot be certainly shown that the Thing is not still existing—a creature born neither of God nor man" (715).

As we are never able to learn what the Beetle "really" is, so we never learn what she really does. We have all the details of the effects she causes—Marjorie's insanity, Paul's hysterical breakdowns, Holt's enslavement and eventual death—but don't know what terrible action she performs to wreak these effects. Like many a gothic text, *The Beetle* makes use of the trope of ineffability which characterizes the presence of the abject. Words fail to represent the dread the Beetle induces, and the magnitude and type of the agony she is able to inflict, so these are left more profitably to the reader's imagination, enflamed by the vague hyperbole which masses itself round the unnamed and unnameable events connected with the Beetle. The Beetle's female victims, Marjorie in particular, are subjected to "unimaginable agony," "speechless torture," "every variety of outrage of which even the minds of demons could conceive" (686, 634). We see the effects of such torture in Marjorie's utter physical and mental debilitation by the end of the novel, as well as in the extremities to which the male victims are reduced—the young English boy's "state of indescribable mutilation" after having suffered "nameless agonies and degradations" (689), Lessingham's lapses into crawling, gibbering idiocy at the mere mention of the Beetle. One does not even know with what instruments the oriental inflicts her tortures. The landlady of the "disorderly house" to which the Beetle carries Marjorie and Holt says she heard no "sounds of struggling, or of blows," only "shriek after shriek" as Marjorie was somehow molested behind a locked door (701). Perhaps the "Arab" hides her instruments of torture in the mysterious "bundle"—the "lurking place of nameless terrors" (686)—she carries on her head about London; perhaps her instrument of torture is her terrible body itself. As Holt lies dying with "two abrasions of the skin" on either side of his neck (696), he gasps out that "[The Beetle] took me by the throat . . . [and] killed me" (698).

All phenomena associated with the Beetle are, finally, shrouded in mystery. The main events of the story remain unspeakable and unexplained. As Champnell writes, since Marjorie recovers with an absolute memory block as to what the Beetle did to her,

> what actually transpired will never, in all human possibility, be certainly known and particularly what precisely occurred in the railway carriage during that dreadful moment of sudden passing from life unto death. What became of the creature who all but did her to death; who he was—if it was a "he," which is extremely doubtful; whence he came; whither he went; what was the purpose of his presence here—to this hour these things are puzzles. (713)

Though all the horrible possibilities which the novel raised seem to be neatly dispatched in Champnell's postscript—the Beetle squashed to death, the subterranean temple of Isis back in Egypt destroyed by some unexplained explosion, Marjorie recovered in health and happily married to Paul—Champnell prefers to leave his ending open. "The Thing," or something like it, he warns, might very well return. It might return and wreak the same havoc because it was never understood, and was destroyed only by accident. Indefinition—a world in which it is possible that there might exist "creature[s] born neither of God nor of man"—is the final condition of the novel, just as the Beetle is, in the final analysis, indefinable.

And yet this heightened sense of indefinition, from which *The Beetle* gains most of its dramatic effect, may be seen as a certain coyness on the part of the text. The text censors itself from speaking of what the Beetle does as effectively as Marjorie's memory censors itself from remembering what the Beetle did to her. Other characters besides Marjorie suffer from lapses of memory: their narratives are interrupted by insanity, or aphasia, or a fainting fit. Holt's narrative ends with an occurrence so terrible his very consciousness gives way: "[the Beetle] leaped, shrieking, off the bed, and sprang at me, clasping my throat with his horrid hands, bearing me backwards on to the floor; I felt his breath mingle with mine . . . and then God, in His mercy, sent oblivion" (488). After his dreadful weeks in the Temple of Isis, Lessingham suffers a long period of "aphasia" and "semi-imbecility" (637); when he recovers he wills himself to forget by trying to bury his memory of the Beetle in hard work.

The characters in the novel cannot bear to recall what the Beetle did to them—or perhaps the text cannot bear to represent it. All one can be certain about is that the Beetle's predations are somehow sexual in nature. The sadistic tortures inflicted on the naked white bodies of English virgins by the priestesses of Isis seem to require, or at least be heightened by, intercourse with a passive and mesmerized English male sex slave—Lessingham, the unnamed English teenager, and later, one may speculate, Holt. The three stalwart Englishmen in pursuit of Marjorie and her captor writhe with horror at "the notion of a gently-nurtured girl being at the mercy of that fiend incarnate" (688). The repeated trope for what she and the other English virgins have undergone is "that to which death would have been preferred," a common Victorian euphemism for rape; and Paul frets that even if they get his fiancée back alive, "she will be but the mere soiled husk of the Marjorie whom I knew and loved" (688), as if the oriental villainess (perhaps with some phallic substitute hidden in her mysterious bag of tricks, her "paraphernalia of horror and of dread") could even deprive Marjorie of her virginity.

One thing is clear from the beginning: the oriental, whatever its gender, has a "savage, frantic longing" for the body of Paul Lessingham. "He is straight—straight as the mast of a ship—he is tall—his skin is white; he is strong—how strong!—oh yes! Is there a better thing than to be his wife? his well-beloved?" (465). This strong sexual desire on the part of the oriental, metamorphosed into vengeance, is what motivates the plot of *The Beetle*. There does exist a certain amount of insistent, posturing sexual desire among the non-supernatural characters in *The Beetle*. As in *Dracula,* several suitors (Sydney Atherton, Lessingham, and Percy Woodville) jockey for the hand of one woman, Marjorie Linden, while an otherwise demure Dora Grayling rather shamelessly pursues Sydney. Most of this sexual rivalry and tension is fairly civilized, often even comic, involving the sorts of mix-ups and awkward situations one might find in a novel like *Barchester Towers*. While the two rivals Atherton and Lessingham snarl and snap at one another, both are adamant about the purity of their intentions toward Marjorie. The novel even indulges in the traditional comic ending of a triple marriage (including the rather gratuitous awarding of a Dora Grayling bridesmaid to the minor character Percy Woodville).

However, this civilized and commonplace comedy of mortal romantic desire is displaced—or perhaps one should say, shown up—by the terrible drama of sexuality brought about by the polymorphously perverse and intense desires of the oriental villainess as she catches the major characters in her snares. Under her hypnotic suggestion, Sydney suddenly finds himself acknowledging a physical longing for Marjorie: "I thought . . . of the delight of holding her in my arms, of feeling the pressure of her lips to mine. As my gaze met his, the lower side of what the conquest of this fair lady would mean, burned in my brain; fierce imaginings blazed before my eyes" (540). However, Sydney manfully shakes off the suggestion and disclaims the desire as his own: "Rage took hold of me. 'You hound!' I cried." Sexual desire, seen by the text as monstrous and violent, is displaced from the romantic relationships and projected onto the depraved oriental. What the novel presents, in her person, is a terrible, rampant sexuality, taken to deviant extremes of sadism, enslavement, homoeroticism, and a general perversion.

And the perversion of the oriental is undeniably connected with her femininity, as we see in the remarkable opening sequence from Holt's narrative of "The House with the Open Window." Seeking shelter, Holt enters this seemingly deserted house through the inviting open window, but no sooner does he enter than he wants nothing more than to leave, for he senses a "presence" in the pitch-dark room, "something strange, something evil . . . . I had a horrible persuasion that, though unseeing, I was seen; that my every movement was being watched"; and this invisible mesmeric gaze holds him and cuts off his retreat by paralyzing him, mind and body (450).

Immobilized and panic-stricken, Holt watches two glowing eyes, six inches above the floor, advance towards him. The creature, emitting an "unpleasant, foetid odour," stalks and climbs him as he stands with unwilling but utter passivity:

> On a sudden I felt something on my boot, and, with a sense of shrinking, horror, nausea, rendering me momentarily more helpless, I realized that the creature was beginning to ascend my legs, to climb my body . . . . It was as though it were some gigantic spider—a spider of the nightmares; a monstrous conception of some dreadful vision. It pressed lightly against my clothing with what might, for all the world have been spider's legs. There was an amazing host of them—I felt the pressure of each separate one. They embraced me softly, stickily, as if the creature glued and unglued them, each time it moved. (451)

The creature, proceeding with an infinitely sickening deliberateness, mounts his "loins" and "the pit of [his] stomach," its odor becoming so intense as to be "unbearable," and slowly proceeds up his neck to "envelope [his] face with its huge, slimy, evil-smelling body, and embrace [him] with its myriad legs," at which point Holt is finally maddened into breaking the paralysis and shaking the thing off (452).

Except for the sight of the two glowing eyes and an occasional "squelching" sound, all Holt has to guide him in envisioning the creature are his senses of touch and smell, which feed him only impressions that nauseate him on a visceral level and quickly dismantle his powers of self-control, volition, and especially, rationality—those powers without which Holt feels himself "unmanned." The creature's teasing advance up Holt's body, the darkness of the setting, the intense, intimate physicality of the contact, combined with the idea of stickiness and overpowering smell, point towards a reading of this as some sort of nightmare of sexual encounter, sexuality at its most primitive and terrible. Where Holt entered seeking warmth, shelter and safety, he is paralyzed and assaulted—emasculated by this unseen thing that is almost a parodic and monstrous version of the female genitalia. This same Beetle that attacks Holt, as we discover later (if we can trust Atherton's amateur orientalist scholarship), is associated with "the legendary transmigrations of Isis," and "the story of the beetle which issues from the woman's womb through all eternity" (546). Lessingham's "Woman of Songs" transmogrified into the Beetle—gave birth to this reduction of herself out of her own death—when Paul Lessingham finally broke free of her mesmeric control and strangled her. Always a sexual predator, a "man-eater," she becomes embodied as her own hungry, emasculating womb—damp, adhesive, and overwhelmingly nauseating.

Holt and the other victims, then, are not so much "taken out of the corporeal body to be plunged into the inner chambers of all nameless sin," as Holt describes his experience (485), as trapped within their corporeal bodies by the spectre of the externalized "inner chambers" of that repository of "nameless sin," a woman's body. Holt and other victims are bestialized, reduced to mere bodies without self-volition, whose speech and actions are controlled by the will of the Beetle. What they then do (what the Beetle makes them do), or what she does to them, is done without reference to their own wishes and desires—each character in the text vehemently proclaims the revulsion that the oriental's caresses inspired in him. Sexuality in the text is displaced onto the body and motives of the oriental woman. Sexuality is rewritten as a hideous, gothic perversion, which then becomes the thing that one cannot name, that one cannot speak of, that one blocks from one's memory, that one cannot represent.

In its depiction of femininity, *The Beetle* employs the set of dark woman/light woman characterizations so common in Victorian literature. The "good woman" is Marjorie Linden, "the daintiest damsel in the land," and the bad woman—the woman who once seduced Marjorie's fiancé—is an oriental. She captivates her male victim with her thrilling melodies as the seductive "Woman of Songs," and she dispatches him, with a combination of powers both occult and sadistic, as the cruel, emasculating votary of the goddess Isis. Here, as in much literature of the supernatural, the femme fatale is reduced to nothing more than an embodiment of sexuality—or perhaps it would be better to say that her sexuality is exaggerated into a monstrous, all-consuming parody of itself. *Dracula*'s Lucy Westenra, whose incipient lasciviousness finds full expression in a slavering vampirism, and Arabella the snake-woman in Stoker's 1911 *Lair of the White Worm* are two such femmes fatales who tempt their male victims with their alluring charms in the hope of devouring them. Each text provides her with a pallid counterpart: Mina Harker and Mimi Watford respectively, in the protection of whose pure-mindedness their menfolk find the strength of mind to resist and destroy the temptress.

Though the traditional polarity of good versus bad woman is presented untraditionally by *The Beetle*—Marjorie is too adventurous and outspoken to be a conventional heroine, and the "Woman of Songs," by the time she appears in London, too hideously ugly to be exactly a femme fatale—the novel does juxtapose a pert, lively, but desexualized heroine with a villainess whose fierce and emasculating sexual aggressiveness has made of her a repulsive, yet sexually potent monster: a "ghoulish example of her sex, who had so yielded to her depraved instincts to have become nothing but a ghastly reminiscence of womanhood" (462). As the narrative progresses, each woman becomes transformed into a sheer parody of the polarity of femininity she represents. The oriental is revealed as a literal monster, cruel, sadistic, castrating, and vile; while Marjorie becomes reduced to complete passivity—physical incapacitation, idiocy, and dependence—by the end of the novel.

Femininity as represented by Britannia is all of the finest and most civilized. Essential femininity, the text continues to insist, is the femininity of Marjorie Linden: pure, high-minded, appealingly winsome, and, metaphorically speaking, disembodied. The embodied female—with her troublesome sexual desires, her problematic gender identity, her terrible avatar of the Beetle—is a thing of abjection; but the text denies that she has anything to do with true Victorian femininity. First, she has become "unwomaned," or masculinized, by her behavior, as in Holt's remark quoted earlier, "it was impossible such a creature could be feminine." Secondly, after her femininity has been proved by the undeniable fact of her naked body, the reader is still free to attribute her unnaturally masculine sexual aggression to her oriental savagery.

IV

> It often happens that male patients declare that they feel there is something uncanny about the female genital organs.
>
> Sigmund Freud, "The 'Uncanny'"

The Beetle is a text obsessed with naked bodies. Robert Holt, Marjorie Linden, Paul Lessingham, the many victims of the Isis cult, all are "stripped to the skin" (the full phrase is always used) and leeringly examined, or tormented, or sexually molested in "unspeakable" ways we only have leave to conjecture. The oriental, too, is briefly displayed to Sydney Atherton and the reader in all her nakedness, and only then, as she metamorphoses from human being to scarab and back again and her robes lie about her on the floor, is the tricky question of her gender settled once and for all. "I had been egregiously mistaken on the question of sex," Sydney informs us; "My visitor was not a man, but a woman, and judging from the brief glimpse which I had of her body, by no means old or ill-shaped either" (547).

When stripped, the Beetle's unexpected essence is her decided femininity; but when stripped, the essence (as the text emphasizes it) of her victims, male and female alike, is their decided whiteness; "What a white skin you have—how white! What would I not give for a skin as white as that," gloats Holt's captor after commanding him to undress (456). Champnell, recalling the rumors he has heard of the depraved Isis cult in Egypt whose "practice" is "to offer young women as sacrifices," remarks that the cult members prefer "white Christian women, with a special preference, if they could get them, to young English women" (690); and Lessingham, an eyewitness to the cult sacrifices, proclaims solemnly of the victims, "they were as white as you or I" (634).

In the ramshackle London house that the Beetle has turned into her headquarters, Marjorie Linden finds, on top of the pile of cushions and rugs that serves the oriental for a bed, a bedspread representing a naked white woman, her writhings and agony depicted with lifelike verisimilitude, in the very act of being burned alive under the pleased scrutiny of Isis. As she watches, the bedspread begins to move, and the Beetle comes out from hiding to seize Marjorie and begin to subject her to some of the same tortures. This is the point to which Marjorie's compulsively rewritten diary leads again and again, and past which it can go no further. Her memory balks after the moment when she meets her oriental captor face to face. This event depicted on the bedspread is both the moment the text is trying to ward off, the narrative gathering momentum as Marjorie's three champions rush to save her from the fate of the woman on the bedspread, and the point to which the text, like Marjorie's diary, compulsively returns again and again: in Champnell's secondhand narration of the ill-fated young Christian women abroad, in Lessingham's hysterical "attacks" or flashbacks in which he recalls what he witnessed in Egypt twenty years ago. There in the temple of Isis, "young and lovely" Englishwomen were stripped naked, "outraged," and "burnt alive," and then their ashes "consumed by the participants" of the Isis cult in a frenzied "orgie" (635). The scene on the bedspread is a sort of icon of the monstrous potential of the orient, an orient which, in its insatiable desire for the whiteness of the West and frenzied envy and hatred of the West, would destroy and engulf it in all its whiteness, consuming its very ashes.

The text dwells obsessively upon the bodies of two naked women: one a victimizer, the other a victim; one a masculine-appearing and masculine-behaving creature, whose nakedness terrifyingly reveals her unexpected femininity, the other a young "Christian" creature whose nakedness reveals, equally terrifyingly, the vulnerability of the white body—a vulnerability the white male victim shares. The feminine "pulchritude" of the stripped Englishwoman is not emphasized by the text. In her victimization, she is less a sexual object than a representation of whiteness at its "best"—a virginal whiteness in its most fragile, most valuable, most cherished state. Her nakedness reveals her as a member of the purest race, subject to the invidious envy and rage of lesser, dark-skinned peoples.

The Beetle inverts its culture's own fascination with "the Oriental experience," its mania for colonization of the desirable orient, into a belief in British (white) desirability, and a fear of aggressive oriental "colonization." At the same time that the novel manifests a terror of engulfment by the orient, it evinces, from a masculine perspective, a terror of an overwhelming feminine sexuality as embodied in the supernaturally potent Beetle-woman.

Even if the sadism of the oriental vents itself most fully on her female victims, the real object of her visit is Paul Lessingham. Her sexuality is directed toward men, and her desire is to consume her object. Aggressive feminine desire is portrayed by the novel as a devouring force which emasculates its male object and literally dehumanizes the sexualized female. For feminine pulchritude (and the lascivious desires that go along with it) does manifest itself in the oriental. But the beautiful body of the Woman of Songs is a trap. Like Duessa in *The Faerie Queene,* or Arabella in *The Lair of the White Worm,* the lovely siren hides beneath her fair form, in her "nether parts," the serpent, the worm, or, in this case, the Beetle: a devouring, emasculating, and abject embodiment of her genitalia.

In *The Beetle,* issues of race and gender come together in the gothicization of the oriental villainess. A Victorian fear of the hidden depravity, the hidden potency, of the female is literalized, in the novel, by a supernatural occurrence: the oriental's transformation from woman into Beetle, from woman into a reductive, compressed, and monstrous embodiment of her sexuality. And a Victorian fear of the orient is given focus by the supernatural powers (mesmerism, transmogrification, control over the natural elements) which the Western mind associated particularly with the Eastern races, and which the Beetle uses to enslave and destoy her white victims. All of the barbarity and primitiveness which, as Said discusses, the West attributed to the orient are borne out by the savage behavior of the Beetle; but that barbarity particularly manifests itself in sadistic sexual behavior directed towards the masculinist West. By casting its villainess as an oriental, the text manages to avoid suggesting that abject female sexuality could inhere in any sense in caucasian women: but by casting its oriental as a woman the text manages to suggest that barbaric sexuality is, in some sense, inherently feminine.

NOTES

CHAPTER 1

1. Julia Kristeva, "Stabat Mater," in *The Female Body in Western Culture: Contemporary Perspectives,* ed. Susan Rubin Suleiman (Cambridge: Harvard University Press, 1986), 101.

2. Jon Stratton, *The Virgin Text: Fiction, Sexuality and Ideology* (Brighton: Harvester, 1988), 43.

3. Harold Garfinkel, "Passing and the managed achievement of sex status in an 'intersexed' person part 1," in *Studies in Ethnomethodology* (Cambridge: Polity Press, 1984), 124.

4. Michel Foucault, *The History of Sexuality, Volume I: An Introduction,* trans. Robert Hurley (Harmondsworth: Penguin, 1981), 26. For the relationship between sexuality and discourse in the 1800s, cf. Thomas Laqueur, *Making Sex: Body and Gender from the Greeks to Freud* (Cambridge: Harvard University Press, 1990), on the period's development of "a radically different rhetoric" to represent the "fundamental differences between the male and female sexes" (5).

5. See Catherine Gallagher, "The Body versus the Social Body in the Works of Thomas Malthus and Henry Mayhew," *Representations* 14 (1986): 90.

6. Michel Foucault, *Discipline and Punish: The Birth of the Prison,* trans. Alan Sheridan (New York: Vintage, 1979), 26.

7. Lytton Strachey, *Queen Victoria* (1921; London: Collins, 1968), 47. Further references will be cited parenthetically in the text.

8. Strachey traces Victoria's increasing symbolic prestige through the jubilee and the rise of imperialism: "The Queen was hailed at once as the mother of her people and as the embodied symbol of their imperial greatness" (256); "The need for a symbol—a symbol of England's might, of England's worth, of England's extraordinary and mysterious destiny—became felt more urgently that ever before. The Crown was that symbol: and the Crown rested upon the head of Victoria" (275). Yet the corollary of this intensified symbolism is an eventual loss of executive authority, "by the end of the reign the power of the sovereign had appreciably diminished, the prestige of the sovereign had enormously grown" (275).

9. Although acknowledging their historical distance, we can compare the impressions created by Victoria's persona to those made by Elizabeth I on her "passage through the citie of London to westminster the daye before her coronation," as she theatrically elicited her subjects' obedient response: "her grace by holding up her handes, and merie countenance to such as stode farre of, and most tender and gentle language to those that stoode nigh to her grace, did declare herselfe no lesse thankefullye to receive her people's good wille, than they lovingly offred it unto her." The writer happily notes the new star's success: "So that if a man should say well, he could not better tearme the citie of London that time, than a stage wherin was shewed the wonderfull spectacle of a noble hearted princesse toward her most loving people, and the people's exceding comfort in beholding so worthy a sovereign, and hearing so princelike a voice." Quoted in *Elizabethan Backgrounds: Historical Documents of the Age of Elizabeth I,* ed. Arthur F. Kinney (Hamden: Archon, 1975), 15–16.

10. See for example, Louis Adrian Montrose's essays, "The Elizabethan Subject and the Spenserian Text," in *Literary Theory/Renaissance Texts,* ed. Patricia Parker and David Quint (Baltimore: Johns Hopkins University Press, 1986), 303–40; and, "'Shaping Fantasies': Figurations of Gender and Power in Elizabethan Culture," in *Representing the English Renaissance,* ed. Stephen Greenblatt (Berkeley: University of California Press, 1988), 31–64; also Peter Stallybrass, "Patriarchal Territories: The Body Enclosed," in *Rewriting the Renaissance: The Discourses of Sexual Difference in Early Modern Europe,* ed. Margaret Ferguson et al. (Chicago: University of Chicago Press, 1986), 123–42.

11. Lady Cook (Née Tennessee Claflin), *Talks and Essays,* 4 vols. (Westminster: Roxburghe, n.d.), 3:112. Cf. Stratton, *Virgin Text:* "Mythologically speaking, the ideal married woman would be a mother and virginal, unsullied by the sexuality which occurs outside the domestic domain" (186).

12. John Ruskin, "Lilies: Of Queens' Gardens," in *Sesame and Lilies* (1864), rpt. in *Essays English and American,* ed. Charles W. Eliot (New York: Collier, 1969), 158. See Adrienne Auslander Munich's essay in this collection for a discussion of lily symbols in the period, and Jeffrey L. Spear's paper for comments on the influence of Ruskin's notions of maternal purity.

13. Cf. Kirsten Hastrup, "The Semantics of Biology: Virginity," in *Defining Females: The Nature of Women in Society,* ed. Shirley Ardener (London: Croon Helm, 1978): "biological categories are always transformed into meaningful categories which are defined by their relationship *to,* and interaction *with,* other categories of society" (63). Although virgi-

nal categories need not relate exclusively to women, Hastrup notes that the development of a concept like male virginity is a type of "back-formation" from the female category (64).

14. Cook, *Talks and Essays,* 3:110–13. On the personal and symbolic "benefits" that may accrue to virginal figures see the essays in Part 2 of this collection, "Virgin Poeisis"; also cf. Foucault, *The Care of the Self,* volume 3 of the *History of Sexuality,* trans. Robert Hurley (New York: Vintage, 1988): "We see then that virginity is not simply abstention as a preliminary to sexual practice. It is a choice, a style of life, a lofty form of existence that the hero chooses out of the regard he has for himself" (230).

15. Sigmund Freud, "The Taboo of Virginity" (1918), in *The Standard Edition of the Complete Psychological Works of Sigmund Freud,* ed. James Strachey (London: Hogarth Press, 1957), 11:198–99. This essay is discussed in more detail below.

16. Cf. Strachey: "the distinction between what is public and what is private is always a subtle one; and in the case of a reigning sovereign . . . it is often imaginary" (66).

17. Cook, *Talks and Essays,* 3:110–11. On the influence of Milton's notions of purity on Pre-Raphaelite texts, see Barbara Garlick's essay in this collection.

18. Freud, "Taboo," 193, 198.

19. Mary Douglas, *Purity and Danger: An Analysis of Concepts of Pollution and Taboo* (London: Routledge, 1966), 115.

20. Ibid., 128.

21. Ibid., 158.

22. Virginia Woolf, *Three Guineas* (1938; London: Hogarth, 1986), 186, no. 38. On the Pauline tradition, see R. Howard Bloch's recent study of patristic doctrines on virginity and their influence on the English literary tradition through Chaucer: "Chaucer's Maiden's Head: 'The Physician's Tale' and the Poetics of Virginity," *Representations* 28 (1989): 113–34.

23. Luce Irigaray, *The Speculum of the Other Woman,* trans. Gillian C. Gill (Ithaca: Cornell University Press, 1985), 27–28.

24. Cf. Bloch's remarks on the two conclusions of medieval religious contemplation of the virgin: "either virginity, as absolute, has no substance, does not exist . . . [or] the abstraction that virginity implies is destroyed by its articulation" ("Chaucer's Maiden's Head," 123).

25. Freud, "Taboo," 191.

26. Ibid., 193, 198, 202.

27. Ibid., 205.

28. Cf. Irigaray's comment that "psychoanalysis needs to recon-

sider the very limits of its theoretical and practical field, needs to detour through an 'interpretation' of the cultural background and the economy, especially the political economy, that have marked it, without its knowledge": "Psychoanalytic Theory: Another Look," in *This Sex Which Is Not One,* trans. Catherine Porter (Ithaca: Cornell University Press, 1985), 66–67.

29. Woolf, *Three Guineas,* 187.

30. Woolf, *Three Guineas,* 188.

31. Woolf, *Three Guineas,* 188. The Bastardy Act allowed a maximum of five shillings weekly support from the child's father.

32. See Foucault, "Nietzsche, Genealogy, History," in *Language, Counter-Memory, Practice,* ed. Donald F. Bouchard (Ithaca: Cornell University Press, 1977), 148 and passim.

33. See "Victorian Sage Discourse and the Feminine: An Introduction," in *Victorian Sages and Cultural Discourse: Renegotiating Gender and Power,* ed. Thaïs E. Morgan (New Brunswick: Rutgers University Press, 1990), 17.

34. Foucault, "Nieztsche, Genealogy, History," 152.

35. Peter Brooks, *Reading for the Plot: Design and Intention in Narrative* (New York: Knopf, 1984), 37.

CHAPTER 2

1. Gerhard Joseph, "Frankenstein's Dream: The Child as Father of the Monster," *Hartford Studies in Literature* 7 (1975): 97–115.

2. *Frankenstein or, The Modern Prometheus,* ed. with Introduction by M. K. Joseph (London: Oxford University Press, 1969), 58, emphasis added. Further references are to this edition.

3. Jaques Lacan, "The Agency of the Letter in the Unconscious," in *Écrits: A Selection,* trans. Alan Sheridan (New York: Norton, 1977), 161.

4. Jacques Lacan, *Speech and Language in Psychoanalysis,* trans. and commentary by Anthony Wilden (Baltimore: Johns Hopkins University Press, 1968), 31–32, 237–49.

5. See for instance, Muriel Spark, *Child of Light: A Reassessment of Mary Wollstonecraft Shelley* (Hadley: Essex Tower Bridge Publications, 1951), 134; Harold Bloom, Afterword to *Frankenstein* (New York: New American Library, 1965), 213; Masao Miyoshi, *The Divided Self: A Perspective on the Literature of the Victorians* (New York: New York University Press, 1969), 84.

6. Norman Holland, "Prose and Minds: A Psychoanalytic Approach to Non-Fiction," in *The Art of Victorian Prose,* ed. George Levine and William Madden (London: Oxford University Press, 1968), 314–37.

7. See James Rieger's edition of the 1818 text (New York: Bobbs-Merrill, 1974), 29–30.

8. Ellen Moers, "The Monster's Mother," *New York Review of Books,* March 24, 1972: 24–28.

9. In the colloquial usage of the day, Mary Shelley would have referred to *notches* as much as *folds.* See her letter to Jane Williams of August 28, 1827: "in fact, dear, except the feminine what is amiable except our pretty N_____"; quoted in Emily W. Sunstein, *Mary Shelley: Romance and Reality* (Boston: Little, Brown, 1989), 272. Sunstein glosses "Notches" as "slang for female genitals." I thank my colleague Rachel Brownstein for calling this citation to my attention.

10. For the distinctions between androcentric and gynocentric criticism and androcritical and gynocritical reading, see Showalter, "Feminist Criticism in the Wilderness," *Critical Inquiry* 8 (1981): 179–205; Jacques Derrida, *Writing and Difference,* trans. Alan Bass (Chicago: University of Chicago Press, 1978), 296. For the Derridean discussion of the textual *hymen* and *fold,* see *Dissemination,* trans. Barbara Johnson (Chicago: University of Chicago Press), 181–226; and for a powerful feminist response, Gayatri Spivak "Displacement and the Discourse of Woman," in *Displacement: Derrida and After,* ed. Mark Krupnick (Bloomington: Indiana University Press, 1983), 169–95. For Lacan's *objet petit a,* that obscure lost object which for the questing subject will never be anything other than a serial displacement of the ever-illusive object *a,* see Lacan, *The Four Fundamental Concepts of Psycho-Analysis,* trans. Alan Sheridan (New York: Norton, 1981), 67–78, 82–90.

11. Moers, "Monster's Mother," 24–28.

12. "The Laugh of the Medusa," in *New French Feminisms,* ed. Elaine Marks and Isabelle de Courtivron (New York: Schocken, 1980), 255.

13. In the essay, "Femininity" (in *New Introductory Lectures on Psychoanalysis,* trans. James Strachey [New York: Norton, 1965]), Freud described the weaving of cloth as one of woman's few contributions to civilization, an invention symbolically bound up with the covering of her "genital deficiency." In weaving, so his argument goes, women restage nature's art of concealment by which pubic hair comes to hide what is missing, what woman "wants." For a discussion of the extension of this weaving metaphor into patriarchal poststructuralist thought in general and the *mise en abyme* in particular, as well as of feminist attempts to reclaim "the voice of the shuttle," see Nancy K. Miller, "Arachnologies:

The Woman, the Text, and the Critic," in *Subject to Change: Reading Feminist Writing* (New York: Columbia University Press, 1988), 77–101.

14. Mieke Bal, "Mise en abyme et Iconicite," *Litterature* 29 (1978): 116–28; and *Lethal Love: Feminist Literary Readings of Biblical Love Stories* (Bloomington: Indiana University Press, 1987), 88. On the appeal of the labyrinthine abyss in (male) critical discourse, see Frank Lentricchia's account of recent critical history, particularly the chapter "History or the Abyss: Poststructuralism," in *After the New Criticism* (Chicago: University of Chicago Press, 1980).

CHAPTER 3

1. Terry Eagleton, *The Rape of Clarissa: Writing, Sexuality and Class Struggle in Samuel Richardson* (Minneapolis: University of Minnesota Press, 1982), 44–45.

2. Concerning the attraction of the genre of gothic romance for its primarily female readership, see Cynthia Griffin Wolff, "The Radcliffean Gothic Model: A Form for Feminine Sexuality," *Modern Language Studies* 9 (1979): 98–113.

3. This may seem to imply that I'm supposing Keats's reader is or needs to be male. I myself, trying to think about what literary evidences suggest, am not so sure what to suppose. I wonder if popular book sales today, or sales of movie tickets, would indicate a significant difference between male and female minds on the issue of the appeal of the Virgin's Tale. Nonetheless, a number of critics now propose that Romantic writing is essentially a male club; see, for example, Anca Vlasopolos, "'Deep Romantic Chasm': Women as Textual Disturbances in Romantic Poetry," in *Power, Gender, Values,* ed. Judith Genova (Edmonton: Academic Printing & Pub., 1987), 31–40.

4. The famous essay that began and remains at the center of this debate is Jack Stillinger, "The Hoodwinking of Madeline: Scepticism in 'The Eve of St. Agnes,'" *Studies in Philology* 58 (1961): 533–55.

5. Arnold Kettle, *An Introduction to the English Novel,* 2 vols. (London: Hutchison University Library, 1951), 1:90.

6. J. E. Austen-Leigh, *Memoir of Jane Austen,* ed. R. W. Chapman (1926; Oxford: Oxford University Press, 1967), 157.

7. Lionel Trilling, Introduction to *Emma* (Boston: Houghton Mifflin Riverside, 1957), ix.

8. There is a pattern in some modern Austen criticism, woven often from feminist thread, that does not find Mr. Knightley a good catch. See, for example, Alison G. Sulloway, "Emma Woodhouse and *A Vindication of the Rights of Women,*" *Wordsworth Circle* 7 (1976): 320–32.

9. Cf. Tony Tanner's remark in *Jane Austen* (Cambridge: Harvard University Press, 1986), that many of the great nineteenth-century novelists found it was "more challenging, more rewarding, more interesting to explore what happens to relationships *after* marriage than to concentrate on the delights and difficulties, the privations and problems, which precede it" (11).

CHAPTER 4

1. William Makepeace Thackeray, *Vanity Fair* (New York: Heritage Press, 1940), 25.

2. Wilkie Collins, *The Woman in White,* 2d ed. (1860; New York: New American Library, 1985), 18–19. Subsequent references to the novel are to this edition and are cited parenthetically in the text by page number.

3. I have chosen to use the term *reference* rather than *referent* for reasons similar to those Robert Scholes outlines in *Textual Power* (New Haven: Yale University Press, 1985): "[T]he problem posed by the poststructuralist theory of textuality . . . is not really a matter of the referent but of reference; it is not a question of whether the world exists but of whether we can perceive it or refer to it adequately" (80). Although Scholes does not extend this point to Derrida, his distinction between *reference* and *referent* is useful when considering the implications of Derrida's now somewhat infamous statement, "There is nothing outside of the text [*il n'y a pas de hors-texte*]," in *Of Grammatology,* tr. Gayatri Chakrovorty Spivak (Baltimore: Johns Hopkins University Press, 1982), 158. As Derrida himself later states, "*text* is not the book"; rather, "the text is always a field of forces: heterogeneous, differential, open, and so on"; see "But beyond . . . (Open Letter to Anne McClintock and Rob Nixon)," tr. Peggy Kamuf, *Critical Inquiry* 13 (1986): 155–70. The referent, then, is always inside the text, and in this sense is always a "reference." Accordingly, I use *reference* to keep this question of poststructuralist textuality clearly in mind throughout my paper. The result: "the referent is lifted, but reference remains," as Derrida would say; see "The Double Session," in *Dissemination,* tr. Barbara Johnson, (Chicago: University of Chicago Press, 1981), 211.

4. Collins is provocative in the way he describes this bit of narrative action; Walter is said to "inflame" Marian's curiosity, and she agrees that they "must really clear up this mystery, in some way" (49).

5. Jacques Derrida, *Spurs: Nietzsche's Styles,* trans. Barbara Harlow (Chicago: University of Chicago Press, 1979), 123, 133.

6. Sandra Gilbert and Susan Gubar discuss the relationship between the white dress and madness in *The Madwoman in the Attic* (New Haven: Yale University Press, 1979). They argue that "the ambiguities of the Victorian white dress extend even beyond the tension between virginal vulnerability and virginal power, though they are implicit in that tension. It is surely significant that doomed, magical, half-mad, or despairing women ranging from Hawthorne's snow-image to Tennyson's Lady of Shalott, Dickens's Miss Havisham, and Collins's Anne Catherick all wear white" (617). However, Gilbert and Gubar's analysis of *The Woman in White* denies the problematic nature of the title figure, in proposing first that "Anne Catherick's white dress, which gives Wilkie Collins's *The Woman in White* its title, suggests the pathos of the Victorian child-woman who clings to infancy because adulthood has never become a viable possibility," and then that "Anne's white dress tells a realistic story of female powerlessness . . ." (620). Gubar also takes up the question of blankness with regard to woman's image of herself as text in " 'The Blank Page' and Female Creativity," in *The New Feminist Criticism: Essays on Women, Literature, and Theory,* ed. Elaine Showalter (New York: Pantheon Books, 1985), 292–313.

7. This is an explosion that, elsewhere in *The Gay Science* (trans. Walter Kaufmann [New York: Vintage, 1974]), Nietzsche locates as the "the eruption of arbitrariness in feeling, seeing, and hearing, the enjoyment of the mind's lack of discipline, the joy in human unreason" (130). For an extended discussion of the relationship between madness and language, see Shoshana Felman, *Writing and Madness: Literature/Philosophy/Psychoanalysis,* trans. Martha Novel Evans and the author with the assistance of Brian Massumi (Ithaca: Cornell University Press, 1985).

8. See Derrida's double consideration of Freud's "The Uncanny" in the footnotes of "The Double Session" (220, 268).

9. Sarah Kofman, *The Enigma of Woman: Woman in Freud's Writings,* trans. Catherine Porter (Ithaca: Cornell University Press, 1985), 223.

10. In effect, the abyssal quality of the figure's referentiality shows how woman will remain in the distance, outdistancing distance. For a developed argument along these lines, see Derrida's discussion of Nietzsche in *Spurs.*

11. In "Freud and the Sandman," in *Textual Strategies,* ed. Josué Harari (Ithaca: Cornell University Press, 1979), Neil Hertz explores this question by turning, at the end of his essay, to Giles Deleuze's connection between the repetition-compulsion and the irreducible figurativeness of language.

12. I borrow this phrase from Walter Benjamin who uses it to describe the effect of world exhibitions. According to Benjamin, "world exhibitions build up the universe of commodities"; see "Paris, Capital of the Nineteenth Century," in *Reflections,* ed. Peter Demetz, trans. Edmund Jephcott (New York: Schocken, 1986), 152. This remark seems particularly appropriate with regard to *The Woman in White.* Collins precisely locates the time-frame of the narrative by having Walter mention: "the year of which I am now writing was the year of the famous Crystal Palace Exhibition in Hyde Park" (560).

13. "Love Me, Love my Ombre, Elle," *Diacritics* (1984): 22. Spivak makes this comment in her attempt to "chart the movement of women in Derrida's vocabulary." She goes on to point out that "Derrida's critique of the legitimation through the patriarchal proper name can be appreciated in the most common-sensical way. The Western metaphysics of everyday life does indeed make a woman's name undecidable. It is either her father's or her husband's. What is her 'own' name?" (22–23).

14. D. A. Miller explores at length what he calls the extensive "gender slippage" within the text and points to the pervasive confusion of gender within characters in "*Cage aux folles:* Sensation and Gender in Wilkie Collins's *The Woman in White,*" *Representations* 14 (1986): 107–36. Nina Auerbach also discusses the confusion of the masculine/feminine as well as biological gender in *The Woman in White.* Her most important point is the parallel she draws between Marian's masculinity and the "unenglish masculine beauty" depicted in the Pre-Raphaelite renderings of women; see *Woman and the Demon: The Life of a Victorian Myth,* (Cambridge: Harvard University Press, 1982), 135–42.

15. See Derrida, *Spurs,* 49, 103–5, 111.

16. Jonathan Loesberg points out "the constant concern with identity and its loss, that is recurrent in sensation fiction." He advances the position that "loss of legal identity entails loss of class identity," and goes on to elucidate the position that "debate over reform was shaped by a prior, ambiguously held attitude toward class structure." However, Loesberg, with his strict focus on class, concludes that "finally the question of the woman in white is more a monumental tangent than a central concern of the novel"; see "The Ideology of Narrative Form in Sensation Fiction," *Representations* 13 (Winter 1986): 115–38.

17. Cf. Roland Barthes, *The Fashion System,* trans. Matthew Ward and Richard Howard (New York: Hill and Wang, 1983).

18. Cf. Derrida, "White Mythology," in *Margins of Philosophy,* trans. Alan Bass, (Chicago: University of Chicago Press, 1982), 207–71.

19. Jacques Lacan, "Seminar of 21 January 1975," in *Feminine Sexuality: Jacques Lacan and the école freudienne,* ed. Juliet Mitchell and Jacqueline Rose, trans. Jacqueline Rose (New York: Norton, 1982), 170.

20. Lacan, "God and the Jouissance of The Woman," in *Feminine Sexuality,* 144.

21. See Nicolas Abraham, "The Shell and the Kernel," *Diacritics* (March, 1979): 16–28.

CHAPTER 5

1. On the ambivalent representation of Mary in Western art and thought see Julia Kristeva, "Stabat Mater," in *The Female Body in Western Culture: Contemporary Perspectives,* ed. Susan Rubin Suleiman (Cambridge, Mass.: Harvard University Press, 1986), 99–118.

2. Letter of 4 January 1939; cited in Robert Langbaum, "Browning and the Question of Myth" (1966), rpt. in *The Word from Below: Essays on Modern Literature and Culture* (Madison: University of Wisconsin Press, 1987), 124.

3. Paul A. Cundiff, *Browning's Ring Metaphor and Truth* (Metuchen, N.J.: Scarecrow, 1972) painstakingly summarizes, abundantly cites, and polemically contends with the substantial body of criticism devoted to the question of truth in *The Ring and the Book.* Chapters 2–4, focusing on the figure of the ring from Book 1, constitute an exhaustively annotated bibliography of a controversy already a century old. The best of recent entrants to the fray are cited by E. Warwick Slinn, "Language and Truth in *The Ring and the Book,*" *Victorian Poetry* 27 (1989): 115–33. My essay is indebted to Slinn's insights that, "as a produced artifact," Browning's ring "is the sign of its own production" (125), and that accordingly "the central focus of the poem is on the production of representational form" (126).

4. I cite throughout the edition by Richard D. Altick, based on the first edition of 1868–1869 (New Haven and London: Yale University Press, 1971).

5. The most recent edition of the poem by Roma A. King, Jr., in *The Complete Works of Robert Browning,* vol. 7 (Athens: Ohio University Press, 1985), calls "repristination" a coinage of Browning's (263). But not even this verbal gold proves virgin: the term occurs in an 1838 essay by Cardinal Wiseman (whom the poem names at 1.446) concerning church history, to which topic the American divine William G. T. Shedd applied it afresh within a year of the poem's publication. The juxtaposition of all three uses in *OED* serves as a reminder that Browning made *The Ring and the Book* a platform for his considered views on the issues

of church tradition and scriptural authority that the Higher Criticism raised to prominence in England during the 1860s.

6. Paul F. Mattheisen, "Uproar in the Echo: The Existential Aesthetic of Browning's *The Ring and the Book,*" *Literary Monographs* 3 (1970), remarks that "Readers have been so accustomed to expect the ring-poem comparison which is worked out later in the poem that it is perhaps difficult now to feel the confusion introduced in the first two paragraphs" (165). That the pertinence of this remark has strengthened with the decades is one justification for the rhetorical reading attempted in the present essay. In one of the few discussions of the passage that attends as closely to rhetorical as to metallurgical detail, George R. Wasserman, "The Meaning of Browning's Ring-Figure," *Modern Language Notes* 76 (1961): 421–22, points out that even the metaphorical vehicle "honey" is momentarily displaced—humanized, and one might add eroticized—by the supplementary metaphor "tear."

7. Richard D. Altick and James F. Loucks, II, *Browning's Roman Murder Story: A Reading of "The Ring and the Book"* (Chicago and London: University of Chicago Press, 1968), describe the poem as "a dense network of association, analogy, and attribution" (226); for W. David Shaw, "Browning's Murder Mystery: *The Ring and the Book* and Modern Theory," *Victorian Poetry* 27 (1989), "It is as if Browning had written a parable about parables" (95), "a nesting structure of sacred books, of commentaries on commentaries" (97). See also Slinn, "Language and Truth": "Only textually produced terms whose meaning is derived from an unceasing extension of textual contexts are available" (115).

8. Since its publication the relevance of Browning's Roman murder story to modernity has been most often conceived in terms of a moralized analogy or metaphor, at the cost of neglecting the causal or metonymic linkages that Browning also asserts between late-Renaissance Italy and Victorian England, at the level of Western material and ideological history. As Lee Erickson points out in *Robert Browning: His Poetry and His Audiences* (Ithaca and London: Cornell University Press, 1984), to view the poem as the expression of an atomized, dehistoricized psychology is seriously to diminish its claim to epic stature (234–38). Alternative views are glimpsed by Henry James, "The Novel in *The Ring and the Book*" (1912), in *Notes on Novelists* (New York: Scribner, 1914), 387; William E. Buckler, *Poetry and Truth in Robert Browning's "The Ring and the Book"* (New York and London: New York University Press, 1985), 256–59.

9. On the interdependence between Caponsacchi and Pompilia see Altick and Loucks, 277; Mary Rose Sullivan, *Browning's Voices in "The*

Ring and the Book": A Study of Method and Meaning (Toronto: University of Toronto Press, 1969), 86, 99–100; Flavia Alaya, "The Ring, the Rescue, and the Risorgimento: Reunifying the Brownings' Italy," *Browning Institute Studies* 6 (1978): 25–26; Paul Zietlow, "The Ascending Concerns of *The Ring and the Book:* Reality, Moral Vision, and Salvation," *Studies in Philology* 84 (1987): 213. The reversal of gender roles that this interdependence implies in the Perseus-Andromeda myth is discussed by Judith Wilt, "The Laughter of Caponsacchi," *Victorian Poetry* 18 (1980): 337–57; Joseph Nicholes, "The Virgin to the Rescue: Robert Browning's Inversion of the Myth of Perseus and Andromeda," *Studies in Browning* 16 (1988): 18–29; and, with general application to Browning's career, Adrienne Auslander Munich, *Andromeda's Chains: Gender and Interpretation in Victorian Literature and Art* (New York: Columbia University Press, 1989), 137–59.

10. Compare an analogous passage from Caponsacchi's monologue, where syntactic ambiguity crystallizes both souls into semiotic transparency: "As I / Recognized her, at potency of truth, / So she, by the crystalline soul, knew me, / Never mistook the signs" (6.931–34).

11. Even in imaginatively annulling the document that has done most to control her life, her bond of marriage to Guido, Pompilia does not just void it as a blank page, but replaces it with a text she can endorse. The blood of her martyrdom "Washes the parchment white" (7.1718), and she pronounces earthly marriage "a counterfeit" (7.1824). Yet at the last she cites Jesus' description of heavenly marriage from Matthew 22:30, affirming at once scripture's priority to ecclesiastical institutions and—with something of a Virgin Mother's mind—her own uncanny hermeneutic priority to scripture: "Oh how right that is, how like Jesus Christ / To say that!" (7.1829–30).

12. Browning often highlights candor by contrasting white with yellow, as in "Fra Lippo Lippi" (1855), 11. 201–02, or "Numpholeptos" (1876), 11. 66–82. The patent contrast between the old yellow book and the new white book into which Browning transmutes it is chromatically complicated by the way "white lies" (1.455) produce a "golden" truth. And there is a sense in which the old yellow book comes to Browning as a text that is virgin because unread: hence his insistence on the historical oblivion into which the Franceschini trial has fallen (1.367–69, 417–58); see Altick and Loucks, 19.

13. See Isobel Armstrong, "A Note on the Conversion of Caponsacchi," *Victorian Poetry* 6 (1968), on the way Browning exploits discrepancies between rhetorical intensity and narrative extensiveness in order "to emphasize the process rather than the climax of conversion," as part of his "study of the process of change" (271, 278). What Slinn says of "truth

and meaning" in the poem may also be predicated of the virginal selves brought forth at its narrative center: they are "fluid features of present discourse" (128). In this sense Browning anticipates his ambivalent admirer Henry James. Both authors represent virginity, as Lloyd Davis puts it, "in terms of processes of transition from one state of knowing to another," so that "the virginal inscribes and is the inscription of ambivalent meanings which both announce and contra-dict the sociosymbolic code": see *Sexuality and Textuality in Henry James: Reading through the Virginal* (New York: Peter Lang, 1988), 79 and 199.

14. On the question of Caponsacchi's celibate priesthood see Sister M. Richard Boo, "The Ordeal of Giuseppe Caponsacchi," *Victorian Poetry* 3 (1965): 179–88; Charles E. Nelson, "Role-Playing in *The Ring and the Book*," *Victorian Poetry* 4 (1966): 91–98; Michael G. Yetman, "Giuseppe Caponsacchi: 'A Very Reputable Priest,'" *Baylor Browning Interests* no. 21 (Waco: Armstrong Browning Library, 1970).

15. Pompilia's modeling herself on the Virgin Mary climaxes with the claim that her son was born by parthenogenesis (7.1762–64), but it occurs throughout the monologue and is repeatedly confirmed during Caponsacchi's. See Sullivan, 81; Buckler, 166; Roy E. Gridley, "Browning's Pompilia," *Journal of English and Germanic Philology* 67 (1968): 64–83, and "Browning's Caponsacchi," *Victorian Poetry* 6 (1968): 281–95; William Walker, "*Pompilia* and Pompilia," *Victorian Poetry* 22 (1984): 47–63; and my "Memorabilia: Mnemonic Imagination in Shelley and Browning," *Studies in Romanticism* 19 (1980): 312–18.

16. E. D. H. Johnson, "Robert Browning's Pluralistic Universe: A Reading of *The Ring and the Book*," *University of Toronto Quarterly* 31 (1961), finds in this passage "language that can only evoke the scene of the Annunciation" (35). See also 3.1530–38, where "The strange and passionate precipitance / Of maiden startled into motherhood" is figured by the simile of a "she-dove." For Altick and Loucks, the bird "is a medieval and Renaissance symbol of the Incarnation" (346n). As for the flies, an early D. G. Rossetti sonnet "For an Annunciation, Early German," in which "The loud flies cross each other in the sun," anticipates Pompilia's lines so closely as to raise a suspicion that Browning may have been revising, if not expurgating, the designs of his junior rival in poetic typology. Munich places Rossetti's sonnet in the context of Victorian analogies between the myths of Andromeda and Mary (97–98).

17. Browning emphasizes this effect intertextually, by packing the virginal initiation scene of the highly literate Caponsacchi with allusions not only to the New Testament (1 Corinthians and Revelation; see *Complete Works* 8:336), but also to Romantic texts that formed part of the

cultural air breathed by literate Victorians. "To spurn the ground, / Soar to the sky" is Shelleyan, as is the figure of the flame-drawn fly; the "weight o' the world" echoes Wordsworth's "Tintern Abbey," 39–40; and the crowning trope of the ungirdled "virgin-band" looks back through Collins's "Ode on the Poetical Character" to the chastity belt in Spenser's *Faerie Queene* 4.7–8.

18. W. C. DeVane, "The Virgin and the Dragon," *Yale Review* 37 (1947): 33–46. Mythological and psychoanalytic challenges to the DeVanean consensus are posed by Claudette Kemper Columbus, "*The Ring and the Book:* A Masque for the Making of Meaning," *Philological Quarterly* 53 (1974): 246–48; and by Munich, 137–60.

19. See Langbaum: "The modern mythical method challenges and re-establishes mythical pattern precisely through realism and through psychology in the modern sense" (126). "Modern," "realism," and "psychology" are, of course, literary-critical terms that remain subject to a revision that is moving at present in sociocultural directions.

20. The episode of the Gorgon's head can remind us that Perseus' victory is in part a trick done with mirrors: his heroism, like that exemplified in *The Ring and the Book,* presupposes crucial skills in the manipulation of empowered images. The prevalence of such skills in the Renaissance culture the poem depicts is reflected in frequent references to paintings, especially of virginal subjects: eg. 3.58–74, 4.367–79, 9.17–70, 11.2112–22.

21. See Shaw: "What kindles faith is not the original but the portrait, not the historical person but the picture" (85). That Shaw is here describing the situation of the poet—and, by implication, of the reader—underscores Browning's habit of extending the dynamics of historiography into even the most vividly experienced events his poem treats. Zietlow infers that even Pompilia hails her Annunciation scene as such only in interpretive retrospect (206–7)—an inference that we may find reinforced by the "painterly" parallel between that scene and Caponsacchi's at the theater. In this connection it is significant that there was no Rafael Madonna in the cathedral at Arezzo (*Complete Works* 8:333).

22. This point deserves special stress where Pompilia is concerned, since the Victorian critical tradition of exalting her purity still survives in the form of an insistence on her complete independence of context: see Buckler, 170; Ann P. Brady, *Pompilia: A Feminist Reading of "The Ring and the Book"* (Athens: Ohio University Press, 1988). For a comparable but less urgent claim about Caponsacchi, see Charles T. Phipps, S.J., "Browning's Canon Giuseppe Caponsacchi: Warrior-Priest, Dantean Lover, Critic of Society," *ELH* 36 (1969): 696–718.

23. In seventeenth-century Italy the cult of the Virgin Mary was

instrumental in the authoritarian reaction (spearheaded by the Jesuits in a second Counter-Reformation) against the liberalizing Jansenist and Quietist movements, which are represented in *The Ring and the Book* by "Molinism." Insofar as Browning portrayed Caponsacchi and Pompilia as Molinist sympathizers, he was subversively appropriating the devotional insignia of their Marianist opponents. See Nicholas Perry and Loreto Echeverria, *Under the Heel of Mary* (London and New York: Routledge, 1988), 32, 49–50; and, on the relations between Marianism and patronage culture, Michael P. Carroll, *The Cult of the Virgin Mary* (Princeton: Princeton University Press, 1986), 28–32.

24. A century of subsequent research has made it clear that the historical Caponsacchi and Pompilia were not the moral paragons of Browning's vision, yet the old yellow book and other sources suggest that their liaison made constant reference to culturally derived models. Beatrice Corrigan, *Curious Annals: New Documents Relating to Browning's Roman Murder Story* (Toronto: University of Toronto Press, 1956), finds Caponsacchi guiding Pompilia to steamy poetry and fiction, and both of them modeling their secret correspondence on characters from Guarini's *Il Pastor Fido* (xxx); in depositions given after her arrest Pompilia "was still translating into the terms of her real life the romantic standards of constancy to a lover which she had learned from her favourite reading" (xliv). It thus appears that Browning's real-life originals did cast themselves as hero and heroine—not of an epic, though, but of a seventeenth-century Harlequin romance.

25. Browning's sacerdotal image, which gets recycled in the poem at 6.148–72 and 12.828–29, may derive from biblical sources like Leviticus 24:4 and 1 Samuel 3:3; it certainly recalls the famous sacrificial soliloquy that opens *Othello* 5.2. See *Complete Works* 7:279; 8:330.

26. My argument about the belated back-formation of virginal truth in the poem thus extends to its genre. The Victorian dissemination of the Higher Criticism of scripture—and of its close, barely secular analogue, the Homeric question—suggested to Browning's generation that the chastity of design and cultural authority traditionally vested in epic texts might be a naive, albeit enabling, literary-historical fiction.

27. On Browning's ringing initial question, see Susan Blalock, "Browning's *The Ring and the Book:* 'A Novel Country,'" *Browning Institute Studies* 11 (1983): 43; Joseph A. Dupras, "Browning's Testament of His Devisings in *The Ring and the Book*," *Victorian Newsletter* 71 (Spring 1987): 23; Adrienne Auslander Munich, "Robert Browning's Poetics of Appropriation," *Browning Institute Studies* 15 (1987): 71. The story of the actual ring(s) behind the poem, and of the "Etruscan" processes discovered and adapted by the Castellani firm, is told in A. N.

Kincaid, "The Ring and the Scholars," *Browning Institute Studies* 8 (1980): 151–59; and in *Complete Works* 7:263.

28. Cited from *The Poems,* ed. John Pettigrew and Thomas J. Collins (New Haven and London: Yale University Press, 1981).

CHAPTER 6

1. According to Alba Warren, *English Poetic Theory 1825–1865,* Princeton Studies in English, No. 29 (New York: Octagon, 1976), one of the "fundamental concepts" of post-Romantic theory of poetry is the notion of genius: "Poetry is what the genius says or makes" (6); "The definition of poetry as 'that which is produced by the poet' rests firmly on the concept of original genius, a concept which was formulated in English criticism as early as 1759" (22).

2. In "Combatting an Alien Tyrrany: Elizabeth Barrett Browning's Evolution as a Feminist Poet," *Browning Institute Studies* 15 (1987), Deborah Byrd explains that Barrett Browning "began to compose poems in which female characters act assertively and independently" (27).

3. See Margaret Forster, *Elizabeth Barrett Browning: A Biography* (New York: Doubleday, 1988), 34. Cf. John Henry Newman, "Poetry, with Reference to Aristotle's Poetics," *The London Review* 1 (1829), rpt. in *Essays Critical and Historical,* vol. 1 (London: 1873), 9; and Warren, *Poetic Theory,* 11.

4. Barrett Browning, *Essays on the Greek Christian Poets and the English Poets* (Plainview: Books for Libraries Press, 1972), 128.

5. *Essays,* 128–29.

6. *The Letters of Robert Browning and Elizabeth Barrett Browning,* ed. Elvan Kintner, 2 vols. (Cambridge: Harvard University Press, 1969), 1:9. Further references to the *Letters* will be included in the text.

7. Cf. the wording in Browning's "Preface": "An objective poet, as the phrase now goes"; "The subjective poet of modern classification"; see *An Essay on Percy Bysshe Shelley,* ed. W. Tyas Harden, Published for the Shelley Society (London: 1888), 11, 13.

8. Dorothy Mermin, *Elizabeth Barrett Browning: The Origins of a New Poetry* (Chicago: Chicago University Press, 1989), observes that Barrett Browning "always refers to poets with the generic 'he,' even in *Aurora Leigh*" (242).

9. *Sonnets from the Portuguese: A Facsimile Edition of the British Library Manuscript,* ed. William S. Peterson (Barre: Barre Publishing, 1977), henceforth cited in the text by sonnet number.

10. Cf. Robert Langbaum, *The Poetry of Experience: The Dramat-*

ic Monologue in Modern Literary Tradition (London: Chatto and Windus, 1957), 76ff.

11. *Poems of Robert Browning,* ed. Donald Smalley (Boston: Houghton Mifflin, 1956). References to Browning's poems are taken from this edition, unless otherwise indicated, and cited by line in the text.

12. *The Poetical Works of Elizabeth Barrett Browning,* ed. Ruth M. Adams (Boston: Houghton Mifflin, 1974), line 54. References to Barrett Browning's poems are taken from this edition, unless otherwise indicated, and cited by line in the text.

13. Mermin points out that bleeding is the mark of both Christ and the mature woman (102).

14. Cf. Cypris's sensual kiss in Barrett Browning's translation of Bion's "A Lament for Adonis" (lines 48–56). The kiss is invested with a lavish sensuality and comes to represent both Adonis and the explicitly sexual relationship between him and Cyrpis.

15. The lily iconographically recalls his initiation from virginity to female sexual experience, which enabled him to understand the true poet's work.

16. *The Seraphim, and Other Poems* (London: 1838); *Poems,* 2 vols. (London: 1844).

17. *Coleridge: Poetical Works,* ed. Ernest H. Coleridge (1912; Oxford: Oxford University Press, 1980), cited by line in the text.

18. Browning's *Bells and Pomegranates* was published in eight pamphlets between 1841 and 1846.

19. Glennis Stephenson explains, on the other hand, that while Bertram narrates most of the poem "the female voice . . . indirectly control[s] the reader's understanding of the text." *Elizabeth Barrett Browning and the Poetry of Love* (Ann Arbor: UMI Research Press, 1989), 56.

20. The two speakers who chose to be alone seem to resemble Barrett Browning, who states in her diary: "My love of solitude is growing with my growth. I am inclined to shun the acquaintance of those whom I do not like & love": *Diary by E. B. B.: The Unpublished Diary of Elizabeth Barrett Browning, 1831–1832,* ed. Philip Kelley and Ronald Hudson (Athens: Ohio University Press, 1972), 155.

21. See Helen Cooper, *Elizabeth Barrett Browning, Woman and Artist* (Chapel Hill: University of North Carolina Press, 1988), for the genesis of the figure of Silence and the significance of the rose in Barrett Browning's interpretation (93–94).

22. In "The Feminine Subject in Victorian Poetry," *ELH* 54 (1987): 385–401, Carol Christ examines a nineteenth-century "feminine mode of verse" in which the female subject becomes increasingly important to poetry "not only as a subject but as a characteristic of the poetic sen-

sibility" (385). In particular, Tennyson "identifies the poetical with the feminine" through acts of appropriation or "theft" (386). Barrett Browning uses an analogous process of appropriation when she identifies herself with the male poet-genius, but to a different end. Initially, she imagines creative genius as a male characteristic, but comes to identify her female speakers with the feminized male poet until, in Aurora Leigh, she represents an autonomous, female poet-genius, who appropriates the characteristics of the male poet.

23. Daniel Karlin, *The Courtship of Robert Browning and Elizabeth Barrett* (Oxford: Clarendon Press, 1985), finds a "link between the poetic and the personal" gratitude (92) that runs through an argument between the two. As the issue of personal gratitude subsides, one of professional gratitude takes its place (78–90). The questions of who was a better poet and who should be most grateful to whom had a "central place in the relationship" (86). "In and through" the "poetry question," Karlin concludes, the question of personal gratitude is continued (86).

24. Dorothy Mermin, "The Female Poet and the Embarrassed Reader: Elizabeth Barrett Browning's *Sonnets from the Portuguese,*" *ELH* 48 (1981), asserts that "critics avert their eyes in embarrassment" when reading the *Sonnets* (351). The twentieth-century reader finds them "awkward, mawkish, and indecently personal" and turns away "from a sight that violates both literary and social decorum" (352–53). Mermin points, for example, to the third sonnet, "which imagines the beloved as a glorious court musician 'looking from the lattice-lights' at the speaker, who is just a 'poor, tired, wandering singer, singing through / The dark, and leaning up a cypress tree'" (353). However, if the sonnets are read with the knowledge that Barrett Browning sees herself in her relationship with Browning as a poet but regards him as a superior poet, then the discrepancy between the "glorious court musician" and the "poor, tired, wandering singer" becomes a continuation of the question of gratitude begun in the letters the two poets exchanged. The sonnet speaker's feelings of inadequacy reproduce Lady Geraldine's feelings of inadequacy.

25. Aurora Leigh reveals that, over the years, she "mixed, confused, unconsciously" whatever she happened to be reading with her mother's face, which remained unaltered, as the eyes in Sonnet 36 do not change: *Aurora Leigh and Other Poems,* ed. Cora Kaplan (London: Women's Press, 1978), 1.128–51, henceforth cited in the text by line number.

26. Diedre David, *Intellectual Women and Victorian Patriarchy* (London: Macmillan, 1987), suggests that these overlap. She points out that because of Barrett Browning's seclusion, inexperience, and restricted "world of reading and writing," her life is a text "which becomes the source of textual production" (101–2). This view seems to be borne out by Barrett Browning's heightened enjoyment of textualized rather than

face-to-face interpersonal communication. On the interconnection between life and text for women artists, cf. Susan Gubar, "'The Blank Page' and Issues of Female Creativity," *Critical Inquiry* 8 (1981): 251.

27. In the 1844 volume, there are 80 occurrences of "poet" (including "poets," "poet's," "poets'"). In *Aurora Leigh,* there are 84 occurrences; but as the female poet-genius replaces the males, Barrett Browning's fascination with the figure of the poet ends. In the 1850 volume there are 3 occurrences; thereafter, 9 in *Casa Guidi Windows,* and 5 in both *Poems Before Congress* and *Last Poems.*

28. Aurora lists various tasks her aunt set her, "And last I learnt cross-stitch" (1.446–47). Tongue-in-cheek, she describes her difficulties with that task, but then meditates seriously on the notion of women's work. "By the way," she begins, "The works of women are symbolical . . . [we] sew, prick our fingers, dull our sight, / Producing what?" They may produce useless items, such as a cover for a stool that a man, presumably a husband, may stumble over and curse (1.457–60). At best, a woman may produce a cushion: "where you lean / And sleep, and dream of something we are not / But would be for your sake. Alas, alas!" (1.461–63). What "hurts most" is "that, after all, we are paid / The worth of our work, perhaps" (1.464–65). Like a woman, poets produce work which is also "symbolical" but is valued for its own sake. Poets are crowned "to their worth" ("A Vision of Poets" [54]), just as women are (ironically) paid the worth of their work. Aurora, the experienced poet and experienced woman, discovers that if she wants to be crowned to her worth, she will have to find a way to crown herself. In "The Queen's Looking Glass: Female Creativity, Male Images of Women, and the Metaphor of Literary Paternity," Chapter 1 of *Madwoman in the Attic: The Woman Writer and the Nineteenth-Century Literary Imagination* (New Haven: Yale University Press, 1985), Sandra Gilbert and Susan Gubar describe the first queen, Snow White's mother, framed by a window while sewing, just as Aurora was. The motifs introduced by this scene, such as sewing and enclosure, "are associated with key themes in female lives (hence in female writing)" (37). At this point, the queen is not without prospects; she is able to look out through the window, even though it is only snow that she sees, unlike the second queen who looks into the patriarchal mirror. Aurora's story revises the story of the first queen in "Snow White." For although she sews with her back to the window, doing women's work while under the influence of her aunt, looking from her window when alone in her room, she sees an extended vision of her woman's space, albeit dominated by male genius in the form of the lime tree. She is able, however, to impose both her vision of the feminine space and her ideas of feminine creativity on the world.

29. As Sandra Gilbert points out in "From *Patria* to *Matria:* Eliz-

abeth Barrett Browning's Risorgimento," *PMLA* 99 (1984), it was not until Romney was able to "read" Aurora—literally read her "texts of female desire"—that she was able to accept him as a husband (202).

30. *In a Balcony,* in *Victorian Poetry and Poetics,* ed. Walter E. Houghton and G. Robert Strange (Boston: Houghton Mifflin, 1968); cited in the text by line number.

CHAPTER 7

1. *Vision and Difference: Femininity, Feminism and the Histories of Art* (London: Routledge, 1988), 94, 111.

2. This is William Michael Rossetti's description of *The Germ* on the title page of his 1901 facsimile reprint of its four issues. Quotations are taken from this edition (London: Elliot Stock, 1901).

3. Cf. Mary Jacobus, *Reading Woman: Essays in Feminist Criticism* (New York: Columbia University Press, 1986): "Another way to pose the question is to explore the extent to which patriarchal representation, by contrast, 'silences' women—the extent to which *woman* or *womanhood,* considered not as an image but as a sign, becomes the site of both contradiction and repression" (30).

4. A more explicit framing appears in D. G. Rossetti's "The Blessed Damozel" in the second issue of *The Germ,* in which the damozel is confined not only by death but by the "golden barriers" of heaven. She leans outward from the window-like frame of "the terrace of God's house" ("rampart" in the 1870 edition), adorned with the visible lilies and white rose of virginity. The 1870 edition of the poem also includes in the eighth stanza the more direct "stooped / Out of the circling charm" instead of the 1850 "stooped / Into the vast waste calm." The framing implicit in the poem is given a high degree of specificity in the most famous version of the later painting (1871–1879) where the damozel is literally enclosed by a narrow frame within the ornate gilt outer frame, cut off from the predella beneath where the lover is shown in the earthly world.

5. For a pertinent discussion of this series, see Larry D. Lutchmansingh, "Fantasy and Arrested Desire in Edward Burne-Jones's *Briar-Rose* Series," in *Pre-Raphaelites Re-viewed,* ed. Marcia Pointon (Manchester: Manchester University Press, 1989), 123–39.

6. John Ruskin, *Modern Painters* (London: Geo. Allen, 1843), 1.448.

7. Note Ronald Parkinson's comment on Rossetti's influence on the Brotherhood as model: "The physical vulnerability, the narrow shoulders, and wide-eyed stare, reinforce the notion that it was as much

the appearance of Christina Rossetti that determined the emaciated and angular style of the Brothers as any return via Lasinio's engravings to the Pre-Raphael frescoes in the Campo Santo at Pisa"; see his essay "James Collinson" in *Pre-Raphaelite Papers,* ed. Leslie Parris (London: Tate Gallery/Allen Lane, 1984), 64.

8. Geoffrey Millais, *Sir John Millais* (London: Academy Editions, 1979), 59.

9. W. Holman Hunt, *Pre-Raphaelitism and the Pre-Raphaelite Brotherhood* (London: Macmillan, 1905), 1:154.

10. Virginia Surtees, *The Paintings and Drawings of Dante Gabriel Rossetti 1828–1882: A Catalogue Raisonné* (Oxford: Clarendon Press, 1971), 1:14. See also Holman Hunt, *Pre-Raphaelitism,* 118.

11. Surtees, *Paintings and Drawings,* 1:13.

12. *The Poetical Works of Christina Georgina Rossetti: With Memoir and Notes &c by William Michael Rossetti* (London: Macmillan, 1904), lxii.

13. Quoted in Surtees, 1:14.

14. Diana Holman-Hunt, *My Grandfather, His Wives and Loves* (London: Hamish Hamilton, 1969), 89.

15. Holman Hunt, *Pre-Raphaelitism,* 307. Pollock also points to the deliberate misspelling of Elizabeth Siddall's name as "Siddal" in literature about the Pre-Raphaelites, *Vision and Difference,* 93.

16. Rossetti, *Poetical Works,* lxii.

17. In a comparison between *Hesterna Rosa* and Hunt's *The Awakening Conscience,* Linda Nochlin comments on "the power of music, an art traditionally associated with erotic temptation"; see "Lost and *Found:* Once More the Fallen Woman," in *Feminism and Art History: Questioning the Litany,* eds. Norma Broude and Mary D. Garrard (New York: Harper and Row, 1982), 233.

18. Rossetti, *Poetical Works,* lxiii.

19. Jerome Bump points to a basic sense of rivalry operating in Rossetti's exclusion from the Brotherhood: "Sibling rivalry can be one of the fiercest forms of competition we know, and Christina could have been perceived as a dangerous rival to Dante Gabriel's dominance in the group, as well as to other members of the Brotherhood"; see "Christina Rossetti and the Pre-Raphaelite Brotherhood," in *The Achievement of Christina Rossetti,* ed. David A. Kent (Ithaca and London: Cornell University Press, 1987), 345; see also 322–23.

20. W. B. Scott records seeing Rossetti in an artisans' drawing class in Camden Town set up in opposition to the Board of Trade Schools of Design; see *Autobiographical Notes of the Life of William Bell Scott,* ed. W. Minto (1892; New York: Kraus, 1970), 1:279.

21. Timothy Hilton, *The Pre-Raphaelites* (London: Thames & Hudson, 1970), 56–57.

22. *The Face of the Deep: A Devotional Commentary on the Apocalypse* (London: SPCK, 1892), 72–73; 99.

23. D. G. Rossetti, quoted in Surtees, 1:14. For a reproduction of this painting, see Figure 2 in Adrienne Auslander Munich's essay.

24. Quoted in E. H. Gombrich, *Art and Illusion: A Study in the Psychology of Pictorial Representation* (1959; Oxford: Phaidon, 1983), 250.

25. *The Works of John Milton,* eds. F. A. Patterson et al., (New York: Columbia University Press, 1931), 4:311.

26. "Three Nuns" was included in Rossetti's early novella *Maude* (written about 1850), but was omitted from the published version in 1897 "on copyright grounds"; see Rossetti, *Poetical Works,* 460.

27. *The Complete Poems of Christina Rossetti: A Variorum Edition,* ed. R. W. Crump, 3 vols. (Baton Rouge and London: Louisiana State University Press, 1979–1990), 3:187–93. All quotations from Rossetti's poems, apart from those first published in *The Germ,* are taken from this edition and will be cited in the text with volume and page number where necessary.

28. Surtees cites many instances of Dante Gabriel's responses to the insistent pressures of the marketplace (1:28, 54, 77, 87). It is also interesting to note the way in which these aesthetico-economic pressures worked to satisfy the commodity fetishism of mid-century capitalism.

29. See Elaine Shefer, "The 'Bird in the Cage' in the History of Sexuality: Sir John Everett Millais and William Holman Hunt," *Journal of the History of Sexuality* 1(3) (October 1990): 446–80, for a discussion of the image in the art of the period.

30. *Christina Rossetti: The Poetry of Endurance* (Carbondale/Edwardsville: Southern Illinois University Press, 1986), 174, 149.

31. Adrienne Munich, *Andromeda's Chains: Gender and Interpretation in Victorian Literature and Art* (New York: Columbia University Press, 1989), interprets the foreshortened space in Dante Gabriel's painting *The Girlhood of Mary Virgin* as a telescoping of "the two spheres [for men and women] at once confirming and denying the convention" (97).

32. Cf. my discussion of the position of the narrator in "My Dream" in "Christina Rossetti and the Gender Politics of Fantasy," in *Victorian Fantasists: Essays on Culture, Society and Belief in the Mythopoeic Fiction of the Victorian Age,* ed. K. Filmer (London: Macmillan, 1991), 145–46.

33. *To the Lighthouse* (1927; London: Dent, 1938), 43.

34. Andrew Belsey and Catherine Belsey, "Christina Rossetti: Sister to the Brotherhood," *Textual Practice* 2(1) (Spring 1988), discuss a similar but later assertion of writerly power and subjectivity in the world of negatives of "Cobwebs," written in 1855 (43).

35. "Femmes Divines," *Critique* 454 (March, 1985): 294–308: "But without a divinity which is appropriate to her, woman cannot accomplish her subjectivity, according to and within an objective corresponding to her [also to it—her subjectivity]. She lacks an 'ideal' which may be for her a goal and a pathway to becoming" (300; my translation). In her use of "objectif," Irigaray puns on its use in optics to indicate the lens farthest away from the eye and nearest to the object being observed.

36. "We look at ourselves in the mirror in order to please others. Rarely to interrogate the state of our body, of our 'soul,' rarely for us and with a view to our becoming. The mirror almost always serves as a means of reducing us to pure exteriority, no matter which. It intervenes as the possibility of constructing screens between the other and me . . . . The mirror, and furthermore the gaze, are frequently used as nontactile, sealed weapons or instruments. Cutting through the tactile as well as through the gaze . . . . The mirror should assist and not reduce my incarnation" (301).

37. "Loving God has often been the recourse of women. They are the guardians of the religious tradition. And alone among them, or almost, certain mystics have achieved an important body of work, notably historic, notably political" (299).

38. Rossetti, *Poetical Works,* lxviii.

CHAPTER 8

1. Patmore published the precocious (in both literary and sexual senses) *Poems* with Moxon, the publisher of poets, in 1844. He greatly revised some of these poems and dropped many while adding others in *Tamerton Church-Tower and Other Poems* (London: William Pickering, 1853)—somewhat revised in the 1854 edition published by John W. Parker (not, as the British Library catalog and other sources indicate, identical). Further revisions and deletions were made until his collected *Poems* (1886 and after) offer little sense of the themes and interest of these volumes.

2. Trans. Robert Hurley (New York: Pantheon, 1978), esp. 147–59.

3. *The Other Victorians: A Study of Sexuality and Pornography in Mid-Nineteenth-Century England* (New York: Basic Books, 1966).

4. Paul M. Fry, *The Poet's Calling in the English Ode* (New Haven: Yale University Press, 1980). For brief histories of the ode see John Heath-

Stubb, *The Ode* (New York: Oxford University Press, 1969); John D. Jump, *The Ode* (London: Methuen, 1974); as well as the older, more specialized English histories, Robert Shafer, *The English Ode to 1660* (Princeton: Princeton University Press, 1918) and George N. Shuster, *The English Ode from Milton to Keats* (New York: Columbia University Press, 1940). Fry's work is by far the most thoughtful and critically provocative.

5. *The Unknown Eros* in Coventry Patmore, *Poems,* ed. Frederick Page (London: Oxford University Press, 1949). References hereafter are in the text, by volume and number, without unnecessary page numbers. Page's text is essentially a reprint of Patmore's final *Poems,* without serious attempt to grapple with the major issue of Patmore's incessant revisions. The Odes were first published privately and anonymously as *Odes* in 1868: only nine odes. They were expanded to 31 in 1877, also anonymous, then to 46 in the acknowledged text of 1878 and 43 in 1879, *Poems*. The final text was established in 1886 *Poems:* 43 odes, including a "Proem." Patmore badly needs a competent bibliographer. All accounts of his texts, including those by J. C. Reid in his bibliography in *The Mind and Art of Coventry Patmore* (London: Routledge, Kegan Paul, 1957), by Terence Connolly, *Mystical Poems of Nuptial Love* (Boston: Bruce Humphries, 1938)—the *only* useful annotation—and by Sister Mary Weinig, *Coventry Patmore* (Boston: G.K. Hall, 1981), have serious errors and/or omissions.

6. As a Catholic convert who read extensively in theology, Patmore did have a general model in a great tradition that converted union of church and God to a sexual union of individual and God, especially in Catholic mystical writers, many of whom he knew. Reid, at pages 90–100, summarizes parallels and possible influences on the odes from St. Bernard of Clairvaux (whose work Patmore and his second wife translated as *St. Bernard on the Love of God* [London: Kegan Paul, 1881]), St. John of the Cross (known before the odes were complete, despite Gosse's observations to the contrary) and St. Teresa of Avila (dear to Patmore's religious daughter and who Reid believes at least offered ideas for the Psyche poems). St. Bernard's sermons on the Canticle could have suggested an interpretation of the Song of Solomon as about the individual's love with God, rather than the conventional reading of these apparent love poems as about marriage of the Church or Israel to God. Reid also suggests St. Augustine (who, with Aquinas, Patmore knew fairly well) for some of Patmore's own assertions of the individual's relation to God as a parallel to the marriage of Christ and Church forecast in the Bible (e.g. 2 Corinthians 11.2–3). Reid's other connections between Patmore and Augustine are interesting but somewhat confusing. Patmore moves from

sexual energy in human love to that with God; Augustine redirects sexual energy, but does so while and by insisting on the dangers of lust's power, since the Fall, over man's rational control (in Augustine, sex before the Fall was a rational act, not one of passion). Reid is probably right in asserting that Patmore took comfort in Augustine's directness about sex in his own attacks on the prudery of parts of Victorian society. Reid mentions Patmore's lesser familiarity with St. Catherine of Genoa, St. Francis de Sales, and St. Catherine of Siena (107–11). He rightly stresses Patmore's tendency to seek his ideas after the fact in Catholic texts and the generally fresh thinking, rather than mere copying, in his use of such sources. Although he identifies some echoes in the odes, mainly the Psyche poems, most of the specific references are in Patmore's late prose work. On a non-Catholic source, Swedenborg, later claimed to be essentially in harmony with Catholic thinking, see Reid, 66–81. Swedenborg's idea of purified marriages in heaven better fits Patmore's more conventional thinking at the time of *The Angel,* when he read Swedenborg, than Patmore's work in the odes.

7. Connolly, 249–50, rightly calls attention to Patmore's transposition of God's love for Israel to the individual soul and the parallel to the same move in St. Bernard's *Sermons on the Canticle of Canticles.*

8. Patmore falls flat wherever he tries to extend his sexual/religious themes to a political realm. His ultraconservative opinions, noble in his prophetic distance from the language and idols of his time (as in the Prologue to Book 1 or the ode "Dead Language") lead him to mere snobbish, often rather brutal rant when he attempts, in a number of political odes, to offer specific jeremiads on the abuses of his age. By contrast, some of his odes on moral issues or on the scientific perspective of his day ("Crest and Gulf," 1.19, "The Two Deserts," 1.18), though not central to the series, are quite good.

CHAPTER 9

1. Joseph Pequigney, *Such Is My Love: A Study of Shakespeare's Sonnets* (Chicago: University of Chicago Press, 1985), 129.

2. I am not directly addressing the equally interesting case of *les jeunes garçons en fleur,* although the figures I mention have masculine counterparts or masculine alter-egos. Salomé, for example, is mirrored in the relationship between Naraboth and Herodias's page, and Sir Claude calls Maisie a fellow and a chap. Little Miles and Flora, taken together, form an androgynous figure. Proust, though beyond the scope of this inquiry, is particularly relevant to the homoerotic interest in virginal desire.

3. Richard Ellman, *Oscar Wilde* (New York: Knopf, 1988), 25.

4. Bram Dykstra, *Idols of Perversity: Fantasies of Feminine Evil in Fin de Siècle Culture* (New York: Oxford University Press, 1986), observes that "even the symbol of purity itself, the lily, became suggestive of the end of innocence" (191). See also his section on "Poison Flowers" in which he traces the metastasis of flowers of innocence to flowers of desire (235–44).

5. I am grateful to Joseph A. Kestner for showing me this picture.

6. If *Leila* portrays a literary character, there are three obvious candidates, all Semitic. Byron uses the name for two characters, the most likely for this picture being a slave girl, beloved of the Giaour, who is killed by her master, Hassan and thrown in a sack into the sea. Byron's Don Juan rescues "little Leila, with her orient eyes / And taciturn Asiatic disposition" (12.27). She is a virgin being prepared for a coming out. Byron observes the commercial value of this enterprise and compares the girl to "virgin honey" (12.31). The third Leila comes from Edward Bulwer-Lytton's novel, *Leila, or the Siege of Granada,* where the heroine is a beautiful and intelligent Hebrew maiden who loves a Moor, and dies as she, converted to Christianity, is about to take the veil.

7. For a further discussion of the sexuality of Rossetti's painting and of aesthetic defloration in general, see Adrienne Munich, *Andromeda's Chains: Interpretation and Gender in Victorian Painting and Literature* (New York: Columbia University Press, 1989), "Typologies of Defloration," 86–131.

8. Judith L. Fisher, "W. S. Gilbert: The Comedic Alternative," in *When They Weren't Doing Shakespeare,* ed. Judith L. Fisher and Stephen Watt (Athens: University of Georgia Press, 1989), 286–87.

9. Among the many analyses of fin de siècle Salomé, Mario Praz, *The Romantic Agony* (1933; Cleveland: Meridian, 1956), considers Wilde's a second rate work; and Rita Severi, "Oscar Wilde, La Femme Fatale and the Salomé Myth," in *Proceedings of the Xth Congress of the International Comparative Literature Association,* eds. Anna Balakian and Tomas Wilhelm (New York: Garland, 1985), considers Wilde's use of tradition (458–63).

10. Oscar Wilde, *Salomé,* in *The Works of Oscar Wilde,* vol. 7 (New York: Lamb, 1909), 19. Further references will be included in the text.

11. Frank J. Sulloway, *Freud: Biologist of the Mind. Beyond the Psychoanalytic Legend* (New York: Basic Books, 1979) cites a tradition in the nineties of linking eating and sex. He particularly notes Wilheim Bolsche's *Das Liebesleben in der Natur* of 1898.

12. There is no suggestion of Herodias's promiscuity in Matthew

14, but the tradition arises from her apparent willingness to marry brothers.

13. Jane Marcus, "Salomé: The Jewish Princess Was a New Woman," in *Art and Anger: Reading Like a Woman* (Columbus: Ohio State University Press, 1985), states that "Virginity is considered Salomé's only asset, and she knows it" (9). Arguing that the theme of the play is "[t]he revolutionary potential of female desire" (8), Marcus also points out parallels between Salomé and Iokanaan different from those I focus on here.

14. Klaus Freweleit, *Male Fantasies,* vol. 2, *Male Bodies: Psychoanalyzing the White Terror,* trans. Erica Carter and Cris Turner (Minneapolis: University of Minnesota Press, 1989), passim.

15. Francoise Meltzer, *Salomé and the Dance of Writing: Portraits of Mimesis in Literature* (Chicago: University of Chicago Press, 1987), 45–46.

16. Henry James, *What Maisie Knew,* in *The Novels and Tales,* vol. 11, New York Edition (New York: Scribner's, 1922), 3. Further references will be included in the text.

17. John C. McClosky, "What Maisie Knows: A Study of Childhood and Adolescence," *American Literature* 36 (1965): 487.

18. Edward W. Wasiolek, "Maisie Pure or Corrupt?" *College English* 22 (1960): 170–172.

19. Sallie Sears, *The Negative Imagination: Form and Perspective in the Novels of Henry James* (Ithaca: Cornell University Press, 1968), compares Maisie's plight to "heroine-victims of pornographic novels . . . . One might call *What Maisie Knew* a latent pornographic novel" (27).

20. For a discussion of the effect of Maisie's perspective and the narrator's consciousness, see Sears, 26–33; and Donna Przybylowicz, *Desire and Repression: The Dialectic of Self and Other in the Late Works of Henry James* (Tuscaloosa: University of Alabama Press, 1986), 31.

21. Child worship, specifically of prepubescent girls, takes many forms, beginning with Wordsworthian idealization of Lucy. Lewis Carroll's interest in girls, as his photographs show, verges on the prurient. The age of consent in London was raised to sixteen in 1885, but before that, it was thirteen, and until 1871, it was twelve. James's story, thus, gestures to more overtly sexualized children. For a discussion of some of these issues, see John Reed, *Decadent Style* (Athens: Ohio University Press, 1985), 225–26.

22. Sigmund Freud, "On the Grounds for Detaching a Particular Syndrome from Neurasthenia under the Description 'Anxiety Neurosis,'" (1895), in *The Standard Edition of the Complete Psychological Works*

of Sigmund Freud, trans. James Strachey (London: Hogarth, 1953–1974), 99. Further references will be included in the text.

23. Sulloway, *Freud,* 310.

24. Sulloway, *Freud,* 279–80.

25. Cf. Mary Douglas, *Purity and Danger: An Analysis of the Concepts of Pollution and Taboo* (London: Routledge, 1966), 7.

26. The frame to the governess's story also suggests that "Douglas," original possessor of the manuscript, who is also dead at the writing of the story, loved the governess, and it may be he who is the story's original sufferer from virginal anxiety. Thus, both the frame and the story distribute the virginal anxiety between the two sexes, a counterpart of the uses of androgyny at the time.

27. Henry James, "The Turn of the Screw," in *The Complete Tales of Henry James,* vol. 10, ed. Leon Edel (Philadelphia: J.B. Lippincott, 1964), 22. Further references will be included in the text.

28. In a personal communication Nina Auerbach suggested buggery as Miles's crime. She suggests that contemporary readers, alerted to this "crime" not only by personal experience but also by the recent (1895) Wilde trial, would understand the ambiguity of the headmaster's reticence about explaining Miles's expulsion.

29. As in Salomé's kissing John the Baptist's head, the scene echoes the famous conclusion of Browning's "Porphyria's Lover" when the lover holds the woman he loves in his arms after murdering her. In little Miles, the virginal girl has become the virginal boy. Hyacinth Robinson in *The Princess Cassimassima* is another character to examine in this respect, as well as in relation to contemporary treatments of the Narcissus myth.

30. Freud, "'Anxiety Neurosis,'" 99.

31. Ellman, *Oscar Wilde,* 342.

CHAPTER 10

1. Thomas Hardy, Preface to the Fifth and Later Editions, in *Tess of the d'Urbervilles* (New York: Norton, 1979), 3. Further references will be included in the text.

2. Jacques Derrida, "White Mythology: Metaphor in the Text of Philosophy," *Margins of Philosophy,* trans. Alan Bass (Chicago: University of Chicago Press, 1982), 229.

3. Derrida, "White Mythology," 211.

4. Ibid., 213.

5. Four layers or separately written prefaces comprise the introductory material to *Tess*. The first, Explanatory Note to the First Edition, dated November 1891, accompanied the initial publication of the novel in

book form and briefly describes the editing history to date of *Tess*. In July 1892 Hardy appends Preface to the Fifth and Later Editions, the lengthiest and most defensive of the four. In January 1895 he adds a paragraph in which he confesses, in a sense, the transgression of responding so warmly to the critical reception of *Tess* "when a spirited public and private criticism of its points was still fresh to the feelings." At the same time, Hardy inserts distance not only between his present comments and "the foregoing remarks," but also by disclaiming, in a sense, "the feelings." Finally, the March 1912 passage for the Wessex Edition discloses yet another textual dismembering and re-membering.

6. Penny Boumelha, *Thomas Hardy and Women* (Totowa: Barnes & Noble, 1982), 118.

7. At Talbothays Dairy, Tess listens to a conversation between the Cricks, Angel, and the dairymaids on the subject of whether a specific fallen woman should have confessed her sexual history to her current lover. What is essentially entertaining gossip to the others nearly chokes her as she eats her bread and butter at the breakfast table: "Yes, there was the pain of it. This question of a woman telling her story—the heaviest of crosses to herself—seemed but amusement to others. It was as if people should laugh at martyrdom" (152). Hardy also suffers martyrdom (see discussion below), and so aligns himself as writer with his heroine, by telling this narrative of transgression that in turn trespasses social decorum about subjects fit for fiction.

8. Many readers suggest that Hardy "identified" with Tess. In *Fiction and Repetition* (Cambridge: Harvard University Press, 1982), J. Hillis Miller contends that Hardy's feelings for this heroine were "perhaps stronger than for any other of his invented personages" and that Hardy "even obscurely identified himself with her" (119). As reported by J. T. Laird in *The Shaping of* Tess of the D'Urbervilles (New York: Oxford University Press, 1975), Bernard Paris believed that Hardy was "in love" with Tess (122). Boumelha argues that the narrative silences of both the rape scene and the initial truncation of marital consummation permit the narrator, whom she identifies as "Hardy," to be the sole "possessor" of Tess (121). Lois Deacon speculates that Tess was modelled after Hardy's cousin (or niece) Tryphena Sparks with whom Hardy may have fallen in love, been engaged, and produced a child during the betrothal period. She subsequently married someone else, and died in March 1890 as Hardy was writing *Tess* (Laird, 120–22). With this parallel, of course, Alec d'Urberville, purportedly Tess's distant cousin, would stand in for Hardy.

9. Thomas Hardy, *The Life and Work of Thomas Hardy,* ed. Michael Millgate (Athens: University of Georgia Press, 1985), 259.

10. Hardy, *Life,* 255.

11. Hardy, *Jude the Obscure* (New York: Oxford University Press, 1985), xxxvi.

12. This is Mrs. Oliphant's phrase in her review of the novel in *Blackwood's Magazine,* March 1892: "We have a great many objections to make to Tess. The fact that what we must call the naughty chapters have had to be printed surreptitiously, in what we presume ought to be described as elderly Reviews, while the rest has come out in the cheerful young newspaper open to all men, is of itself a tremendous objection to our old-fashioned eyes." The review is included in *Thomas Hardy: The Critical Edition* (New York: Barnes & Noble, 1970), 203–14. These "naughty chapters" of the rape and baptism scenes were published separately as sketches: "Saturday Night in Arcady" in a Special Literary Supplement of the *National Observer,* 14 November 1891, and "The Midnight Baptism, A Study in Christianity," in *Fortnight Review,* May 1891.

13. Boumelha uses this phrase in arguing that the repeated absence of Tess's consciousness in the text (she falls asleep before scenes of disaster—both Prince's death and her rape) enforces her indeterminacy as a speaking subject (*Thomas Hardy,* 127).

14. Laird, *Shaping of* Tess, 18. Laird does posit an Ur-text in his discussion of the novel's bibliographic history. But his own observations about Hardy's writing process and strategies of revision also belie the material existence of such an "original" document. The status of textual purity becomes hypothetical only.

15. Hillis Miller observes that "the novelist in his own way repeats the fate of his heroine" (*Fiction and Repetition,* 125).

16. Julia Kristeva writes about this designation of the writing subject in *Revolution in Poetic Language,* trans. Margaret Waller (New York: Columbia University Press, 1984), defining the authorial "I" as "a projection of the paternal role in the family," whereas the writing subject points to the complicated "subjectal space" that the network of enunciations structures (90–91, 209). In *Tess,* this "subjectal space" traverses both the "mere tale-teller" of the prefaces and the narrating perspective, often hard to delineate or fix carefully, in the novel itself.

17. Substituting a J for the first person, Joan Durbeyfield writes to her daughter: "But with respect to your question, Tess, J say between ourselves, quite private but very strong, that on no account do you say a word of your Bygone Trouble to him. J did not tell everything to your Father, he being so Proud on account of his Respectability, which, perhaps, your Intended is the same. Many a woman—some of the Highest in the Land—have had Trouble in their time; and why should you Trumpet yours when others don't Trumpet theirs? No girl would be such a Fool,

specially as it is so long ago, and not your Fault at all" (160). Although her mother encourages Tess to withhold her "Bygone Trouble" from Angel, she also insinuates that the problem of confession is not so much the "Bygone Trouble," something many women, even "the Highest in the Land" have had, but masculine pride and the dubious "Respectability" of paternal privilege.

18. Boumelha cites Mary Jacobus's findings of discrepancies between earlier and later versions of Angel's confession. Evidence suggests that initially Angel was to confess a loss of faith rather than a sexual fall. This earlier rendition would have underscored "the varieties of heterodoxy available to (intellectual) man and (sexual) woman" (*Thomas Hardy,* 122). In any case, the vestiges of this dichotomy remain since Angel's confession appears in words, while Tess's is displaced onto a description of transmogrified physical objects.

19. Again and again Angel reads (and in a sense writes) Tess through the appearances of her body and face: "Clare regarded her attentively, conned the characters of her face as if they had been hieroglyphics" (147). Repeatedly Angel fashions Tess into the imaginary romantic mold he has construed, so that this line about his future intentions are ironic: "after I have made you the well-read woman that I mean to make you" (159). Indeed, Tess is already the much *read*—if not accurately or "purely"—woman.

20. Julia Kristeva, *Powers of Horror,* tr. Leon S. Roudiez (New York: Columbia University Press, 1982), 4. Cf. Kristeva's other definitions of the abject: "A massive and sudden emergence of uncanniness . . . radically separate, loathsome . . . . A weight of meaninglessness" (2).

21. Catherine Belsey, "Constructing the Subject, Deconstructing the Text," in *Feminist Criticism and Social Change,* eds., Judith Newton and Deborah Rosenfelt (New York: Methuen, 1985), 56.

22. See Textual Notes to *Tess of the d'Urbervilles,* ed. David Skilton (New York: Penguin, 1978), 512–13.

23. Skilton, Textual Notes, 503.

24. Tess stands out among Victorian fallen women in literature as the only one who is raped. In other depictions, the women seem complicitous, even if the fall is the consequence of so-called seduction. Besides Carry Brattle, other fallen women include Esther in Gaskell's *Mary Barton* (1848), Ruth in Gaskell's *Ruth* (1853), Lady Dedlock in Dickens's *Bleak House* (1854), Lady Audley in Braddon's *Lady Audley's Secret* (1861), to name just a few. Of course, many readers still prefer *seduction* to *rape* in reading Tess's fall, while the close of Chapter 11 is often cited as "the seduction scene." Roman Polanski's film version of the novel makes

this interpretation of seduction as Tess appears to wake to Alec's kiss and responds in kind.

CHAPTER 11

1. See Geoffrey Wall, "'Different from Writing': *Dracula* in 1897," *Literature and History* 10 (1984): 15–23, for a discussion of *Dracula* as an "anxious text."

2. *The Annotated Dracula,* ed. Leonard Wolf (New York: Ballantine Books, 1975), 21. Hereafter cited parenthetically in the text.

3. "Suddenly Sexual Women in Bram Stoker's *Dracula,*" *Literature and Psychology* 27 (1977): 113–21. Reprinted in *Dracula: The Vampire and the Critics,* ed. Margaret L. Carter (Ann Arbor: U.M.I. Research Press, 1988). This collection contains most of the significant articles on *Dracula* that appeared prior to its publication.

4. *The History of Sexuality,* vol. 1, trans. Robert Hurley (New York: Vintage, 1980), 128.

5. For an account focused on literary history, see Richard Dellamora, *Masculine Desire: The Sexual Politics of Victorian Aestheticism* (Chapel Hill: University of North Carolina Press, 1990).

6. "The Censorship of Fiction," *The Nineteenth Century* (September 1904): 486.

7. D. A. Miller, *The Novel and the Police* (Berkeley: University of California Press, 1988), viii.

8. Franco Moretti, *Signs Taken for Wonders,* trans. Susan Fischer, David Forgacs, and David Miller (London: Verso, 1983), 102.

9. "'Kiss Me with Those Red Lips': Gender and Inversion in Bram Stoker's *Dracula,*" *Representations* 8 (1984): 107–33 (reprinted in Carter, *Vampire and Critics*). There are, of course, other approaches to *Dracula.* For a broad survey of sources and categories of interpretation, see Clive Leatherdale, *Dracula: The Novel and the Legend* (Wellington: Aquarian Press, 1985). For the literary history of the English vampire, see James B. Twitchell, *The Living Dead: A Study of the Vampire in Romantic Literature* (Durham: Duke University Press, 1981), and Carol A. Snef, *The Vampire in Nineteenth-Century English Literature* (Bowling Green: Bowling Green University Press, 1988).

10. Alan P. Johnson, "'Dual Life': The Status of Women in Stoker's *Dracula,*" in *Sexuality and Victorian Literature,* ed. Don Richard Cox (Knoxville: University of Tennessee Press, 1984), 20–39. Stoker's reference to "dual consciousness," noted by Johnson, refers specifically to a double awareness on the part of the actor of both method and emotion, but Stoker gives one example in the work of Ellen Terry where the perfect

action was enacted by "unconscious celebration"; see *Personal Reminiscences of Henry Irving,* vol. 1 (New York: Macmillan, 1906), 265.

11. "Of Queen's Gardens," from *Sesame and Lilies,* in *The Works of John Ruskin,* eds. E. T. Cook and Alexander Wedderburn, vol. 18 (London: Allen, 1903–1912), 125; 114.

12. The most elaborate reading of *Dracula* in relation to the New Woman is given in Snef, *Vampire in Nineteenth-Century.*

13. See Ethel S. Person, "The Omni-Available Woman and Lesbian Sex: Two Fantasy Themes and Their Relationship to the Male Developmental Experience," in *The Psychology of Men: New Psychoanalytic Perspectives,* eds. Gerald I. Fogel, Frederick M. Lane, and Robert S. Liebert (New York: Basic Books, 1986), 71–94. Person cites the Fantasy Project at the Columbia Psychoanalytic Center for Training and Research which found that 11 percent of the men they surveyed had fantasies of torturing a sexual partner; 20 percent of whipping or beating her, and 44 percent fantasized forcing a partner to submit to sexual acts: "The comparable figures for women are 0 percent, 1 percent and 10 percent" (74). For other views of male sexuality in *Dracula,* in addition to those already cited, see Stephanie Demetrakopoulos, "Feminism, Sex Role Exchanges, and Other Subliminal Fantasies in *Dracula,*" *Frontiers: A Journal of Women's Studies* 2(3) (1977): 104–13; Gail B. Griffin, "'Your Girls That You All Love Are Mine': *Dracula* and the Victorian Male Sexual Imagination," *International Journal of Women's Studies* 3(5) (1980): 454–65 (reprinted in Carter, *Vampire and Critics*); George Stade, "Dracula's Women and Why Men Love to Hate Them," in Fogel et al., *Psychology of Men,* 25–48; Richard Astle, "Dracula as Totemic Monster: Lacan, Freud, Oedipus and History," *Sub-stance* 25 (1980): 98–105, and "Evolution and Information, or Eroticism and Everyday Life, in *Dracula* and Late Victorian Aestheticism," in *Sex and Death in Victorian Literature,* ed. Regina Barreca (Bloomington: Indiana University Press, 1990), 144–57.

14. Such an execution is depicted in a watercolor dated c. 1640 reproduced in Robert Held, *Inquisition: A Bilingual Guide to the Exhibition of Torture Instruments from the Middle Ages to the Industrial Era* (Florence: Qua D'Arno, 1985), 141.

15. For examples, see Bram Dijkstra's chapters on "The Collapsing Woman" and "The Lesbian Glass" in *Idols of Perversity: Fantasies of Feminine Evil in Fin-de-Siècle Culture* (New York: Oxford University Press, 1986).

16. Person, "Omni-Available Woman," 91.

17. Richard F. Burton, "The Tale of the Bull and the Ass," in *The Book of the Thousand Nights and a Night,* vol. 1 (New York: The Burton Club, n.d.), 24.

18. Because it would link the vampire neatly to Lucy, some commentators persist in stating that Lucy is blond. There is one description of her hair having "sunny ripples" in the light (147), but the only specific reference calls her "a dark haired women" (189). Elaine Showalter is the latest to make this link. She also moves the attack on Harker by the three women from their bedroom to his; see *Sexual Anarchy: Gender and Culture at the Fin de Siècle* (New York: Viking, 1990), 180.

19. "Carmilla," in *Best Ghost Stories of J. S. LeFanu,* ed. E. F. Bleiler (New York: Dover, 1964), 292.

20. *The Man Who Wrote Dracula* (London: Michael Joseph, 1975), 233–34.

21. The effect of syphlitic marriage on women both historically and as reflected in literature has been a concern of Elaine Showalter's since *A Literature of Their Own* was published in 1977. She picks up the theme again in *Sexual Anarchy.* See also Sander Gilman's *Difference and Pathology* (Ithaca: Cornell University Press, 1985), and *Disease and Representation* (Ithaca: Cornell University Press, 1988).

22. *The Bonds of Love: Psychoanalysis, Feminism, and the Problem of Domination* (New York: Pantheon, 1988), 92.

CHAPTER 12

1. The British Library Catalogue indicates that *The Beetle* went through numerous editions between 1897 and 1907, but I have not been able to determine how many copies of the text were sold. Everett F. Bleiler, in his *The Guide to Supernatural Fiction* (Kent: Kent State University Press, 1983), writes that "With the exception of *Dracula,* this was probably the most popular horror novel of the 1890s" (344). Surprisingly enough, after summarizing the plot of *The Beetle,* Bleiler concludes that "most of the novel is a bore" (344). Contemporary reviews of *The Beetle,* like Bleiler's comment, tend to be brief and dismissive.

2. For lack of space, this essay elides the problematics of male sexuality that are articulated by the text. For a discussion of male hysteria in *The Beetle,* see my "The Novel of the Gothic Body: Deviance, Abjection, and Late-Victorian Popular Fiction," diss., Stanford University, 1988, chap. 6.

3. Richard Marsh, *The Beetle,* in *Victorian Villainies,* eds. Graham Greene and Hugh Greene (New York: Penguin Viking, 1984), 580. Further page citations from *The Beetle* have been incorporated within the text.

4. Edward Said, *Orientalism* (New York: Vintage Books, 1978), 1–2.

5. *Orientalism,* 3.

6. I will confine myself to references to two works discussing the relationship between nineteenth-century theories of race and theories of physical and cultural evolution: Stephen Jay Gould, *The Mismeasure of Man* (New York: Norton, 1981); and George Stocking, *Victorian Anthropology* (New York: The Free Press, 1987).

7. For overviews of British colonial relations with Egypt, see Peter Mansfield, *The British in Egypt* (New York: Holt, Rinehart and Winston, 1971); and Ronald Robinson, John Gallagher, and Alice Denny, *Africa and the Victorians: The Climax of Imperialism* (Garden City: Anchor, 1971), chaps. 8–10.

8. For a similar argument about *Dracula,* see Stephen D. Arata, "The Occidental Tourist: *Dracula* and the Anxiety of Reverse Colonization," *Victorian Studies* 33 (1990): 621–45. Patrick Brantlinger also discusses the late-Victorian phenomenon of gothic novels of inverse colonialism, or "invasion fantasies," in chapter 8 of *Rule of Darkness: British Literature and Imperialism, 1830–1914* (Ithaca: Cornell University Press, 1988).

9. Said, *Orientalism,* 206.

10. Said, *Orientalism,* 188, 190.

11. Carol A. Senf argues a connection between 1890s feminism and fin de siècle representations of gothicized female sexuality in "*Dracula:* Stoker's Response to the New Woman," *Victorian Studies* 26 (1982): 33–49.

12. Julia Kristeva, *Powers of Horror: An Essay on Abjection,* trans. Leon S. Roudiez (New York: Columbia University Press, 1982), 4. For Kristeva, the ultimate abjection occurs at the moment of birth, when the child begins the process of separating from the body of a mother with whom she is still intimately connected: "Abjection preserves what existed in the archaism of pre-objectal relationship, in the immemorial violence with which a body becomes separated from another body in order to be" (10). One could argue that the attacks by the Beetle-avatar, that walking vagina, as described later in the essay, reconfigure this "pre-objectal relationship," that is, the simultaneous desire for and revulsion from the maternal womb, in its engulfing, adhesive dampness.

CONTRIBUTORS

Susan David Bernstein is assistant professor of English at the University of Wisconsin. Her publications include articles on feminist theory and nineteenth-century British and American literature. She is finishing a book entitled *Confessional Subjects* on confession and the construction of female subjectivity in fiction and feminist theory.

Lloyd Davis teaches English and cultural studies at the University of Queensland. He is the author of *Sexuality and Textuality in Henry James* and articles on Walter Scott, Renaissance literature, and language theory.

Dolores DeLuise is a doctoral student in English at the Graduate Center of the City University of New York. She is currently completing a dissertation on Elizabeth Barrett Browning's *Sonnets from the Portuguese.*

Diane Elam is assistant professor of English at Indiana University. She is the author of *Romancing the Postmodern* and essays on literary theory, feminism, and British fiction. She is currently working on a book on deconstruction and feminism.

Barbara Garlick teaches English and is the present coordinator of women's studies at the University of Queensland. She has published on French Renaissance poetry and nineteenth- and twentieth-century British and Australian literature.

Kelly Hurley is assistant professor of English at the University of Colorado at Boulder. Her teaching and research interests include Victorian studies, feminist and film theory, and popular culture, and she is currently at work on a book entitled: *Gothic Embodiments of the British Fin de Siècle.*

Gerhard Joseph, a professor of English at Lehman College and the Graduate Center of the City University of New York, has published widely on nineteenth-century subjects. His most recent book is a critical study entitled *Tennyson and the Text: The Weaver's Shuttle.*

John Maynard is professor of English at New York University. He has published *Browning's Youth, Charlotte Brontë and Sexuality,* coedited *Nineteenth-Century Lives,* and is coeditor of *Victorian Literature and Culture.* He is completing a study of Victorian discourses on sexuality and religion.

Adrienne Auslander Munich, associate professor of English, is director of women's studies at State University of New York at Stony Brook and coeditor of the annual *Victorian Literature and Culture.* Her recent work includes *Andromeda's Chains: Gender and Interpretation in Victorian Literature and Art* and *Arms and the Woman: War, Gender, and Literary Representation.*

Jeffrey L. Spear is an associate professor of English at New York University. He is the author of *Dreams of an English Eden: Ruskin and His Tradition in Social Criticism* and numerous essays on Victorian topics.

L. J. Swingle is professor of English at the University of Kentucky and has written widely on nineteenth-century English literature. He is the author of *The Obstinate Questionings of English Romanticism* and *Romanticism and Anthony Trollope.*

Michael Timko is professor of English and chair of the Victorian Committee at the City University of New York. He has published extensively on major figures and movements in Victorian literature. His most recent book is titled *Carlyle and Tennyson,* and he is currently writing a study of Carlyle, Robert Browning, and Shaw. He serves as editor of the *Carlyle Annual.*

Herbert F. Tucker, professor of English at the University of Virginia, is the author of *Browning's Beginnings: The Art of Disclosure* and *Tennyson and the Doom of Romanticism.* He is currently at work on a study of epic in the nineteenth century.

INDEX